# BUCKETS, SHOVELS, GHOST AND WORMS

Alvin Bell

Copyright © 2025

All Rights Reserved

https://www.bookwritingexperts.com/

# Other Book's by Alvin Bell

*I Cant Remember*

*The Impulse of Rage*

*Buckets Shovels Ghost and Worms*

*In Perfect View*

*Jasmine*

Page Blank Intentionally

# Preface

Callie Devereaux, a Southern Belle with a distinct personality all of her own. She eventually takes charge as the only remaining heiress of a family estate previously owned and dominated by men of the Southern Confederacy. But Callie, a rare Creole native-born of wealth, beauty, and a humongous appetite for sex, is no pushover. Men find that, although she's what fantasies are made of, keeping her subdued is an illusion as well.

She has a daughter, a daughter whose best friend is quite a mystery. And a butler so witty and outspoken he's sometimes more nerve-wracking than he is helping around the house. He's been with the Devereaux family for what seems like forever, and as a father figure, loves Callie dearly regardless of how borderline insane he thinks she might be.

Eventually, a husband comes along at just the right time in Callie's life when settling down in marriage does seem ideal. He's got kids, too, and together, they become a happy family. However, love, hardship, and tragedy come in all forms and fashions. And as it is with anything else in life, nothing will last forever, including what some would consider to be a perfect marriage.

*"Johnny, wait... don't shoot!!! It's all my fault!!!" she yelled.*

*But Johnny didn't listen, and pulled the trigger anyway,*

*splattering the night with the loud sound of the gun, and with Blu's blood.*

# Prologue

**Dec. 1959**

Far inside the dark and, at times, delusional backwoods of Southern Louisiana, upstairs in the master bedroom of what was then considered a house of luxury, a mansion by simple Cajun standards.

Chivalry was all but lost, subdued by a man and woman's unbridled desire to please each other sexually. This, when the only light was from an old kerosene lantern, added both romances and the allured mystique of not knowing what would happen next. As well, the double doors of the balcony were open, and a breeze from outside blew in and made the curtains and the flickering flame of the lantern dance violently, an indication of how the night would end.

Callie, lying across the bed with only a red negligee on to cover the exquisite feminine treasures hidden beneath it, spoke in a soft, sensual tone,

"My, My, what a surprise…Blu Roy Jenkins Junior.

Mon Cheri," she said, emanating pure lust from being so excited and fond of the person in front of her, smiling all the while and watching intently while Blu got undressed, thinking,

*"It took you long enough."*

Nevertheless, what she said was something totally different.

"So… to what do I owe the unexpected pleasure of havin' you here at the Devereaux house this evenin'?" she asked, pretending as if she didn't already know and was, at the same time, becoming more and more aroused with every stitch of clothing Blu took off.

She missed him dearly, the wild sexual experiences, the way he once held and stroked the passion trapped inside of her... passion held in by fear, fear that her father might find out and that Blu might be blamed and punished for it. The thought of such danger, even from so long ago, was still a serious turn-on.

"Let's not pretend or waste time, Missy. You want this just as much as I do. Probably more. Don't you?" Blu asked, not bothering to hide or disguise the sarcasm and arrogant tone of voice, speaking words only an inkling less than what he thought he knew for sure. All the while, stacking each item of clothing, he took off neatly across an armchair.

"Besides...," he said, sharing with her a cunning smile, extending more arrogance, "...it's New Year's Eve. And I guess you can say I wanted somethin'...different. Somethin'...special," he said, in short, prolonged sentences, waving a hand around at the same time as if searching for the right words to say.

"Somethin' like me, Blu?" Callie spoke up and asked while smiling, playing along with Blu in a way that made her seem gullible and naïve in return for him being so bold and arrogant. The response made both of them smile.

Callie, all the while, was hot and bothered inside and didn't mind letting him know by showing off one of her long, pale, ivory-colored legs and thighs. Thin, red panties underneath the silk, red gown she was wearing were also shown and exposed.

Callie was thinking,

"*An extra treat...just for you, Blu.*" It was a celebration, and nine other girls were in the house and they were all wearing silk gowns with what ever color sexy panties to match underneath.

"Yeah, somethin' like you, Callie," said Blu, standing there naked for a while, taking it all in, now wearing only a handsome smile of pearly whites with a single gold tooth showing.

He then took the few necessary steps it took to get closer, placing himself beside the bed.

"What I really wanted was the experience of havin' a real jewel again," he said, admitting the truth...he missed her too, the way she touched and kissed and moaned with him deep inside of her.

"Yeah, well… you sure picked a hell of a night for it," said Callie, giving in to being so excited, extending the leg and thigh, allowing Blu to catch it, but not before the ball of her foot found Blu's private.

Whether it be a brothel or not, of all the men who visited the Devereaux house, Callie very rarely made herself available for any of them. However, in this particular case, with it being Blu, he would be made an exception. The only problem was that the gangster, Johnny Le Fleur, the man in charge of security and the one Callie had promised herself to, was never far behind. But just moments before Blu walked in, spirits were high with a few drunk men, and a fight had broken out. A man had been stabbed, which meant that for a while, Johnny would have his hands full, securing the place and getting things calmed down and back in order. Even so, people who knew him knew that Johnny was very observant—nothing ever seemed to get him, not even something as minute as a careless whisper.

"I've missed you," said Callie, still using the ball of her

foot and soft, manicured toes with red painted toenails to massage Blu's private until the length of him grew and got rock hard, solid.

The risk was immense and obvious to both of them,

"...thrilling and so exciting, yet dangerous as hell," a thought the two of them both shared.

Blu had given up life as a field hand long ago after being forced to move near Baton Rouge, where life became a lot easier...he didn't have to break his back, bending to pick cotton or any of the other seasonal, cultivated land items the Devereaux farm had planted and grown for harvest. Instead, he slept most days and spent the evenings with a different woman almost every night of the week.

To him, this lifestyle was a lot more rewarding, especially when the women all worked and brought home to him what little money they might've made. In return, he found himself driving a nice automobile, wearing rare, expensive jewelry and new suits of clothing every day. In addition, he handled the money right; he could have just about anything else he wanted as well.

"Living the life" was what he called it. "…the easy life."

Being as dark as night was how he'd gotten such a name as "Blu." But being six foot three and good-looking was how he became such a lady's man. And with that came the reputation of how well-endowed he was, which altogether was what drove most women crazy and made them do some of the things they did for him.

On the other hand, Callie Devereaux, at five foot ten, was rather tall for a woman. And the fact that she was extraordinarily pretty and voluptuous made her a very attractive person as well. It just so happened to be that she was also the great-granddaughter of Colonel Luke Devereaux, a pure white breed Confederate soldier from way back in the days of slavery and the Civil War conflict. Keep in mind that the Colonel and many like him in the South were instilled with hatred and intolerance towards black people, an accepted normality during times back then, especially in the state of Louisiana.

After the war, the Colonel died, and his grandson, who later became a high society playboy, hired Bessie McIntyre, Callie's mother, supposedly to cook and clean around the house. But Bessie was considered "a black beauty," and for good reason…regardless of being a woman of color, she was probably the most beautiful woman in all of Louisiana. Of course, it was against everything the Devereaux name stood for to have Callie's father fall in love with such a woman. Nevertheless, that's exactly what happened…Bessie McIntyre was a woman Ted Devereaux just had to have.

Somewhat of a romance developed, and eventually Callie, a baby of color, was born a Devereaux too, something nobody thought would ever happen: a Creole, a child with negro blood in its veins, given the Devereaux name. It was said that screams could be heard from the Colonel's grave the night that it happened. Nevertheless, over the years, after all the other blood relatives had either died or been killed, the house, the Devereaux name, and everything else was passed down to Callie. Since then, Callie, after a long bout with an acute psychological breakdown, had turned the house into a high-class brothel and business second to none other in the sacred backwoods of Southern Louisiana.

The house itself was historical: a two-story brick mansion, the first of its kind in those parts of Louisiana. It had eight bedrooms, including the master bedroom, all of which were on the second floor.

The first floor had two big living rooms, one on each side, along with a pool hall and a dining room parlor used mostly for serving guests and having formal meals. The kitchen, with two pantry and storage areas, was behind it. Servant quarters were behind the kitchen.

The front of the house was lined with four huge white pillars and two often used rocking chairs, all of which were enclosed by a beautifully manicured lawn and a tall, black, wrought iron gated fence. From there, as far as the eye could see were prime, Southern Louisiana sugar cane, cotton, and/or tobacco fields. Even so, you'd better have on boots stepping out the back door because behind the house was nothing but miles and miles of deep swamp land, the Louisiana Bayou.

* * * *

After seeing him walk through the front door, and when she thought nobody was looking, Callie maintained her composure of being excited and overwhelmed, calmly made her way over, and whispered to Blu.

"Meet me upstairs, the first bedroom on the left, in about five minutes."

The ploy was meant to be inconspicuous, but the house was filled with all sorts of people, some of them the most prominent people in the area, all celebrating the New Year, which made it hard to miss Callie whispering something seductively in the ear of what turned out to be the only black face in the crowd there, to patronize a business.

Like everything else about the house, the master bedroom was huge, too. It had a king-size bed in it along with an old-fashioned French provincial living room set that Callie had arranged neatly around an antique fireplace, the kind that stood almost as tall as a human being.

"You do realize we're takin' a hell of a chance bein' up here together like this, don't you, Blu?" asked Callie once she'd made sure the bedroom door had been closed and locked behind them.

"If he comes up here, Johnny'll probably shoot and kill us both."

"Stop your worryin', girl…he's gotta catch us first," said Blu with the same slick smile on his face while depositing on the couch the hat and then the jacket he'd been wearing.

Callie and Blu had been taking the same kind of chances since when the two of them were teenagers, sneaking around like two horny dogs in heat, having sex whenever and where ever they could while everybody else, including Callie's father and both Blu's parents, worked the fields.

Back then, it was a cardinal sin in Louisiana for any man of color to be with a white woman. Many men had been found beaten and hanging from trees for just the assumption. In Callie's case, regardless of the fact that she had a black mother, which made her a negro as well, the danger was just as existent. The only thing that mattered was that she had smooth, pale, ivory skin, with long, straight hair flowing down her back. Not to mention that she was the daughter of Devereaux, a rich, white landowner, who insisted that Callie be treated as if she were white. But back then, all Creoles, *"light-skinned black folks,"* thought of themselves as white or that, although they were indeed Negroes, they were at least better than those with darker skin. It all spelled trouble for any man of real color who came along wanting to court her.

Blu's father had caught them both naked in the barn once. He beat Blu half to death for it, thinking that Blu needed to be taught a lesson. Thinking,

*"It could've and would've been a lot worse if anybody else had caught them."* Blu more than likely would've been hanged, shot, or maybe even beaten to death for real. Nevertheless, regardless of the danger, Callie and Blu seemed helplessly enthralled, to a point past infatuation, and obviously unable to stop. Especially Callie; when it came to Blu and sex, it was as if she could never get enough of either.

Finally, Blu's parents got fed up with the worry and sent Blu away to live with other relatives in another part of Louisiana, which was where he stayed, in an area outside of Baton Rouge, until after he became an adult.

Not much had changed since then other than the fact that years had passed, and while Blu was away manipulating women in another part of Louisiana, Callie had become somewhat of an unrestrained woman there in the same part of Louisiana where they were both from.

\* \* \* \*

Thirty minutes had gone by since Blu and Callie had gone upstairs, and things had gotten out of hand with the echoing sound of Callie's moans and groans flowing through the fireplace almost loud enough for everybody else in the house to hear, quite an embarrassment for Johnny Le Fleur.

"Oh, Blu...*Mon Cheri*," Callie was heard saying, panting, crying out after having yet another orgasm with Blu still working on the first. But a moment later, Blu, in a state of rapture himself, yelled out as well.

To stir up trouble, one of the more ornery, bigoted patrons yelled out,

"A nigger's upstairs givin' it to her good. Yeah, your girl Callie. What'a' you gonna do about it, Johnny?" the man asked.

That's when Johnny, being so embarrassed and angry, ran upstairs and began to kick the locked bedroom door. Three kicks later, the door came flying open. By then, Blu had gotten out of bed, had gathered all his belongings, and was climbing over the railing of the balcony.

But, before Blue could jump, a shot rang out from Johnny's gun, and Callie screamed, watching Blu collapse over the side, but not before his flesh was split, punctured, and torn apart with blood splattering the night.

Blu hit the ground below hard like a rock—you could hear it clearly. Even so, by the time Johnny had made it to the balcony and looked over the railing, Blu was gone.

# Chapter 1

Typically, a night in the Louisiana Bayou was silent, minus the distinct sound of bullfrogs, crickets, Katydids, and the occasional splash of water by fish, birds, alligators, and other wildlife living abundantly in the Louisiana swamp lands. But this was a night when Callie could be heard as well, screaming and shouting things like,

"Please, Doc…JUST GET IT OUTTA ME!!!"

"I will, but you gotta push a lil' harder," said Doc Elliott, positioning himself professionally as an obstetrician between Callie's long legs.

"Now, come on…PUSH!!!" he said, with both hands opened and held together like a catcher's mitt while Callie screamed and suffered, pushing as hard as she could. Callie had been in labor for almost thirteen hours, and everybody there with her, including Doc Elliott, was starting to get a little tired and impatient.

Doc Elliott, the only licensed medical doctor within fifty miles or so, had been around the Devereaux family for what seemed like forever. And for over fifty years, if there was a baby born in the area, and if midwives didn't deliver it, then Doc Elliott would've been the one to deliver it.

Two black nurses were there to assist, wiping Callie's brow, the blood, and all the feces…Callie was giving them a hard time, too. Finally, the baby's head popped out, which made it even more painful…Callie could barely take it.

With sweat pouring and not knowing what else to do, Callie looked directly at Doc Elliott and yelled again. "Don't just stand there…DO SOMETHIN'!!!"

"Oh, no you don't, Missy," said Doc Elliott, addressing Callie by the childhood nickname he'd given her,

"…don't blame this shit on me. If you'd kept your legs closed and stayed off your back once in a while, then maybe somethin' like this wouldn't have happened."

"Fuck you, Doc Elliott. FUCK YOU!!!" Callie yelled, straining and baring down even harder.

The whole time, Johnny Le Fleur had been standing at the back of the room like a shadow, arms folded, waiting and watching. Occasionally, he'd light a cigarette, reminding everybody in the room that he was still there. In nine months since the night he shot Blu, Johnny had been mostly nonresponsive, hardly saying a word to anybody. He seemed unstable, and people were afraid of him, thinking that at any moment, Johnny might snap and shoot them, too.

Things got even worse when Callie screamed one last time, and then the baby came out.

"It's a girl," one of the nurses said after Doc Elliott cut the umbilical cord and spanked the child, hearing it cry before passing it on.

"Awwwwww, Ms. Callie…she's beautiful," said the nurse after cleaning it and turning the baby so Callie could see it too. But it wasn't what Callie wanted to see; the baby looked nothing like Johnny Le Fleur or her, either. It looked almost exactly like Blu, with the same dark skin complexion and everything.

"Uh uh…no…that's not my child," she said, refusing to even look twice at the baby. The Devereaux name had already been tarnished and became a disgrace, and after the New Year's Eve incident, people, especially the white people in the area, were all starting to realize and take notice of Callie's true ethnicity, which meant the social status that she'd been able to maintain for so long, pretending to be a Caucasian, was over. Having Blu's baby would only make things worse.

Johnny saw the baby and began a tantrum, throwing, kicking, and knocking things over. Doc Elliott, along with both nurses, one holding the baby, took cover on the other side of the room in a corner until the tantrum was over. By then, Le Fleur was tired and out of breath, and the room had been turned into a complete mess.

"I can't believe you've done this, you and your nigger lover," he said, French accent intact, helping to express the torment,

"And to think I actually loved you." Johnny had known all along from the very beginning how promiscuous Callie was as a woman. He just hoped that one day she would change, which she had. It's just that since childhood, she'd been in love with Blu, and seeing him again made her lose all control...she couldn't help herself.

"I guess once a whore, always a whore," said Johnny once he'd calmed down enough to think things over and pack all his belongings.

"Madame...I'll tell you what. Have a good life...all of you," he said on his way out the door.

"Wait, Johnny...don't go...please," said Callie, but by then, Johnny Le Fleur had already walked out. They all heard it when the front door was slammed shut and when the car that he owned cranked. And then it took off with Johnny in it, driving away.

Callie lay on the bed, unable to move or do anything else but cry. Doc Elliott, with his experience in the medical field as both a physician and psychiatrist, thought it was time to comfort Callie and by setting things straight. He began by taking a seat on the bed beside her, taking a gentle hold of Callie's hand.

"Missy…you've lived your entire life pretending to be somebody that you're not...for so long until you've convinced yourself that the lie is true. Well…I hate to be the one to tell you, but it's over—it's time to accept the truth. You're not white, Missy, and you never have been. So, face the facts and care for your child…she needs you."

There was nothing that Callie could say—all she could do was cry. And whether what her good friend and personal physician said was right or wrong, the life that she'd lived and known for so long was indeed over.

*"So, as Doc Elliott said, I might as well face it,"* she thought with what little dignity she had left.

But then the baby started crying again, and so did Callie.

# Chapter 2

"A-B-C-D-E-F-G…H-I-J-K-L-M-N-O-P…Q-R-S…T-U-V…W-X…Y and Z. Now I know my A-B-C's, tell me what you think of me."

At two years old, Dominique was the smartest, sweetest little girl ever, walking around singing nursery rhymes and songs, as happy as any child should be. As expected, by the time she'd turned four, Dominique was still advancing, even more so actually, doing what she could to help in the kitchen, wanting to learn how to cook, and so forth. At six, she'd learned so much until she'd earned the right to be given responsibilities...she was given her own list of chores to do around the house. But Callie wasn't impressed, and to be mean, she would yell and say things like,

"You're not my daughter—you're too black and ugly. I wish you'd go someplace and hide your face…standin' there lookin' like your damn daddy." Nothing was ever said or meant as a compliment.

It all boiled down to Callie blaming and accusing Blu of being the cause of all that went wrong, including how she still longed for him.

And then there was the drinking, almost every day, whole bottles…vodka, gin, tequila…whatever there was available and wet with a content of alcohol in it…all Callie wanted was to get drunk enough to numb the bad feelings.

There was also the problem with Johnny; when he left, so went the clientele and most of the other girls, which basically destroyed the business of having a brothel. Eventually, profits from the crops gathered in the fields became the only source of revenue, which was way more than what she needed to live on, not to mention the millions she'd already inherited…interest alone paid her a hefty monthly income. Therefore, Callie, even without the profits from the brothel, still could afford a live-in maid, a butler, a cook, and anything else she wanted. Consequently, people who knew Callie didn't care that she might be suffering from some form of mental depression…nobody felt sorry for her. All they knew was that the silver spoon she'd been born with was still feeding her and feeding her well.

Other than that, Callie's daughter, Dominique, was the only one that people really cared about, which was something that made Callie's bad behavior and resentment grow even more.

# Chapter 3

Callie made it a habit of sleeping late, past twelve in the afternoon. And Mary Owens, the West Indian housekeeper, never let her live it down.

"Well, good mornin' to ya', Ms. Callie…or should I say good afternoon?" said the housekeeper after giving Callie a stern look and then starting in on her just as Callie was coming out of the bedroom.

Mary, a plus-sized woman, was a Jamaican immigrant who spoke heavily in patois, so much so that, at times, what she said was hard to understand.

"I hope you know it's Thursday, not Saturday or a holiday, no? And yes, I did the child's hair already and sent her off to school in one of those pretty little dresses you bought for her."

"Good…then you did your job. That's why I'm still payin' you," said Callie, not particularly fond of Mary and giving her very little time and attention. Instead, wrapping a heavy house coat around the nightgown she was wearing and hurried to make it down the staircase.

After a long night of drinking, Callie's insides were like a hot box, and the only thing she was thinking about was the kitchen, where she might find a cold glass of water to drink and cool things off.

"Hey…good mornin', Emma," she said, once she'd gotten there, in the kitchen, still behind on time though, and hung-over stricken, dying of thirst.

"What're you makin' for dinner?" she asked in casual conversation. She got a clean glass from the dish rack, and a pitcher filled with cold water was in the refrigerator. After drinking as much as she wanted, Callie then found an aspirin bottle on one of the counters and, in the cabinet above it, found some matches and a Lucky Strike pack that only had one cigarette left in it.

"I made gumbo for lunch; you can have some of that now if you want. I haven't decided on dinner yet.

"But why? Was there somethin' special you'd like to have?" asked Emma, knowing how temperamental Callie could sometimes be, especially when it came down to what she wanted to eat.

Emma and William had been working for the Devereaux family for more than fifty years, since before the Colonel died, long before Callie had been born. Later, when she was hired, Callie's mother and Emma became friends; both cooked and worked in the kitchen. William served as butler and chauffeur, which included driving the family car to run errands. But as of lately, the main thing he'd been doing was driving Dominique back and forth from school.

"Emma...do you remember how momma used to go fishin' and catch all those Brims and Crappies?"

"Of course I do. Most of the time, I wouldn't go with her, not when she went back there in the swamp, but what she caught, I would shol' help clean and fry 'em," said Emma, smiling at the thought of old memories.

"Yeah, well...that's what I have a taste for, some fresh fried fish."

"William's out runnin' errands, but I'll be sure to send for some when he gets back."

"Have him bring back another bottle of gin, too, and a carton of cigarettes," said Callie on her way back upstairs.

* * * *

Outside, the rain was pouring a lot more than just cats

and dogs—it seemed to be coming down in buckets. On the floor beside the bed, Callie found an opened bottle of gin. Only about a quarter of the bottle's contents were left, which was enough after turning the bottle up and downing it to get a buzz on and make Callie feel a whole lot better.

She'd lost the robe and was lying in bed again, reminiscing, thinking not only of the first lover she'd ever had but of the one who she thought had been the best.

"Blu…hands down," she said, smiling mischievously, wishing Blu was there now to fulfill the need.

"Oh, wow…how long has it been?" she asked, unable to remember.

"Too long," she said a moment later, sliding down the white undies she'd been wearing and discarding them on the floor beside the bed.

The rain was still coming down hard, and the room was quiet and still, and just dark enough, but not too dark to see. Light from the flame of a lantern was making a shadowy silhouette of Callie's opened legs appear on the wall. The picture was enticing, even for the person the legs belonged to.

The heat was on, that was for sure, with the way Callie was being turned on. The room was getting warmer and warmer by the minute, all caused by thought and tender emotions.

And then it all started to happen.

"Oh, my God," she said, crying out softly after the penetration of two soft fingertips. "Blu…hands down," she said, again, imagining things as if he was there, but at the same time sending the fingertips deeper until both entire fingers were wet and buried within.

"Oh…my…God," it didn't take long—she was almost there, an orgasm just seconds away with both fingers working wonderfully, massaging, thrusting, and exploring at intervals.

"Oh, shit!!!" she said, finally in one last cry, but not before the door burst open, sending in the light. And then Dominique came walking in right afterward, spoiling the moment.

"Mommy, look," she said, holding a piece of paper up in front of her, "Got a good grade today."

"Mommy?" asked Callie, as if Dominique had just broken a cardinal rule. "First of all, don't ever come in here again without knockin'…you hear?

"And second…what the fuck did I tell you about that

'mommy' shit? My name is Callie…Ms. Callie to you, understand?

"Now, GET THE HELL OUTTA HERE, and close the damn door behind you," she yelled, breaking Dominique's poor little heart.

The tears didn't come right away, that's because she couldn't believe that somebody like her mother could be so mean. But then, when the tears finally did come, so did an explosion of all the hurt and pain that had been building for so long. That's when Dominique turned and ran.

"CLOSE MY DAMN DOOR!!!" Callie yelled, but Dominique kept running down the hallway and straight down the staircase. The back door was opened, and Dominique ran through that, too, outside in the rain.

Emma was in the kitchen and saw it when Dominique ran by. It was too late to call for her, so Emma called William—he was at the kitchen table, nursing two sore knees.

"William…she just ran out the door. Go get her," Emma said, sounding stressed and upset.

"Go get who, Emma?" William asked, wishing to be left alone for a while—it was one of those days when he was in a lot of pain.

"Who was it that ran out the door?" he asked, gathering himself.

"Dominique…there's no tellin' what her mother has said or done to make her feel bad this time. All I know is that she took off runnin' and ran in there," said Emma, pointing towards the thick brush of the swamp.

But the rain was still coming down hard, and arthritis was giving William, the seventy-two-year-old man, a fit. After thinking about it for a moment, William got up slowly, walked outside on the back porch, and called out.

"DOMINIQUE!!! It's gon' be alright…come on back in the house, baby…it's rainin' out here." But there was no response or sound other than the continuous pitter-patter of raindrops.

Five minutes went by, and then ten. Thirty minutes later, William and Emma were both worried and scared half to death, afraid something terrible might've happened. The swamp land could be a very dangerous place if you weren't careful or familiar with the terrain. And even then, with being familiar with it, big, strong, grown men had been known to disappear in swamps and never come back, regardless.

*"Which leaves very little chance for a small child like Dominique,"* thought Emma, becoming even more worried

## Buckets, Shovels, Ghost and Worms

and terrified.

# Chapter 4

Ms. Ladeaux

The idea was to run and keep running and get as far away from the house and her mother as she could. Being out in the rain just wasn't supposed to be a part of it. So, at a moment's notice, Dominique decided to run for the shelter in the woods. When she did, the rain still came down on her, just not nearly as much. However, the darkness and all the eerie sounds that she heard were more frightening than anything she'd ever imagined. But even so, the stubbornness, or the resolution of hearing it when William first yelled out, calling her by name,

"DOMINIQUE!!!" meant that she still hadn't gone far enough. So, she kept running and running anyway until finally she got tired and couldn't run anymore. But as soon as she stopped, that's when both feet started sinking, and in no time at all, Dominique was stuck in the mud.

Right after that, things started falling from trees, creepy crawlers like spiders and snakes…big snakes…three of them, slithering quickly over the water towards her.

When Doc Elliott passed away, Callie took Dominique to the funeral, so she knew what a dead body looked like…like a person sleeping peacefully, actually. But from the way that people cried about death, even like how Callie cried at the funeral, Dominique imagined dying might really hurt badly.

And when it came to snakes, William had already warned her about them. One day, after picking her up from school, he'd killed one in the front yard,

"Gotta be careful with these things," he said, holding it up so Dominique could see it,

"They dangerous as hell…the poison from one bite can kill you," he told her, which made it just that much more frightening, thinking about how she might get bit now by one of the ones she saw crawling towards her.

So, in fear, she yelled out,

"MAAAAAA!!!" even the thought of seeing 'Ms. Callie' again was more entertaining than the sight of the three slithering reptiles in front of her.

One of them had actually gotten close enough to bite, within striking distance—its body had curled up and everything. Its head reared back, but just before the snake and the lightning quickness of its venomous fangs could strike, the spade of a shovel came down hard on it first, killing it. The others were killed as well.

"You have to watch your step and be very careful when you walkin' back here, sweetie," said the old gray-haired woman holding the shovel.

Looking from the ground up, the first thing Dominique saw was a pair of galosh boots and then the long skirt the woman was wearing, which made it kind of weird, seeing a woman in the swamp wearing a skirt. But then, looking down at herself, Dominique was still wearing the same sweater and dress that she'd worn at school that day, which, to the woman, probably didn't make any sense either.

The woman also had on a thick, gray sweater and a red hat, the kind that most women only wore out at parties or nightclubs—this was something Dominique knew from watching Callie get dressed to go out.

"What made you come all the way out here?" asked the woman, with the spade part of the shovel stuck down in the ground while she leaned on the handle of it.

"My momma was bein' mean. So, I got mad and ran out

of the house."

The woman chuckled, her way of laughing.

"Honey…there'll be a whole lotta other mean people in the world that you'll see too. But that doesn't mean you have to take off runnin' every time you see one," said the woman, ending what she was saying on a note of all seriousness,

"Now come on here and let me get you outta there," she said, reaching out, taking hold of Dominique under both armpits and pulling until she came straight up out of the mud.

"What about my shoes?" Dominique asked afterward, seeing that both feet were dangling bare, "…they still stuck in the mud."

"Don't worry 'bout 'em…tell ya, momma, to spend some of that money she got and buy you some more," said the woman, walking off, leading the way with the shovel in one hand and a bucket of freshly dug worms in the other.

"Hey…you never told me your name," said Dominique, barely able to keep up, walking as fast as she could in bare feet,

"And where're we goin'?" she asked.

"My name's Ladeaux…Ms. Ladeaux.

"What's yours?" the woman asked, still in stride, sloshing through mud and water, walking forward at a quick pace.

"My name's Dominique…Dominique Devereaux."

"Alright then, Little Ms. Devereaux…nice ta' meet 'cha. And as far as where we're goin'…I don't know 'bout you, but I'm goin' fishin'."

# Chapter 5

Over an hour had gone by since Dominique first ran out of the house. Mary and Emma were both pacing the kitchen floor, worried sick.

"Lord…please don't let nothin' happen to that poor lil' child," said Emma, feeling somewhat responsible and sorry, thinking she should've somehow been able to stop Dominique when she first ran out the door.

And Mary,

"Oh Lord," she said, on the verge of crying,

"…just bring her back safely," it was all the two women could do: worry themselves and pray.

\* \* \* \*

The rain had stopped, so William, after loading the shotgun, decided to finally go look for her.

Callie was still upstairs, nursing a bottle of vodka that she'd found stashed away, totally unaware of what was going on downstairs.

William had just stepped off the back porch, gun in hand, when Dominique came out of the swamp, dragging behind her a whole string of freshly caught Brim and Crappie.

"Look," she said, smiling as if there was nothing wrong, "...look what I got."

At first, William didn't say anything, thinking that if it were his child, he would've taken a strap to Dominique right then and there. But he didn't. Instead, he reached down and took the fish.

"Gimme these...and go on in the house," he said, speaking somewhat angrily, too upset to really talk much,

"... got us all worried 'bout you."

It wasn't until after he'd taken the string from her and tried to lift it himself that William finally started wondering about how and where Dominique might've gotten so many fish.

The kitchen had a double sink. The fish that were on the string damn near filled one of them up completely.

"Girl...you almost gave me a heart attack," said Mary once Dominique had gotten inside. For most of her young life, Mary had been more of a mother to Dominique than anybody else, including Callie, and the love she had for her was genuine and true.

"What I wanna know is this," Emma said, pointing at the sink, still amazed by what she saw William put in it,

"...where did all these come from?" she asked.

"Ms. Ladeaux caught 'em. I helped, but most of 'em she caught," said Dominique, proud of what she'd done.

William and Emma looked at each other; both were in shock after hearing Dominique's explanation. Images of people had been known to materialize and vanish in the swamp all the time, images of people who didn't actually exist.

"Where's Ms. Ladeaux at now?" William asked, quizzing Dominique, sure that she was either lying or mistaken or that maybe it was just a coincidence and a woman had, in fact, taken Dominique fishing for real. People, former slaves and others running from the law, and some who just refused to accept the more modernized ways of the world, were known to sometimes take refuge in the swamp. But then, what Dominique said next gave Emma and William even more reason to wonder.

"I was lost and stuck in the mud, and Ms. Ladeaux got me out. After we went fishin', she showed me how to get back home, but when I turned to say goodbye, Ms. Ladeaux was gone. I looked around but didn't see her anywhere."

William and Emma looked at each other again, but this time, Mary had a curious look on her face as well; she'd also heard weird stories of unexplainable phenomena that happened in the swamp.

"Come on, child…let me get you cleaned up," Mary said, deciding to leave it up to the elders, William and Emma, to figure things out.

But before they left, Emma leaned down and told Dominique,

"Look, baby…don't tell ya' momma 'bout this, ok? Let's just keep what happened between us here in the kitchen, alright?"

"Ok…yes, ma'am," said Dominique before she and Mary walked away.

After they were gone, William asked Emma,

"Why don't you want Callie to know 'bout this?"

"Because…it was just earlier this afternoon when she was standin' right in here wit' me, talkin' 'bout the same thing, how her mother used to go catch Brim and Crappie, and that fresh fish was what she had a taste for.

"You know Callie's mind ain't right…hearin' 'bout somethin' like this might be all it takes to push her over the edge again."

"Yeah, you might be right. But you don't think the woman Dominique saw in the woods today actually had anything to do wit' Callie's momma, do you?" asked William,

"Her name wasn't Ladeaux—it was McIntyre…Bessie McIntyre."

"I know…but I have heard of a woman they called Ms. Ladeaux…a voodoo woman. She supposedly died a long time ago, but some say she might've come back. I can't say that I know that for sure, but I have heard of things a lot crazier that's happened," said Emma, turning the water on in the sink.

"Yeah, I have too, and I know that anything's possible. But I doubt very seriously if the woman Dominique saw back there in the woods had anything to do wit' Bessie.

"We gon' find out, though…I'm'a go in there tomorrow myself, then I'll know for sure."

As an afterthought, William asked Emma,

"Hey…I guess I don't have to go buy no fish now, huh?"

"No, but Callie still wanted you to get her some more gin and cigarettes."

William thought about it and then told Emma,

"Alright, but I shouldn't go get nothin'. That's her problem…she drinks too much. And one day she gon' end up burnin' the whole house down wit' all that damn smokin'."

"Let's pray that she don't," said Emma, holding a knife, already starting to clean fish.

"…don't forget, we live here too."

# Chapter 6

The next morning, William was up bright and early, as usual. He had the shotgun loaded and ready, leaning against the wall, a cup of coffee in hand, and was sitting on the back porch waiting for Emma to finish making breakfast.

As usual, Eddie Lauren, the field hand supervisor, had already been by to report in. But since Callie didn't get up early anymore, all communications were done between him and William. Actually, Emma, William, and Mary were depended upon to do just about everything, which included taking care of Dominique and running the house and farm.

"What you 'bout to do?" Emma asked after William sat down at the kitchen table; she noticed he hadn't dressed himself in the black pants, jacket, and white shirt he usually wore, presenting himself decent enough as a butler or chauffeur. Instead, he had on a dark red sweater, jeans, and black boots,

"If you don't mind, I think I'm'a eat first," he told Emma, sharing a smile, kidding with her. But Emma didn't think what he said was funny.

"Alright, alright…I'm'a drop Dominique off at school first like I always do," he said, speaking more seriously. "When I get back, though, I'm'a go walk around back there in the swamp for a while, see what I can see."

"You takin' anybody wit' you?" asked Emma, ignoring William's sarcasm and smile, showing concern instead.

"Nah…I figure I'll be alright as long as I got a gun. Ain't nothin' gon' get me."

"That ain't what I'm worried about. You are almost seventy-three years old, William. What if you get back there and get stuck in the mud or somethin' like Dominique did, then what?"

"I won't…she's a child, remember?" said William, taking offense,

"…and I might be old, but unlike Dominique, I know what to look for, where to walk, and where not to walk.

"I'll be alright," he said, William's way of ending the conversation. For over forty years, even before the two of them were married, they'd been having the same kind of early morning conversations. And William, being dominant, always found a way to end them…his way.

Nevertheless, what he said was true; the swamp wasn't something he didn't already know about.

"Not after all the gators and hogs I've gone back there and killed," he thought, saying what he had to say under his breath but feeling somewhat insulted by Emma's doubt and mistrust.

"I used to go back there and fish, too. I'm the one who first took Bessie back there and got her started fishin'."

\* \* \* \*

In town, he dropped Dominique off at school and then bought himself some chewing tobacco before making the drive back home. Surprisingly, when he got back, although dressed in only a gown and house coat, Callie was awake and sitting on the front porch in one of the rocking chairs, smoking a cigarette.

"I would say it's gon' rain, but it already did yesterday," said William, teasing her about being up so early.

"I know, right," said Callie, exhaling smoke, finding it funny too.

"While you playin', it's probably gon' storm again with

how early I'm up this mornin'."

The two of them shared a laugh. But on a more serious note, Callie told William,

"I couldn't sleep…I was thinkin' 'bout momma. It's like she came to me in a dream, wanting, wishing, and even asking me to do better, especially wit' Dominique.

"She made me feel real bad."

"She probably did," said William, noticing that Callie had been crying.

"Me and your mother knew each other very well, and I know for a fact that if she was here, she wouldn't be happy…not at all.

"You know what you gotta do to straighten things out, though, right?" asked William before turning to walk away.

"Yeah…I do," said Callie, starting to cry again. "…and I will, you'll see."

"I sure hope so. But it ain't me you gotta prove it to. It's that child of yours; she needs you," said William. And with that, he turned and walked away. He had a lot on his mind, too—things he refused to share or talk about with anybody, not Callie or Emma either. It was better if he could just be alone for a while, and William knew the perfect place.

\* \* \* \*

Every few feet, a cypress tree standing thirty feet tall or better, covered with lichens and Spanish moss, was planted deeply in muddy water, which altogether was what the swamp mostly consisted of. Because of it, very little light shined through. Nevertheless, when William walked in, the nighttime chirping and croaking of bullfrogs and crickets had been replaced by a symphony of early morning quacking ducks.

Every so often, a pair of keen alligator eyes would surface and peep over large bodies of standing water. And from up above, an owl would hoot. But it all fit well and in harmony with what nature had in mind for this part of the country. William sure thought so, enjoying it and only then realizing how much he missed the scenery and tranquil sound…but still not as much as he missed Bessie.

# Chapter 7

**Sept 1911**

As ancient history goes…both were seventeen and meeting each other for the very first time, William and Bessie, long before either of them worked for the Devereaux family. As a matter of fact, back then, it was Jack Le Roux that they both worked for and in the northern parts of Louisiana, near Shreveport, far from the Bayou.

A tear ran down the cheek of William's face with him thinking about it, remembering things as terrible as they were and had been back then, but also wishing he could start time all over again and do things differently.

* * * *

Jack Le Roux, as it was and had been with the Devereaux family and many of the other white landowners in the South, initially ignored the freedom laws against slavery,

"Something that President Lincoln and the Union Army are still trying to force upon us," the land owners would say...this, even after the Civil War was over. And some of them, for as long as they could, had, in some form or fashion, kept the slave practice alive.

Even so, some Black Americans, in remembrance of rebellious leaders like Nat Turner, who, no matter how brutal he was, gave blacks the idea and courage to revolt and stand up for themselves, demanded to be freed.

In the eyes of some land owners and overseers, all that did was label those involved as "trouble makers," and for it, they were either shot or hanged, illegally, of course. But then, for Blacks, there was always the refuge and sanctuary of northern states, or even Canada and Europe, where every man was free and given more of a chance to earn his or her stay and keep. The only problem was getting there.

Eventually, things would change, but until then, living in a depressed state was just something that poor black folks in the South had to deal with; even the so-called house niggas and sharecroppers weren't protected or shielded from the unfair and sometimes inhuman practices.

* * * *

Jack Le Roux, whose grandfather had also been a Colonel in the Confederate Army, had just returned home from Mississippi, and with him, he'd brought back over a dozen black men, women, and children, most of whom he wanted to work the fields. Their travel had been long and quite uncomfortable; that's because Jack had most of them, the women and children, bunched together as passengers in one single wagon. One particular passenger on the wagon was Bessie McIntyre.

Once he'd gotten there and stopped the wagon in front of the house, Jack climbed down and immediately started spewing orders.

He told William,

"Help 'em get everything unloaded and show 'em all to their quarters. After that's done, then take the horses' 'round back and put 'em in the field to water and graze."

"Yessir," said William, as obedient as ever...Jack's right-hand man and the only worker Jack felt that he could trust and depend on to get things done the way he wanted them done.

After every return trip, as if on cue, William would be standing there, right in front of the house, waiting to carry out any order Jack had to give. There was something different about this return trip, though, and it had nothing to do with Jack. It was the way that William responded. For one thing, he and Bessie couldn't seem to take their eyes off each other. And then, William moved a little slower than usual, carrying out Jack's orders. And when the two of them got close enough, William carried on casually as if it was alright, asking Bessie,

"You hungry? I got some food if you are." Actually, William didn't think anybody besides Bessie had heard him, and actually, nobody hadn't, but Jack was watching and saw everything, which was just as bad.

"Thanks for askin'. Yes, I'm starvin'," said Bessie, sharing a smile.

"Believe it or not, I ain't had nothin' to eat in two whole days."

"Don't worry, I'll get you somethin'," said William, showing more interest in Bessie than he was in what Jack told him to do.

Even at seventeen, Bessie had already grown into a very lovely, sensual, curvaceous young woman and knew what men liked, especially a young stud like William.

With him helping her down off the wagon, Bessie smiled again, but mischievously, and lifted the long skirt that she was wearing, not only to step down without tripping over it but also so she could tease William, showing him a little of what she had underneath it.

She figured that if William was Jack's right-hand man, then surely he would have access not only to as much food as she wanted but also to anything else she might want or need.

Later that night, after sharing a good meal, Bessie rewarded him with some of the best sex he'd ever had in hopes that from that point on, he'd be locked in and would not only answer to Jack's every beck and call but would answer to hers too.

Over a length of time, the plan was carried out and worked to perfection. The only problem was that, eventually, the two fell in love, and then Bessie got pregnant.

As a single man, Jack had acquired Bessie mainly in hopes that she would not only cook and clean for him around the house but would also become his occasional bed warmer on lonely nights. But he felt that that had all been ruined when Bessie got pregnant, thanks to William.

So, to punish him, Jack, a man who stood a towering six foot six, whipped and beat a poor, average-sized William until blood oozed. And then he banished William off the property. In the end, things couldn't have been any worse, especially not for William.

Only a few days later, William, traveling incognito through forest and woods, ran into a group of other blacks traveling through the woods...the most unusual situation, with them being led by a woman, Ms. Harriet Tubman.

After hearing William's story and explanation of what had happened, Ms. Tubman promised that if he went back and got Bessie and rejoined the group, she would then lead them all to freedom and a much better Northern life. This was after the emancipation and Juneteenth, June 19th, 1865, when slaves were supposed to have been freed already anyway. For some, freedom wouldn't come until President Lincoln's Union Army actually showed up to make the landowners free.

William laughed and thought it to be hopelessly insane...ridiculous, and maybe even suicidal for him to even think about stepping foot back on Jack Le Roux's property again.

He thought the same thing about "this woman" and what she was saying,

"...whoever she is," he thought, with all the people who were there with her believing that she was some sort of savior with the answer to all their problems.

"You would first have to cross highly prejudiced states like Mississippi, Alabama, and Georgia, not to mention the Carolinas and Virginia, and that's just to get you across the Mason-Dixon Line," said William, laughing afterward.

"Huh…good luck," he said and walked away. But then, there he was some fifty-odd years later, wishing he'd taken Ms. Tubman up on the offer, especially after hearing about "The Underground Railroad" and about how famous Ms. Tubman had become for leading so many other enslaved black people to freedom.

He was so caught up in the reverie of past days that he almost didn't see or hear it when out of the thick brush came a wild boar hog, charging right at him. It was just pure instincts that gave William the ability to turn and lower the barrel of the gun in time enough to kill it with one single blast.

The boar had a set of four-inch tusks that would've done him a lot of serious damage had William not killed it.

"I bet Emma would'a never let me live that one down," he said, thinking out loud after the smoke cleared and he'd somewhat regained his composure.

He was just about over it when another hog and three small pigs came out of the brush as well, squealing as if they'd been shot too but scurrying off in the opposite direction.

"They tryin'a' give me a heart attack," thought William with the way the heart in his chest was pounding, fast and harder than a drum beat.

Emma was right; he had no business in the swamp alone. The next time, he might not be so lucky.

Later, after having two field hands retrieve, skin, and dress the hog, William decided that having a barbecue was in order.

# Chapter 8

Of all people, it was the old man, Colonel Luke Devereaux, who eventually came along and saved William. Albeit not intentionally, that's for sure, but nonetheless, that's exactly what happened, which, in the end, turned out to be a good thing for both of them.

\* \* \* \*

Weeks had gone by since William had been banished from Jack's property, and he still hadn't found any place else to go yet. He'd been living, more or less, out in the woods the whole time, enduring the constant threat of alligators and snakes, the constant buzzing and bites of mosquitoes, all while surviving on virtually nothing perishable to eat. Well, on this particular day, an over-intoxicated, half-asleep Luke Devereaux was in a hurry trying to get home; the first Devereaux grandchild of his was expected to be born soon, something that Luke didn't want to miss. The only problem was that he'd stayed up drinking most of the night, and not only was he exhausted, but he was dead drunk, too.

Luke, a big man at six foot three, two hundred and eighty pounds, was burly and a little thick around the waist and so drunk that he could barely walk, not to mention drive. This was all something that happened during a return trip home from Little Rock, Arkansas, where leaders of the Confederate Army still met once or twice a year.

Early that morning, Luke got behind the wheel and tried driving home anyway. Somehow, he made it all the way back across the Louisiana state line before finally veering off the road, running smack into a willow tree,

"BAM!!!" the crash sounded.

Luckily, the tree hadn't grown to its full extent yet, and it gave way as soon as the car hit it. Therefore, the impact wasn't too great, and nobody got hurt, not Luke or the other person riding with him. The car wasn't damaged much either.

Right away, as soon as he heard the crash, William came running as fast as he could to find out what happened and see if anybody needed help.

When he got there, the first thing he did was look inside the car.

"Sir...you alright?" he asked after seeing a gray-haired Luke Devereaux slumped over on the steering wheel. Luke hadn't shaved in a while, and the whiskers he had on his face were gray as well.

"What does it look like, huh? Does it look like I'm alright? Jesus fucking Christ," said Luke, coming to his senses more from being drunk, tired, and sleepy than it was from him having a bad head injury.

"Tell me this, though, boy...have you ever driven a car?" asked Luke, slurring each word badly and smelling as if he'd drank the entire contents of a whiskey barrel,

"Chester, back there, is too damn drunk to drive, and so am I."

"I'm not, though, sir...I ain't drunk...and yes, I can drive...I've driven many automobiles," said William, knowing a good thing when he saw one. It didn't take long to realize that the drunken old man sitting there before him might be the only meal ticket he'd see come around for a while.

So, he told Luke,

"I'll take you anywhere you wanna go, sir...just let me know when you ready."

"Boy…you must have the brains of a jackass, tellin' me to let you know when I'm ready.

"Damn it, I'm ready now.

"Well…? What the hell are you waitin' for? Mr. 'Let me know when I'm ready.'

"Get in," said Luke, opening the door for him and then sliding over on the seat before William could say another word.

"Head southeast, and keep goin' 'till I tell ya' to stop."

"Yes, sir," said William, eager to get going. The next thing he knew, Luke was fast asleep, snoring loudly.

* * * *

In the back seat was Chester, the butler/chauffeur, another gray-haired old soul, even older than Luke presumably, but with what looked to be a mouth of all new, white dentures, which was what made William take notice, seeing him in the rear-view mirror, smiling as if the happiest man alive.

"He definitely ain't feelin' no pain, that's for sure," said William, thinking to himself.

But after paying closer attention, William realized that

although Chester was smiling, he really didn't look so good. He was rail thin for one thing; both the black pants and white shirt he had on draped his body. And his skin was awfully dark, too dark actually; the color of Chester's skin seemed to blend right in perfectly with the black color of the pants he had on and with the black car seat.

William had seen Chester smile, nod his head a few times, and look around, but other than that, Chester hadn't said a word or moved any other part of his body. It was obvious that he'd had his fair share of what they'd been drinking—Luke had even said so himself.

"Aw, he's alright, probably just got a little too drunk," thought William, dismissing any other concerns he might've been having to make him feel sorry for Chester. From that point on, he kept his eyes focused more on the road and his mind on where they were supposed to be going.

It wasn't until hours later that William came across several men on horseback blocking the road. Each of them wore big Stetson hats and shiny law enforcement badges and bore arms of large pistols and long-barreled rifles.

"SIR!!!" said William, on the verge of panic, nudging Luke to wake him out of his sleep.

Only one of the men got off his horse and came over,

## Buckets, Shovels, Ghost and Worms

"Where'n' the hell you think you goin', boy?" he asked, stone-faced, showing authority.

"We're headed home, Jennings," said Luke, still very much intoxicated and sleepy but leaning over a little so the officer could see him.

"Oh, Mr. Devereaux…sorry," said the officer, crouching to get a better look inside the car and then apologizing sincerely and as quickly as he could when he saw Luke.

"Dang…I swear…I didn't see you sittin' there. It's my fault…I should've at least recognized the car.

"Again, sir…my apologies."

Although big, strong, and armed to the tee with other men there to back him up, the officer still seemed to melt in the presence of Luke Devereaux, and understandably so. Luke knew most high-ranking law enforcement officers by name and knew all the mayors and deputy mayors personally. He even knew the Governor of Louisiana himself and was well-liked and highly regarded by all who knew him, which meant that at the drop of a hat, with one word from Luke, the officer crouched down beside the car would be out of a job, and the officer knew it.

So, if he had to kiss a little ass, "So be it," thought the

officer, "...at least I'll still be employed."

"It's not a problem, Jennings," said Luke, honored by the respect the officer had shown him.

"...but if you don't mind me askin'..., why are you all out here like this anyway, blockin' the road? Has somethin' happened that maybe I should be aware of?"

"Oh...no, sir. We're just doin' random searches of wagons and other vehicles to catch those transportin' alcohol illegally.

"And they're also havin' a meetin'," said the officer, averting his attention as well as Luke's to a clearance a hundred yards or so off the road where a giant wooden cross had been erected and sat on fire. Men in hooded white robes were gathered around it.

"To hell with Lincoln and his proposal to free slaves," one man shouted. "In Louisiana, we make our own laws."

"Ahhh...I see. A Klan rally...and you're lookin' for bootleggers," said Luke as if he understood clearly.

"Ok, well...have a good time...and I hope you catch 'em."

"Don't worry, we will," said the officer, speaking with confidence but relieved that Luke was understanding and not upset about being stopped,

"And you have a good evenin' too, sir," he said before backing away.

And with that, they were waved through. And it's a good thing because William had just about peed his pants.

However, they hadn't got ten feet away when Chester, speaking for the first time, said,

"I'm glad he ain't ask to look in the trunk…we'd all be in trouble if he did."

Chester then burst out laughing, thinking that what he said was so funny. But not William or Luke, either. As a matter of fact, Luke turned in his seat and told him,

"Aw, be the quiet, old man, and let me be the one to worry 'bout them and what's in the trunk of this car. You hear?" Luke asked.

"Yes sir…you the boss," said Chester, and with that, he got quiet again and remained that way.

Luke's trip to Arkansas wasn't just to discuss strategies or to reminisce old times with former soldiers of the Confederate Army. He'd gone there to buy liquor. In the trunk were thirty-six individually wrapped gallon jugs of some of the best moonshine ever made, illegally, of course.

They'd been wrapped individually to keep the jugs from breaking but also to keep them from making too much noise rattling together.

An hour or so later, Luke was directing William where to turn on a dirt road and then into the Driveway of the Devereaux house.

"Alright, old geezer," said Luke, yawning and stretching in the front seat when William stopped the car.

"Show William, here, what to do so you and him can unload and stash all the liquor. Be careful, though; I don't want a single bottle broken, you hear?" he said, turning in the seat to make sure that Chester was paying attention.

When he did, he saw that Chester still had a smile on his face, and his eyes were opened, but he seemed to be looking off into space.

William saw it, too, in the rear-view mirror. And when Luke reached back and touched him, Chester was cold and as stiff as a board. Somewhere between the time when they'd gone through the roadblock and getting home, Chester had died, and rigor mortis had set in.

Other than the times when Luke had gone off to fight in the war, he and Chester had known and been around each other all their lives. And, despite the fact that Luke had once owned him, over the years, he and Chester had become the best of friends.

Luke turned back around in the seat and stared out the front window for a while. Although short-lived, it was his way of grieving. There was an awkward moment of silence, and then, after gathering himself, Luke turned to William and said,

"There's a small lil' shack about a mile or so down the road on the left-hand side. His folks live there. They'll wanna give him a decent funeral.

"Take him down there…when you get back, go around the house and come in the back door…Emma'll feed you and show you where your quarters are."

"What…you givin' me a job, sir?" asked William, surely bothered by Chester's demise but more concerned about himself.

"A job?" asked Luke, "Yeah, if you want it. Chester was both the butler and chauffeur and since he's gone…well…the job pays a dollar and a half a week plus meals, room and board. Take it or leave it."

Luke didn't wait around for an answer; instead, he got out and stumbled on towards the house, leaving William there with a dead man in the car.

# Chapter 9

Club Watts, one of New Orleans's most popular and elegant night spots, was where the one and only Ms. Billie Holiday was on stage giving a live performance, singing all of her songs, including the new hit,

"Good Mornin' Heartache."

It just so happened Bessie was there too, a dream come true for her. But unfortunately, she was stuck backstage in a dish pit with a sink filled with soapy, hot water. Almost every cup, glass, and plate, along with all the silverware that was there at Club Watts, not to mention several big pots and pans, were all stacked high, waiting to be washed. Therefore, the best she could do to enjoy it while Billie sang was hope, from backstage, that she'd be able to hear while she worked, trying to finish before the performance was over.

But then, even that got interrupted,

"Come on, now, girl…we ain't got all day. You need to

hurry up," this was said by Ethel, the same heavy-set black woman who hired Bessie and told her that working there wouldn't be so bad,

"Can't none of us leave 'til everything's done back here…and I got other things to do besides wait on you."

"Alright…I'm hurryin'," said Bessie, wanting to hurry and be finished more than anybody.

The place was packed, standing room only. Thankfully, every person who was there that night had already been fed before the show started.

"Thank God," said Bessie, tired of seeing more dirty plates and things being brought in.

The rest of the kitchen help, including the wait staff and cooks, were all out front waiting to be told they could leave.

"At least while they wait, they get to hear and watch Billie sing," thought Bessie, wishing she could see it too; Billie Holiday, one of the first female Black Americans to become a renowned singer, was somebody that Bessie idolized.

"Good Mornin' heartache, you old gloomy sight.

"Good Mornin' heartache thought we said goodbye last night…

"Wish I'd forget you, but you're here to stay.

"It seems I met you when my love went away…

"I've got those Monday Blues straight through Sunday Blues…

"Good mornin' heartache, here we go again.

"You're the one who knew me when.

"Might as well get used to you hangin' around.

"Good mornin' heartache…sit down."

With only a few lines of lyrics, the song seemed to tell Bessie's whole life story, which in nineteen years had been nothing else other than heartaches.

\* \* \* \*

Jack Le Roux became the meanest son-of-a-bitch ever, taking the anger he had against William out on everybody else.

One night, he told Bessie,

"You either go in there and take your clothes off, or you can high tail your ass right out the door. It's up to you," the whole time, he was standing directly in front of her, but yelling and pointing in each direction as he gave her the options of what to do.

Then, as an added measure, hoping to sway Bessie's decision, he told her,

"It's a long way back to Mississippi, especially walkin' along a dark road this time of night."

Later, she thought she would die with him on top of her, humping and grunting like a wild animal. Each time, Bessie's mind would be elsewhere. She did the same thing when the man her mother was married to used to do it, which was why she eventually ran away from home. Except this time, she had a baby inside of her, William's baby.

She dreamed of one day having a family, a real family that included not only having children but having a husband, too.

So far, William had been the only man she wanted to marry. The only thing was that William was long gone…to where? She didn't know, nor did she have the means to go look for him, which was what made her want to go to New Orleans; it's where William said he always wanted to go.

\* \* \* \*

Bessie was just about to finish, rinsing off the last pot,

when she heard a voice speaking behind her,

"Excuse me…am I too late to get a bite to eat?"

Bessie turned around and saw that the voice belonged to none other than Lady Day, Ms. Billie Holiday, standing there smiling and gleaming, wearing black shoes, a black and white polka dot dress, and a red hat.

Bessie stood there in awe and didn't say anything. She couldn't…seeing Billie Holiday up, close, and in person had taken her breath away.

Billie came over, gently grabbed Bessie by the shoulders, and told her,

"Breathe, child…Breathe…it's gon' be alright."

Bessie finally smiled and relaxed a little.

"I was just finishin' up the dishes," she said, in a low voice barely audible but loud enough to expose a sweaty southern accent.

"I have a plate of food here, though, if you want it. I was savin' it for later.

"But you're more than welcome to it. I can always eat somethin' else when I get home."

"I have a better idea," said Billie, coming over and taking charge,

"Why don't we do this," she said, taking a plate off one stack of dishes Bessie had washed and then a couple of forks from the silverware rack.

"Why don't we share it while you tell me about yourself? You look like you can use a friend, back here doin' all this work while everybody else is up front havin' themselves a good time.

"What's your name?" Billie asked, leading the way over to a small table and chairs.

On the plate were collard greens, candied yams, cornbread, baked ham, and fried corn. Billie got busy dividing it while Bessie took in a deep breath and then started talking and talking.

She eventually got to the part when she and William first met, how Jack had responded, beating and banishing him, and everything else, including the parts about how badly Jack had treated her after William was gone.

Billie ate as if famished but listened intensely.

\* \* \* \*

Jack was drunk and mad because another man, a friend

of his, had slapped Bessie on the ass.

"You got a nice 'un here, Jack," his friend told him; both men had been drinking for a while and were nearly drunk already,

"You should let her come spend a night or two with me, spread the wealth, you know what I mean," Jack's friend said, winking at Jack while he laughed.

Jack laughed a little, too, and didn't really show that it bothered him, not until after his friend was gone. That's when Jack suddenly became furious, blaming the whole thing on Bessie.

"You made a pass at him, didn't you?

"Answer me," he said, grabbing Bessie's hair and dragging her through the house.

"No sir, I didn't," said Bessie, absolutely terrified…she knew what was coming next.

"Don't you fuckin' lie to me, bitch," he said, slapping Bessie hard across the face, so hard it made her spin around before falling on the floor.

What came next was more of a serious beating, almost as bad as what he'd done to William. In the end, Bessie was left laid out on the dining room floor, unconscious and bleeding from everywhere, which was how Jack left her. His next mistake, though, was going to bed, where he fell asleep almost instantly, thinking that it was over.

"After that, all he knew when he woke up was that his ass was on fire, the whole house, actually."

Bessie had already caught a ride by then and was long gone, but not before emptying Jack's pockets and afterward pouring kerosene everywhere on him, too, and finally striking a match on her way out the door.

Two soldiers on their way to Shreveport had stopped and given her a ride. From there, she caught a bus and ended up in New Orleans. The rest is history.

"You did look around and made sure that nobody else was in the house, though, didn't you?" asked Billie, the only concern she had.

"Yeah…he was there by himself."

"Good, then…served his ass right," said Billie, finishing what was on the plate.

"I would'a' left him there to burn up too, or worse…I might'a' beat his head in wit' a hammer," said Billie, laughing but paying close attention to Bessie; she seemed saddened after finishing the story about Jack Le Roux.

"Honey...you alright?" Billie asked, noticing the discomfort.

"Yeah, I'm fine," said Bessie, willing to smile but only pretending to be happy. She never mentioned to Billie how, because of Jack beating her, she'd had a miscarriage.

"...it's just so good to meet you," she said instead, smiling while hiding the pain.

"Well, don't look so sad about it," said Billie, taking Bessie by the hand,

"I got another show to do, but lookin' at you is makin' me feel sad, too.

"Tell you what...why don't you come out front and have a drink...anything you want, I'm buyin'," and just like that, Bessie had made a new friend.

The other employees were in shock watching Billie Holiday walk out of the kitchen with Bessie in tow. And when the second show was over, Billie came over and hugged Bessie, telling her,

"Goodbye," and then taking off the hat she was wearing, placing it gently on top of Bessie's head. The hat instantly became Bessie's prized possession.

# Chapter 10

George's wife, Connie Devereaux, gave birth to a healthy baby boy, and they named him Theodore...Théodore Lucas Devereaux, but in conversation, their son was referred to simply as Ted.

Even so, when the baby was born, it was as if a transformation had taken place between him and his grandfather, as in when one life began, another life ended; that's because the very next day, Luke Devereaux had a heart attack and died.

Luke had lived to reach the ripe old age of eighty-four, ten years more than his wife Sarah had lived, and seven years less than how old Chester was when he died, which turned out to be quite a long life regardless.

Nevertheless, his untimely death left those who knew him terribly saddened. At Luke's funeral, tearful Connie spoke first,

"He wanted so much to be a granddaddy. It's disappointing to know he won't be around to enjoy it." She was the only female to speak during the eulogies and did a good job, but as usual, as it was with most situations in their marriage, George was content to remain quiet and let Connie do all the talking.

Next was Doc Elliott. He began with,

"Don't know 'bout y'all, but the old coot still owes me a drink," which created laughter, cheering up sad faces, with everybody knowing how much Luke liked to drink. However, the good humor was short-lived,

"Nevertheless," said Doc Elliott, continuing in his part of the eulogy, "...like a brother, I loved him and always will." The faces were all saddened again.

The governor of Louisiana spoke next, and like a true politician, he went on and on and on communicating self-recognition and promises but ended with,

"For all of us who knew Luke Devereaux...he'll be missed, that's for sure," and so forth. The ending was perfect.

After the minister spoke, Luke was finally carried out and laid to rest.

## Buckets, Shovels, Ghost and Worms

\* \* \* \*

George had been the youngest of Luke's four sons and the only one of them who hadn't been killed during wartime. Unlike anybody else in the family, George was short, chubby, and balding on top, but was extremely kind and very passionate, which was what made Connie, a tall, dazzling, outspoken starlet, fall in love and say yes immediately when George asked her to marry him.

They met during George's senior year at Louisiana State University; Connie was just a freshman. George had taken all the basic classes along with a few classes on agriculture, but his true love was not only Connie; he also loved mathematics, of which he was a genius.

Connie never graduated nor felt the need to, not after George went home and turned the Devereaux farming business into an enterprise. In no time at all, he'd tripled the farm in size and, with the right investments, took them from making only small yearly profits to the point of raking in millions.

Luke retired after that and spent most of his time drinking while George built a farming empire. Connie became a homemaker and an expectant mother…never mind that it took years for it to actually happen. But then, one day, she finally did get pregnant and then came Ted.

Ted was like George, as smart as a whip, and like Connie: tall, handsome, and dazzling. But with Ted, the two different distinguishing features inherited from both parents didn't seem to mix, and a mischievous personality developed that nobody understood.

As a child, Ted didn't cry a whole lot but stayed quiet and alert, watching while making himself familiar with everything around him.

Quickly, he learned what buttons to push, not only for the sense of knowing the mechanics of how things worked but also to know how to control people. And with that, he became very manipulative, especially toward his parents.

The Devereaux family was rich, and Ted was treated like royalty, given everything that George and Connie could imagine he might've wanted, which was just what Ted had planned.

By the time he was a teenager, he began to pour on the charm, becoming a lady's man. But Ted, for some reason, only liked older women, women who had something to offer intellectually but also financially; even at a young age, Ted felt he should be compensated for some of the things he could do.

He thought the girls in high school were childish and naïve. So, Ted set his sights a little higher on teachers and other faculty. Connie insisted that one particular woman at school be fired when, through the grapevine, she heard that the woman and Ted had been staying late some evenings having sex in classrooms.

It was the same scenario at Louisiana State University; as a freshman, he only went out with juniors and seniors. And then, as a senior, it was only professors and other successful women of the alumni, married or otherwise; it didn't matter as long as there was something for him to gain.

At twenty-two years old, a quick learner, Ted Devereaux finished school early and graduated with honors and a bachelor's degree. He missed two semesters but returned, earning a master's degree as well.

It was then that Connie was diagnosed with Leukemia, a rare form of cancer that doctors knew very little about. Doc Elliott recommended she be taken to see specialists in places as far away as St. Louis and Chicago, but the cancer spread quickly, and there was nothing or nobody who could save her.

It drove George crazy, hearing Connie scream from being in so much pain, knowing that there was nothing he could do either. And when Connie died, George couldn't take it and killed himself, too.

"I'd rather be dead than live without her," he said, in a

solemn note that was left behind.

They were found lying in bed together, side by side: Connie with an expression of relief and George with a hole in his head made by the .38 caliber pistol that eventually had to be pried away from his hand. Sadly, the two of them were both dead before either of them ever reached the age of fifty.

The grieving period didn't last too long for Ted, though. Actually, it was Emma and William who took it harder than anybody. They'd been married for over ten years by then. At the wedding, Connie had been the maid of honor, and George was the best man.

But to Ted, everything else other than himself was irrelevant. All he knew was that suddenly, he was a millionaire and the most eligible bachelor in the whole state of Louisiana,

"So, let the good times roll," he said, preparing himself, "Laissez le bon temps rouler."

# Chapter 11

The first thing Ted did, after waiting out the legal process of having everything turned over to him, was to buy himself a new car, the most expensive one on the market at that, which had to be specially ordered from Europe.

A month later, after the car had been delivered, Ted pulled William outside and extended a hand forward.

"There it is," he said, with a big smile on his face…it was clearly Ted's proudest moment.

"Nice," was all William would say, though, and even then, it was said in a way that was less than enthusiastic.

"You still haven't seen it yet…come on out here," said Ted, insisting that William go even further, down off the porch to see it, which William did very reluctantly.

The car itself, black in color with a white convertible top, was indeed an eye-catcher, starting with the huge front grill, which was made almost entirely of pure chromed metal, including the manufacturer's emblem emblazoned on top.

Long, glossy fenders with fake-mounted tires traveled along both sides, encasing the automobile's big, powerful engine. White leather encrusted the only two seats, but a short rear end afforded very little trunk space.

The interior, however, was adorned with an instrument panel that set it ablaze as well, with multiple dials and gauges meticulously set in stained mahogany, which was all trimmed in even more chrome.

"Well...how you like it?" asked Ted as if on pins and needles, waiting for William's appraisal.

"It's a bit fancy for my taste," said William, "...but nice," he said again, but with only a shrug after looking the car over from front to back.

"But don't mind me," he said, turning to face Ted with a smile that showed more pity than anything else.

"I'm just an old-fashioned guy, plain and simple.

"For instance...take that ole' truck of mine. As long as it cranks up in the morning and rolls on all four wheels, then I'm happy and satisfied." Actually, William was a little agitated and disappointed because Ted hadn't shown more compassion or grief toward the recent death of both his parents,

"Instead, he's out spending their money," said William to himself, criticizing Ted for what he thought was bad behavior. But then he thought, "Who knows… maybe buyin' a car is just his way of gettin' over it."

Even so, everybody who knew Ted knew that he was not only a womanizer but also quite arrogant and selfish; nothing except what Ted wanted ever seemed to matter.

"Whatever," said Ted, ignoring William's antics.

"Anyway…me and a few college buddies are headed for New Orleans." It was mid-March, Marti Gras time, and Ted's twenty-fifth birthday.

"Sounds like fun," said William, smiling a little more as not to be a total party pooper, spoiling the moment. After all, it was Ted who'd taken over as the new Devereaux boss, and pissing him off was probably not the best thing to do.

Nevertheless, William told him,

"I know y'all gon' be doin' a lotta drinkin', celebratin' your birthday. So, have a good time, but be careful on the road drivin' back…wouldn't wanna hear 'bout nothin' bad happenin' to you."

Ted might've been the one who owned everything, but it was William who acted more responsibly and took the initiative to actually become the man of the house.

"Alright, ole' man, I will," said Ted with a smile, enjoying the fact that William cared so much.

"Don't worry 'bout me, though…I'm always careful," he said after getting in, starting the car, and then revving the engine.

"Yeah, Ted, I know…that's why I'm standin' here remindin' you," said William, watching Ted spin-off, leaving him there in a cloud of dust,

"…BECAUSE YOU'RE ALWAYS SO DAMN CAREFUL!!!" he yelled afterward, fanning the dust away.

\* \* \* \*

The morning was cool and crisp but with bright rays of warmth shining down from the bright, extremely warm sun, which made the weather feel almost perfect, even with the top down and with Ted driving sometimes as fast as the car would go.

Along the way, on both sides of the road, heavy doses of busy backsides with faces, the color of night, dotting the cotton fields as if, instead, they themselves had been planted and were ripe and ready for harvest. Mile after mile, these people all worked hard for Ted. It made him feel powerful knowing that he either owned or controlled everything around him, even those he saw working.

* * * *

The hundred or so miles that it took to get there was driven with disparity, and in what seemed like no time at all, Ted was there at a bar with a cold beer in hand. It wasn't until several hours later before either of his friends showed up. By then, Ted had had a few too many, especially after he and the bartender made everyone else at the bar aware of what day it was.

The motto became, "It's my birthday, and as long as people are buyin'…what the hell…Ted's drinkin'." There were so many drinks bought that Ted could hardly get them all down.

They were in the famous French Quarters, the part of New Orleans that people came from around the world to see and visit. Along Bourbon Street, Ted and his friends stopped and visited almost every wall-to-wall bar, bordello, and first and second-floor brothel that was open and would allow them inside. The streets were full, and so were all the establishments. It was a party like none other, and people were having the times of their lives.

Men in uniform were there too, from the Army, Navy, Air Force, and Marines…either just before or after returning home from the sea or the crude battlegrounds of World War II. The tide had turned, and the gallant effort of the United States was paying off; we were finally winning, which gave plenty of reasons to celebrate, especially for those still in the military.

At one particular club, Ted and his friends had gone in and ordered more drinks. Obviously, the cocktail waitress who took their orders wasn't as young as they were, but didn't look to be too much older either.

"What'll you have?" she asked, speaking pleasantly with a smile when it was Ted's turn to tell what he wanted. But for the first time, Ted was mesmerized and left speechless. That's because the waitress, whether Ted was drunk or not, happened to be the most beautiful woman he'd ever seen in his entire life. It didn't matter that the woman was black.

"We'll all have beers," said one of the friends he had with him, speaking up for Ted after moments went by and Ted still hadn't said anything. Ted instead sat there staring at the waitress with a silly grin on his face.

After the waitress was gone, another of his friends said,

"Ted… you alright?"

"Yeah… why?" asked Ted without hesitation as if suddenly awakened from a dream.

"Because… just in case you hadn't noticed," his friend said, leaning in, lowering his voice, "…the woman you're gawking at happens to be black.

"She's a nigger."

"Aw, he's just drunk," said one of his other buddies, dismissing it as if maybe Ted was too drunk to know what he was doing.

Yes, Ted was drunk, but he was also fully aware of how he felt about the waitress, and it surprised even him just as much as it had everybody else being so attracted to a woman of color.

His attraction was confirmed, though, when the woman came back and brought them their drinks. Ted, again with the silly grin on his face, couldn't help himself; the waitress was considered tall at five foot nine and, at roughly a hundred and forty pounds, had all the right curves in all the right places, just how Ted liked a woman. Not only was she pretty, she was absolutely gorgeous, and carried herself in such a feminine way that was above and beyond being enticing.

Ted ended up tipping her a hundred-dollar bill, which

was several times more than what their drinks cost. He hadn't noticed before, but when they were leaving, outside, in bright neon lights, the sign above the door said,

"Club Watts." Coming back again was then put at the top of his agenda.

* * * *

"Somebody sure has eyes for you," said one of the other waitresses when Bessie returned to the bar and placed another order.

"Girl…I ain't payin' him no mind. That fool just drunk, tippin' me a hundred-dollar bill when he probably only meant to give me a single dollar."

"You ain't complainin', are you?"

"No, not at all," said Bessie, smiling and then leaning over to make their conversation a little more private, "…be nice if everybody else here was so drunk. Maybe then you and I would be able to make ourselves some real money."

The two women both laughed.

"Ain't that the truth," said the other waitress, walking away with a smile on her face. In the twenty-plus years since working there, the furthest that Bessie had been able to advance was from the dish pit to become a cocktail waitress, and only because Maggie, the other waitress she was talking to, who happened to be white, had spoken up for her.

Although thankful for having a job that didn't include working in the fields or being somebody's bed warmer, Bessie still wanted more: a family, for instance. But the only men she ever seemed to meet were always too drunk to tell whether they were sincere or not when they came on to her.

"The white boy was kind'a' cute, though," she thought, smiling from thinking how taken Ted had been with her. But she knew the young white guys who came to Bourbon Street were usually only looking for one thing: a quick lay before returning to school or back home to be groomed to take over the family business.

"Which don't include marryin' no black cocktail waitress from Mississippi.

"Probably'll be the last I'll ever see of him," thought Bessie, the reality of it coming clear.

And with that, Bessie went on to the next table.

"Hi," she said, smiling, "…what'a' ya' havin'?

# Chapter 12

Whether it was a decision he'd made all on his own or not wasn't ever determined, but the very next day, Abner Kaminski, the owner of Club Watts, decided to call it quits. For years, gangsters from Chicago had shown an incredible interest, but Abner, even at the age of eighty, was still much too stubborn and courageous to be intimidated. Bessie was thinking that he eventually just got too old and tired and finally decided on his own to sell out.

In the end, the gangsters got exactly what they wanted: possession of the property. The name stayed the same, but overnight, the whole nostalgic concept of it being a jazz club changed, which, for the city of New Orleans, had been a historic trademark. The music they played was more upbeat. The bartenders, along with the entire wait staff, were all replaced with raunchy but sexy women who didn't mind stripping down...they all wore clothing that revealed a lot more skin while they worked. They weren't against being propositioned either; in fact, it was encouraged and became a big part of the business.

"So, what're you gonna do now that things have changed?" asked Maggie, presenting the question of the day, which was something she wondered about for both of them.

"Well… I know I'm not goin' back to work at Club Watts anymore," said Bessie, eliminating the possibility and sounding sure of it.

"Neither am I," said Maggie.

"…not interested in becomin' a whore," she said, which left a bad taste in her mouth.

It was the time of day when they'd usually both be at work, but instead, they were in Bessie's one-room apartment, drinking sodas and sitting on the only piece of furniture there was to sit on, Bessie's queen-sized bed. There was also a nightstand in the room and a dresser with a mirror attached, which was about all that would fit, along with Bessie's clothes and shoes that were all lined up neatly against the wall and in the one and only closet.

"I'm actually thinkin' 'bout goin' back home," said Bessie, sounding sure of this decision as well.

"Back home?" asked Maggie, as if she couldn't believe it. "Where? Mississippi?"

"Yeah, girl… Meridian. For the first time in my life, I'm feelin' kind'a' homesick. And yeah, I miss my lil' town."

"Ok, but what're you feelin' home-sick for, boredom? You told me yourself that you left because nothin' was really there, 'cept for that gropin' ole' stepfather of yours who couldn't seem to keep his hands off you."

"Yeah, I know…but that's been over twenty years ago when I was still just a young girl.

"My step-father's dead and gone now, though, and I kind'a' miss the quiet and serenity of bein' in the country.

"It's kind'a' hard to explain…you gotta be from there to understand what I'm sayin'," she said, with Maggie looking on perplexed,

"And besides…I wanna meet a hard-workin' man with simple values, the same as mine."

"Oh, and you think you gon' meet him in Meridian, Mississippi?"

"I might," said Bessie, more hopeful than optimistic but willing to take a chance either way.

"I sure as hell haven't met one here in New Orleans," she said afterward, speaking in terms of it being a fact.

"It wouldn't hurt to see some of my folks again either," she said, hoping Maggie, a girl from New Orleans, would understand, being that she was from New Orleans. Maggie made it a point and took full advantage of being able to visit family and friends as often as possible, which was usually all the time. Bessie was always welcome to go along with Maggie, but all that did was make Bessie miss and think about her own family.

"Sounds like you've got your mind made up," said Maggie, understanding fully.

"I do," said Bessie, smiling as she said it, glad that Maggie understood; the last thing she wanted was for Maggie to be disappointed.

"I've given it a lotta thought, I really have…and what I've decided is that it's just time for me to go home."

"Awwwwww, girl…it's not gonna be the same around here without you.

"You know I'm gon' miss you, though, right?" said Maggie, smiling as well and thinking how wonderful it was to have met somebody like Bessie; the two of them met and became friends the night Billie Holiday was in town.

"Yeah, I know…I'm'a' miss you too, girl…you've been nothin' less than a true friend…my only friend," said Bessie, breaking down in tears, and so had Maggie.

"That's right, and I'll always be your friend; don't ever forget it," she said while Bessie looked on and cried,

"…and if you ever change your mind and wanna come back, or if you need me for anything, I mean anything, just let me know."

"Okay, I will," said Bessie, still crying when she reached over and gave Maggie a big hug.

"Take care of yourself, you hear? And find yourself another job… someplace decent," she said while the two of them still embraced.

"Oh, don't you worry 'bout that…I will," said Maggie, baring a smile through all the tears that were falling,

"You do the same. And write and let me know that you've made it there, alright?"

"Okay, I will," said Bessie, knowing that she wouldn't but agreeing to do it anyway. That was the last time the two of them ever saw each other.

The next afternoon, Bessie was waiting in line to board a bus headed for Meridian, Mississippi. At the same time, Ted was making his way back to see Bessie at Club Watts.

"What'a' you mean she doesn't work here anymore? She was just here last night, and so was I," he said later that evening before the crowds came out.

"Nobody who was here last night works here anymore. They've all been replaced with even more girls, prettier too if you ask me," said the bouncer, standing at the bar beside two nearly nude waitresses.

"So…what're gonna do, buy another drink or what?"

"No thanks," said Ted before walking away in disgust, mad at himself for worrying about what his friends would've said about him asking a black cocktail waitress out for a date and for also being so taken by her.

"Never in my life have I ever been so soft-hearted and gullible," he thought, making his way down Bourbon Street in a fury.

But what he was really mad at himself about was that he'd been too embarrassed to ask the woman out in front of anybody else.

He kept thinking,

*"I should've followed my first mind and said something to her last night when I had a chance."*

However, a man of Ted's caliber just wasn't supposed

to date black women back then, at least not according to Southern society and the friends that were with him.

    His buddies had already left and gone home, and at that moment, Ted decided that it was time for him to forget what did or didn't happen and go home, too.

## Chapter 13

"Those going to Meridian, Mississippi," announced the tall, slim driver in need of a sun tan. He was standing at the door of the bus with a dark blue uniform on, inviting those with tickets to go on board.

Along with Bessie, four other men in uniform, proud Black American sailors going home on leave, and six other women, four white, two black, each of them with at least one child, came aboard some time or another before the bus took off.

It was a surprisingly warm day at seventy-eight degrees, mostly sunny with very little wind blowing, but Bessie wore a tan sweater anyway,

"Just in case it gets cool later on," she said, wearing it over the brown dress and flats she had on, looking her usual gorgeous self, hair pulled back with a pair of dark sunglasses on as well.

Since they were all sitting in the back rows together, the guys in uniform wondered if she'd mind having one of them sit beside her. But neither of them felt confident that they could start a decent enough conversation without embarrassing themselves. Therefore, Bessie rode alone without being bothered while the four sailors daydreamed and looked on or out the window like everybody else.

The bus seemed to have made a stop in every small town along the way, which took hours before the bus even made it a hundred miles to Lafayette, Louisiana, where it then had a scheduled one-hour layover.

Bessie was outside, waiting in line at a hot dog stand, when she recognized a familiar face, one that she'd been hoping to see for over twenty years. The only problem was that they were fifty or so yards away from each other and on opposite sides of the street, a street that had a constant flow of automobiles driving by between them.

The excitement of it all took Bessie's breath away, and so did running, trying to catch up to him before he got in the pickup truck that he'd just finished loading with supplies. He'd gotten in, and just as fast, the truck was about to pull off when Bessie, still on the opposite side of the street but standing directly across from it, started waving frantically.

A break in traffic came, and then the man she was waving at finally looked over and smiled, blind now to everything else except for her…a car had to jam on brakes to keep from hitting him when he ran across the street.

The first thing he did when he got close enough was grab Bessie up, off her feet in a hug, laughing and smiling all the while.

"Put me down, fool… can't you see I'm wearing a dress," said Bessie, but actually wishing he'd never let go.

Afterward, not knowing what else to say, William asked her,

"My God… what're you doin' here?"

"What'a' you think…lookin' for you like I been doin' for the last twenty-some years," said Bessie, with a big smile on her face…there couldn't have been a reunion any happier.

Bessie told him, "Man, I see you still lookin' good," which he did…he'd aged well; he had a few gray hairs here and there, but other than that, he still looked the same.

"Thanks, and so do you," he said, finding himself suddenly mesmerized. Bessie looked absolutely stunning, even more beautiful than she had been the last time he had seen her.

For so long, William had tried his best to forget about Bessie and what had happened to him on Jack Le Roux's property. But even after he and Emma got married, his mind still went back to Bessie once in a while. And certain scars he had on his back wouldn't ever let him forget Jack.

"So, is this where you've been livin'?" he asked, wanting to know that and a whole lot more.

"New Orleans," said Bessie, looking up at William earnestly, "I've been livin' there the whole time, ever since about a month after you left. I just happened to be here today because the bus I'm ridin' on had a layover.

"I'll never forget you tellin' me that if you could go anywhere in the world, New Orleans was where you would go, which was why I went there. Like I said, been lookin' for you the past twenty-some years."

"So, where you supposed to be goin' now, ridin' on Greyhound?" asked William with one question to ask after another.

"Back to Mississippi. I had enough of the fast life.

"But, what about you," Bessie asked, changing the subject, wanting to know more about him too, "…where've you been all this time?"

"Where I've been livin' is actually not too far from here…been there the whole time." He went on to tell her about the day he met Luke and Chester, Emma, George, and Connie, and then their son Ted, of whom he now worked for.

"Uh huh…and I see that you've gotten married," said Bessie, noticing the ring on William's finger,

"Congratulations," she said, meaning it.

It wasn't what William expected.

"Yeah, me and Emma.

"Thanks," he said, looking away, at a loss for words.

There was an awkward moment of silence before either of them spoke again. Bessie finally asked,

"So, are you happy?" It was a question she'd asked from the heart, something she really wanted to know. She knew that after twenty years, anything could've happened, but the love she felt for William was sincere, more than just for sex or having a monogamous relationship with him. William was a friend, first and foremost, and was, in a way, very much like family. So, it didn't take much convincing when he asked Bessie to come home with him to meet Emma, especially not after he mentioned something about possibly getting her a job there, too.

"The house is nice, the food is always good, and the Devereaux family has been more generous than anybody

I've ever known.

"Plus, we have a separate bathroom in the house, one just for us, complete with a sink, commode, and bathtub, all with runnin' water," said William, which was the icing on the cake…back then most rural homes still had out houses that the owner themselves had to use, not to mention the servants.

"Ok, so when are we leavin'?" Bessie asked, thrilled about the notion.

Twenty minutes later, after having the driver unload all of Bessie's things off the bus, she and William were on their way, riding down the road together.

"You're gonna like it at the Devereaux house," he told her, "…you'll see."

# Chapter 14

About forty-five minutes later, after making a right and then a left turn on various two-lane highways, William told Bessie, "The Devereaux property starts here."

"Where?" she asked, looking around from side to side, expecting to see something other than just fields...at least a house.

"From right here on down, on both sides," said William, emphasizing while he drove along at a moderate speed, making sure that Bessie could see all there was to see.

"What about all these people?" Bessie asked, becoming amazed by what she saw; in every direction, fields were stretched as far as she could see, and people, she noticed, were working in all of them.

"Every last person out here, regardless if they're white or black, all work for Ted Devereaux," said William, thrilled that Bessie was so impressed.

"…and we still got ten more miles to go," he said with a proud smile on his face.

"Good Lord," said Bessie, more excited than impressed,

"This Ted Devereaux fella must be filthy rich."

"Yeah, he is," said William, boasting a little,

"He's really not a bad guy, though. Wait'll you meet him," he said, smoothing things over.

Ten minutes later, William was turning the truck onto a dirt road and then in the driveway between a big, black, wrought iron gate.

Three men, one driving a small tractor, the other two with gardening tools, were carefully manicuring the lawn and shrubbery. It wasn't quite the time of year yet for roses, but Bessie noticed red, white, and yellow buds on bushes planted all around the house and imagined how beautiful it would be when the time for them to bloom did come.

"Wow…you were right. This is a really nice house," she said, looking around at everything, even at one of the muscle-bound men gardening the lawn,

"He's nice too," she thought, thinking back on younger days when she might've had the nerve to walk over and ask him his name.

"Don't worry 'bout gettin' your things off the truck," William said, "I'll have one of them get it. You just come wit' me so we can find out what Emma's doin'…cookin' more than likely," William said, smiling along the way. And he was right about Emma.

"I'm in the kitchen," she shouted after William came in, calling for her.

After the formal introduction was made, Emma became the gracious host, showing Bessie around the house as if she and William were the ones who actually owned it.

She told Bessie,

"Ted's hardly ever here anymore, so everything that needs to be done is usually left for William and me to do."

By the time Ted came home, they were all at the kitchen table, enjoying what Emma had cooked.

"I'm tellin' you…I haven't had a good meal like this in ages," said Bessie, complimenting Emma on everything just as Ted walked in.

"Ah…Ted. Good…glad you're here," said William, pushing the chair back from the table and standing while he talked.

"I'd like you to meet a good friend of mine…Ms. Bessie

McIntyre.

"She came to visit us from New Orleans."

The recognition was made right away by Ted and Bessie. Neither of them said anything, though.

"Oh…ok…well…it's good meeting you, Ms. McIntyre," said Ted, nervous as hell but able to extend a hand that had a charming smile at the end of it.

"No loss for words this time around," he thought after they had shaken hands, with him noticing that Bessie had an even lovelier smile than what he remembered.

"You plan to be here long?" he asked, hoping she'd say yes.

"Actually, Ted…that's somethin' I wanted to talk to you about," said William before Bessie could answer or say a word.

"Bessie's in need of a job. I figured we could use her to work 'round here wit' us…you know…she could help Emma wit' the cookin' and cleanin'."

"Good idea," said Ted, becoming convinced a lot easier than William expected.

"Actually, I'm gonna be havin' a lot of other people

visitin' here real soon: other farmers and a few hunters. So, yeah, we could sure use your help if you're willin' to stay," he said, speaking directly to Bessie.

"Yes sir… your offer's mighty generous, Mr. Devereaux…and thanks, I'd love to stay."

"Well…I haven't actually offered you anything yet, but you're welcome," he said, sharing a big smile,

"And please…call me Ted. Everyone else does."

"Alright then, Ted. And you can call me Bessie," she said, which made them all laugh.

"Sure thing," said Ted, laughing right along with everybody else.

"We'll talk more in the mornin' about the pay and livin' arrangements. But in the meantime, consider yourself hired.

"William and Emma'll show you around and get you all settled in."

Then Ted turned to Emma, "What's for dinner?" he asked, looking around at all their empty plates, "Whatever it was, sure must've been good."

"I fried some Quail. I also got some smothered in gravy and onions. Then there's rice, snap beans, and biscuits."

"Oh, my…sounds like my kind'a' meal," said Ted,

"I'm'a freshen up a bit first.

"Gimme about thirty minutes. I'll dine in the parlor at the dining room table."

"Yes sir," said Emma,

"I've got some bath water ready for you, too, if you want it."

"That'll be fine… yes, bring it on up." New hot water tanks were being installed at the Devereaux house. In the meantime, water was boiled on the stove for baths.

"And it's nice meetin' you, Bessie. Like I said, we'll talk more in the mornin'."

"Yes sir," she said, and right then and there, Bessie became a part of the Devereaux household. She was just as surprised and nervous as Ted and wondered what the good fortune of seeing him again would lead to.

* * * *

At first, Ted thought he would faint when he walked in and saw Bessie.

"...here, at my house...at the kitchen table having dinner

with Emma and William.

"There is a God, after all," he thought, taking the stairs up two at a time, tripping on one of them.

His intentions were to come home, bathe, change clothes, and then meet some friends of his in Lafayette. But finding out that Bessie was there made him change his mind and stay home, thinking,

"Wherever she's at, I wanna be there too."

Little did he know, his whole life was about to change.

# Chapter 15

Sleep came only sparingly as Ted lay in bed wide awake most of the night, caught in a whirlwind of helpless thoughts that wouldn't shut off. Bessie, on the other hand, slept soundly, better than she'd slept in a long time.

"It was the fresh air and good food that did it…along wit' finally gettin' outta that darn city, thank you, Jesus," she said, while turning over a couple of times to get more comfortable.

For so long, she'd missed the open fields of agriculture wonder. And trees, lots of them, separating houses, both large and small, that at most times were spaced miles apart from each other.

"That and feelin' so safe that sleepin' wit' the doors open at night wouldn't worry me," which was something else she missed, being able to live virtually free of crime.

"Yep, I'm a country girl, alright, and proud of it," she

said, summing it all up before falling fast asleep. "…and as the sayin' goes, 'once a country girl, always a country girl.'"

Of course, it helped a lot being around good people like Emma and William and even Ted, who seemed a lot more grown up and mature than he did the night in New Orleans when she first saw him. All those things together made Bessie feel welcomed and quiet at home.

Nevertheless, she still didn't know for sure what Ted's intentions were or what he might've had in mind for her, which she figured had to do with a lot more than just her cooking and cleaning around the house. Even so, the attraction was obvious and very mutual, which to her was what mattered most.

"Who cares that he's white and I'm black…I know I don't," she said while thinking aloud about what others might say.

"He's rich and well respected. So really, people shouldn't say nothin'."

At the same time, on a more personal note, she was thinking,

"The only problem might be that he's so much younger than I am. It does help that he's such a handsome young man, though," she said, smiling about it, wondering how good Ted might be in bed.

She remembered,

"Maggie has a much younger friend, too, and talks all the time about how good he is."

Then a decision was made,

"If Ted's kind and treats me good, then…oh well," she said, hoping for the best, "…let's see where it goes."

\* \* \* \*

Getting out of bed the next morning, Bessie noticed a note had been slid under the door. It read,

"Good morning.

Not sure how late you'll be sleeping, and didn't wanna wake you. Had to run an errand early this morning. Won't be back until around nine. Hope you'll join me for breakfast.

Ted."

Reading it made Bessie smile; she couldn't remember a man ever taking the time out to write her a note or a letter. She thought Ted's style of approach was very romantic.

Later that morning, in the parlor, at the formal dining

table where the two of them met for breakfast, a dozen roses were there in a vase for her as well.

They had breakfast together almost every morning afterward and then spent evenings together in Lafayette at places like the drive-in movie theater or at a park, ignoring those who stared or whispered things around or about them.

Those dates turned into long weekend getaways at the beach, mostly in nearby Galveston, the Texas Gulf Coast, or as far away as Fort Walton Beach on the Florida peninsula, where on each occasion, the two made love savagely as if for the very first time.

Eventually, Bessie got pregnant again.

"Girl… at forty years old, this baby's gon' kill me, I know it. But guess what…I'm havin' it anyway," she said, talking while she and Emma spent their usual time together in the kitchen.

"Don't worry, girl…you'll be alright. I know plenty of women your age who've had babies and lived to tell about it," said Emma, laughing, thinking Bessie was being quite silly.

"I hope you're right," Bessie said, suddenly worried that, for some reason, something else might happen to make her lose this baby,

"...like it did the last time."

So, to be on the safe side, for the next eight months, Ted kept a close eye on her and had Doc Elliott make regular visits there to see Bessie, so much so that eventually, Ted gave Doc Elliott his own room for overnight visits. And when the baby came a beautiful, healthy baby girl, everything turned out just fine.

Because of the era and history of Ted's confederate family, Bessie feared that Ted might not want the child to have the Devereaux name. She suggested they name the baby Eleanor Ladeaux after Bessie's grandmother. But Ted wasn't having it; he insisted she be called Callie... Callie Devereaux.

"She my daughter, and she'll have my name," he said, feeling proud of himself.

And so it was, and Callie became Daddy's little girl. Ted fell in love the moment she was born. He loved Bessie, but the love he had for his daughter was more extraordinary.

# Chapter 16

Nobody ever thought that a child being born was all it would take to make a man like Ted slow down. But it was.

"Not the playboy, Ted Devereaux," people had started saying,

"…a baby? You're kidding, right?"

Nevertheless, Ted was a different man than what he once was. He'd gone from being out all the time, sleeping with different women every night, to becoming a dedicated father with no time for anything other than work and his precious little girl.

The relationship he had with Bessie was still ongoing and wasn't a secret, but after Callie came along, the time that Bessie and Ted spent together out and about came almost to a halt. Therefore, most people really didn't know who the baby's mother was or that she was black; Callie's pale, almost white skin complexion sure didn't give it away. All people knew was that seeing Ted with such a little bundle of joy made their hearts melt, especially with how Ted and Bessie kept Callie dressed in all the nicer things a baby could wear.

It helped that Callie was always smiling, as if life was just so grand.

"Missy," said Doc Elliott, for the first time, calling her by the name he thought was more appropriate,

"...you're the smilingest little baby I've ever seen," he told Callie during one of the many times he'd come to do follow up exams...both mother and daughter always checked out satisfactorily. Callie was only five pounds eight ounces at birth, which was why she was always referred to as being little.

After about two years, Ted started taking her everywhere with him, even when he went out in the fields to work. And in no time at all, Callie had learned everything there was to know about farming. At twelve, she'd learned how to drive tractors, and at fourteen, she was doing payroll. She learned that the business end of it was simple: make a profit at the end of the year.

Of course, while Ted worked, Bessie worked too, around the house, but at most times, you'd find Bessie out by a pond somewhere, fishing; it's what she liked doing more than anything, especially in swamps where she usually caught buckets of fish.

William showed her the perfect place in the swamp behind the house, an old wooden boat dock that nobody had used since the Civil War. Schools of fish harbored themselves around it constantly, which made for easy prey. The only problem was an infestation of mosquitoes, something that was always a problem with being in the swamp, which was why Bessie wore long skirts and sweaters, keeping most of her body covered.

As simple as it was, though, Bessie was finally enjoying life and, for the first time, felt happy and absolutely free.

# Chapter 17

"Good mornin' heartache, you old gloomy sight.

"Good mornin' heartache, thought we said goodbye last night.

"I turned and tossed 'til it seemed you had gone,

"But here you are with the dawn."

It wasn't just a song that Bessie sang for sad occasions. It became sort of a theme song, one that she sang all the time, so much so that everybody else in the house knew the words to it just as well as she did.

"Wish I'd forget you, but you're here to stay.

"It seems I met you when my love went away.

"Now, every day I start by saying to you, good mornin' heartache, what's new?"

# Buckets, Shovels, Ghost and Worms

The melody was catchy, which was what most people liked about it. Everybody there at the house thought that the more Bessie sang it, the more she was starting to sound just like Billie Holiday, which still didn't mean they weren't tired of hearing it.

"Stop haunting me now,

"Can't shake you no how just leave me alone.

"I've got those Monday Blues straight through Sunday Blues."

Even with the kind of lyrics associated with sadness, like Billie Holiday, Bessie had a way of singing them happily regardless of the way she felt inside.

"Good mornin' heartache, here we go again.

"Good mornin' heartache, you're the one who knew me when.

"Might as well get used to you hangin' around.

"Good mornin' heartache…sit down."

Early that morning, after Bessie had finished singing the last verse, Callie knocked and then opened the bedroom door a little.

"Hey, momma…good mornin'. You up yet?" she asked, peeping in and then giving Bessie one of her best smiles after seeing that Bessie was up and making the bed.

"I see you're singin' your favorite song again," said Callie, making her way inside the room.

Bessie laughed and smiled before saying,

"Yeah, well… you know me… I'm a fanatic."

"Tell me about it," said Callie, warming to the good feeling she got from being around her mother,

"You've told me the story about Billie Holiday and the hat so many times I could write a book about it myself and would probably sell a million copies."

"That'll be the day," said Bessie, laughing and smiling even more, but in deep thought, thanking God for giving her the strength to make it through the hard times back then.

She wasn't trying to be rude when she told Callie,

"I think your father's waitin' for us at the breakfast table.

"Why don't you go on down? I'll be there shortly," she said, finishing the bed and immediately afterward starting to pick things up from off the floor, showing signs of not really wanting to be bothered.

She told Callie,

"You two go on ahead and start without me."

What she really wanted was more time alone. She was thinking,

*"There's so much to be thankful for, including Callie and all else that God has given me, but there's very little time left to thank him;"* a premonition from a dream had given her a feeling that she wouldn't be around very much longer to thank him later.

"Alright, momma...but make sure you come and eat somethin' too," said Callie, insisting as if she was the one who was the mother, "...and don't wait too long, or else everything'll be cold."

"Alright, yes, ma'am, I won't," said Bessie, still smiling but waiting for Callie to leave.

And when she did, Bessie started singing the same song all over again, except this time with tears in her eyes,

"Good mornin' heartache…"

\* \* \* \*

Friday, January 1955, a month before Callie's sixteenth birthday. Ted was expecting guests, farmers from other Louisiana counties. A friend from college had invented a new irrigation system, one that would surely become a savior and, in most cases, a farmer's best friend.

Ted became a financial partner in hopes that sales of the invention would skyrocket and the money he invested would turn into millions for both him and his partner. However, they decided that the invention would first only be offered to Louisiana farmers before being made available to anybody else in the world.

Invitations had been sent out, and a demonstration was scheduled for later that afternoon during a winter month so that the system could be ordered, installed, and already running by summer, the time when it would most be needed.

\* \* \* \*

"...good mornin' heartache thought we said goodbye last night."

Bessie was still singing and tidying things up when the door opened again. This time, it was Ted who walked into the room,

"Honey... is everything alright?" he asked, a bit worried. "You missed breakfast and been up here singin' that same ole' song since early this mornin'.

"Now, why don't you tell me what's wrong."

"Nothin', baby…don't worry 'bout me…everything's fine," she said, not letting on about how much she hurt inside, afraid that what she dreamed might really come true.

"What time is everybody supposed to get here?"

"In about an hour," said Ted, putting both arms around her, hoping that a little love and affection might do the job of bringing Bessie out of the funk she'd been in all morning.

"You need to be gettin' yourself ready then, and I need to go help Emma in the kitchen, make sure all the food's ready," she said, giving Ted a quick kiss on the lips before breaking free, straightening the sweater and long skirt she had on, and making her way out the room and down the stairs, leaving Ted there in a moment of passion all alone.

"Okay…love you too," he said, still confused after she was gone.

* * * *

The first guest arrived around ten. The rest trickled in between ten and ten thirty. The invitation suggested they all be there by eleven.

In the kitchen, Bessie was telling Emma,

"Girl…I dreamed a man came at me wit' a knife, and I couldn't get away…it seemed so real, that's why I been up in the room all mornin'; I was afraid to come out."

Emma laughed, as usual, thinking Bessie was being silly again.

"What, man? Who was he?" she asked, showing very little patience, "…it sure wasn't Ted or William."

"I know, but…you know how those kinda dreams are…you never get to actually see nobody's face, but it's as if you know what's about to happen."

"Can't say that I do," said Emma, disagreeing, hoping to put an end to it,

"…don't 'member ever havin' one of those kinda dreams. You gon' be alright, though, trust me…we ain't gon' let nothin' happen to you," she said, but all along dismissing it as pure nonsense.

But not Bessie; she'd been superstitious since she could ever remember, and so had everybody else where she was from. Bessie's grandmother, the late Marie Catherine Ladeaux, had been known to practice voodoo, something that all the women in Bessie's family had believed in and practiced. They also believed that dreams were a sign of things to come.

"If you don't mind cuttin' the cabbage for cole slaw, I'll go ahead and start fryin' fish," said Emma, bringing Bessie back from bad memories of black magic and superstition.

An hour later, the men were back from the field demonstration and were all standing around on the front porch, talking and making deals. Emma had already made sweet tea, and after she poured it in glasses over ice, Bessie loaded them on a tray, walked them out, and began serving.

One at a time, the men all took a glass and thanked Bessie, all except one. And with him, it was like seeing a ghost from the past with Jack Le Roux standing there snarling, scaring Bessie half to death. She was terrified.

The jacket and long-sleeved shirt that Jack had on couldn't hide all the scars and burn marks that showed around the neck and on both hands. You could tell that the right side of his face had been badly burned as well.

"Is everything alright over here?" Ted asked, walking over after noticing the look on both their faces.

"Yeah, I'm fine," said Jack, taking one last look at Bessie before drinking from the glass he'd taken.

"Why don't you bring a pitcher back with you, and we'll help ourselves," Ted said to Bessie, not knowing what to make of what he'd just seen, but there was clearly something going on, something wrong, something he needed to find out about.

* * * *

Back in the kitchen, Bessie told Emma,

"SHIT!!! It's him. He's here," she said, all frantic and fidgety...a nervous wreck.

"Bessie...who's here?" asked Emma, standing by the stove, fork in hand, maneuvering fish frying in two separate big skillets of hot grease.

"Jack Le Roux," she said, pacing the floor, trying to figure out what to do. Then she thought of something,

"You're gonna need more fish," she said, headed for the back door.

"Wait...we got plenty," said Emma, but Bessie was already gone.

On the back porch was a bucket already filled with live bait. After grabbing it, a shovel, a long cane pole from a stack piled in a corner, and slipping on a pair of galosh boots, Bessie darted off the back porch, headed for the swamp, but only to run right into Jack Le Roux again.

"Where'n the hell you think you're goin'?" he asked, taking hold of Bessie's arm and wrist so tight that it hurt and made her drop everything she'd been carrying,

"I thought you'd try to run," he said, pleased with himself.

There was no breaking away, so Bessie turned and looked back at the house, hoping that Emma would be looking out the window, which she was.

Jack pulled Bessie in closer, "You think she gon' be able to save you? Uh uh… say your prayers, darlin'. This is payback," he said before letting go of one of Bessie's arms and then brandishing a big hunter's knife.

"No!!! Please don't," said Bessie, beginning to cry hysterically,

"You killed my baby."

"No…I only told you the baby was dead," said Jack, pulling Bessie close again but yelling, "I gave that bastard child of yours away!!!"

"No!!!" said Bessie, becoming hysterical again but unafraid and angry. Then she lunged at Jack and clawed his face.

"You fuckin' bitch!!!" said Jack, yelling at her,

"Do you know how many damn painful surgeries and skin grafts I had to have because of what you did? Too many," he said, plunging the knife into Bessie's midsection again and again.

"Die, bitch," he said, taking pleasure in what he'd done.

It happened so fast that she had no time to scream and collapsed just as fast. For a while, Jack's strong arm held Bessie up until her body eventually went totally limp. With both eyes rolled back, she was lying on the ground, all but dead.

Over twenty years had passed since the last time he'd seen him, but when Jack looked up, right away, he recognized William standing there on the back porch, shotgun in hand, looking confused and angry, stunned by what he'd heard Jack say;

"I gave that bastard child of yours away."

The bastard child that Jack was referring to was William's son, too.

And then, Jack started coming toward him, yelling while he asked William,

"What the hell you doin', boy?"

He was about to say something else,

"Give me that…"

But before he could get the word,

"…gun," out of his mouth, William had raised the barrel and pulled the trigger.

The blast blew Jack upwards and back about five feet from where he'd been standing. Death came instantaneously. Bessie, however, was still gurgling blood, struggling to breathe, and didn't die until a few minutes afterward, with Ted crying, holding on to her.

\* \* \* \*

Ted made sure that no charges were filed against William for shooting Jack, a white man, and four days later, Bessie's funeral was held at a nearby old southern Baptist church; black minister, choir, and congregation, all of whom worked for Ted, including Emma and William. Ted cried and wept the whole time while Callie continuously cried, screamed, and yelled.

"Momma… NO!!! No, momma." She couldn't be consoled. Doc Elliott eventually had to give Callie a sedative, something to make her calm down and sleep for a while.

# Alvin Bell

A New Orleans-styled quartet of jazz men blew horns and played at the site of the Devereaux Mausoleum where Bessie, at last, was laid to rest.

At the house, while Callie slept, Ted thanked family members and friends for coming. Emma fried more fish, Bessie's favorite, and people ate before walking away, still confused about why Bessie had to die.

# Chapter 18

Unfortunately, alcoholism was part of the Devereaux heritage, something they all seemed so proud of. All except George, Ted's father, who never drank at all. Ted started drinking every day, though, after Bessie died, especially when Callie became dependent upon psychiatric treatment.

At times, she'd be fine, talking and responding, totally comprehensive, and at others, becoming spellbound and detached. It happened once too often when Callie became incoherent and then eventually stopped talking completely. Things had gotten so bad that she couldn't focus, and instead of looking at you, she'd look around or through you and wouldn't even blink an eye until it was time to go to sleep.

It became to be a big burden for all of them when Ted refused the recommended hospitalization for Callie.

"Shock treatments are outta the question," he said after finding out about what they wanted to do. He kept her home instead and hired nurses to be there around the clock.

"I think if I had enough time with her, she'd be alright," Doc Elliott had told him, which was what Ted depended on; they all did, Emma and William too.

"I'll bring her out of the broken-down state she's gone into. But like I said, it's gonna take some time," he warned, letting them know that it wouldn't happen overnight, which it didn't…in all, it took about five years.

By then, everything had changed; Callie wasn't a child anymore, for one…she'd grown into a very beautiful young woman. And then Ted was dead too, died in a car wreck.

The day it happened, he'd gotten so drunk he could barely walk. William begged him not to drive, but he did anyway, and a few miles off the property, he ran head-on into a semi-truck. Those at the scene said he died instantly, but those who knew him said that Ted had died years ago, right along with Bessie.

Callie had asked to see him, but when Doc Elliott told her how he died, Callie just stared at the wall for a while and then drank some water without ever crying. Her next words were,

"Tell Emma I'm hungry…a bowl of gumbo and rice'll be fine."

"Right away, Missy," said Doc Elliott, pleased with what he'd heard her say, thinking that after five long years, his work with her was just about over.

Later that night, Callie was awakened from a deep sleep. And standing beside the bed was a glowing image of Ted. Telepathically, he told her,

"Take care of yourself, baby. Daddy still loves you and always will." She saw it when he smiled. She smiled too, but Callie blinked once, and then Ted was gone, never to be seen again.

## Chapter 19

Although very much impressed with Callie's sudden improvement, Doc Elliott still wasn't quite convinced that she'd progressed enough or that the recovery stage was over,

"No…not yet…if anything, it's just beginning, the most important part of it at least," he said, being optimistic but making the determination that in Callie's case, nothing would be rushed. Therefore, further therapeutic treatment and sessions were stretched out over even longer periods and intervals, which worked out fine. It took a little longer, but in the end, Callie showed all signs of being completely sane and normal again and was finally given a clean bill of health.

During the whole time, William stuck close by, giving all the support that he could possibly give. Emma would make the gumbo, but William was the one who would put it on a tray and bring it up to Callie's room. Oftentimes, he'd sit and talk and watch while she ate. And on good days, he would put Callie in the car and drive her around just so she could get out of the house once in a while. On the way back, he might stop and get them both an ice cream cone, but he always made sure that she was returned home safe and in a timely manner as well.

Nevertheless, things changed the day that she was finally able to get out of the house without him. It was as if Callie's sex drive had been kicked into high gear. She became a regular at different bars and nightclubs and brought home a different guy almost every night of the week. She eventually met bad boy Johnny Le Fleur, and then things changed once again.

Johnny was a local gangster, well-known in the area. But regardless of what anybody else might've said or thought of him, Johnny considered himself more of a businessman than anything else. Actually, he did own a nightclub at one time or another, that is, until a man inside the club got killed, an employee whom Johnny accused of stealing. No other employee came forward as a witness, and no formal charges of murder or anything else were ever filed against Johnny. However, the state attorney's office decided to revoke his liquor license, and so went the business.

Callie had a weakness for men like Johnny, who didn't shy away from danger or trouble. It was a similar situation with Blu, a Negro field hand who took chances sneaking around with her. Of course, for what he'd done, Blu could've been killed. But with Callie, even as a teenager, the adventure of how they could possibly get caught someplace while in the midst of sex was what turned her on. So consequently, to her, it was worth taking a chance…never mind if they'd been caught and the next day Blu had been found badly beaten and hanging by a rope from a tree.

"William…just gimme the keys," she said, hand held out, losing patience the one afternoon in question when William kept insisting that he be the one to drive or at least tag along.

"I'm fine… I am, really… and I probably'll be back in time for dinner. But if not, then have Emma save a plate for me." William's love and concern for her were greatly appreciated, but Callie resented being smothered, which was how she felt with William always being around, in the way,

"…cutting things short," as she would say to no one in particular but in private thoughts.

On the other hand, William didn't think Callie's mind was quite right yet and that at any moment, she might go back into what Doc Elliott had referred to as being a broken-down state.

One thing was for certain: she'd changed a lot; she wasn't the same sweet little, innocent young girl walking around smiling all the time. In William's opinion, she had become brash and much more reserved, so much so that he felt he didn't know her anymore, which he didn't.

"How long has it been since you've driven a car, Callie?" he asked to prove a point after she'd taken the keys and started out the door with him right behind her, following step for step in spite of being ignored.

"Uh huh… can't even remember, can you? That's why you need to let me drive," he said in a last-minute attempt at reasoning with her.

But Callie, clearly the one in charge, wasn't hearing it,

"Bye, William…tonight I won't be needin' a chauffeur," she said a minute or two later, being a sarcastic bitch before driving off with him still standing in the driveway, looking on.

"Lord, help her," said Emma, looking on too, but from behind the screen of the front door, "…help them both."

Years ago, William, who was a lot more than just a mere employee, had been welcomed and, as far as the Devereaux family was concerned, had become an actual part of the family after Luke brought him home and introduced him to everybody. And so had Bessie once she and Ted got together.

But they'd all died or had, in some kind of way, been killed. This was what made William want to become more of a savior to both Callie and Emma...they were the only ones he had left. And if protecting them might cost him his life,

"Then so be it," he thought.

The way he figured, he had nothing else better to live for than to make sure they were alright. The only problem was Callie, who, by law, after being medically cleared, had just inherited everything.

\* \* \* \*

Outside, nature's symphony blared the harmonic sound of insects and other living creatures while the nighttime sky, littered with glistering stars and brightened moonlight, stood still.

"A penny for your thoughts," said Callie, whispering softly in Johnny's ear after creeping up behind him, wearing only a smile and the white, long-sleeve shirt that Johnny had just taken off. He'd taken his shoes and socks off, too, and was standing there with just a pair of pants on.

It was the first time that she'd brought him home, and there they were in the doorway of Callie's opened bedroom balcony, enjoying each other as well as the nighttime tranquil sound and scenery. Other than a few burning candles, everything else in the house was pitch black, dark, and quiet.

"The thoughts I have are all of you, Madame," said Johnny, turning just in time to get a kiss and have Callie's long arms thrown around him.

"Awwwwww…Monsieur. And mine are all of you," said Callie, simulating Johnny's blatant French accent. The accent was what she liked most about him.

Nothing else stood out; Johnny wasn't extremely handsome or extravagant, nor did he dress exceptionally well, and wasn't an impressionable physical specimen either, not with him and Callie being about the same height and weight. But the rough edge and French accent seemed to be enough.

"…now take me to bed and fuck me, Johnny," said Callie, leading the way with a hand on Johnny's crotch.

Turns out there was something else about Johnny that Callie found out before the night was over, and that was that Johnny was very passionate and a beast in bed. He wasn't very well endowed, but for that, he made up with other things he could do.

"At last, I've found a worthy lover," said Callie,

mimicking the French accent even more after several hours of good sex.

"Yeah, well…you better find yourself some sleep," said Johnny, collapsing on the pillow beside her, snoring a minute or two later.

Callie kissed him once more and then closed her eyes and dozed off, too. It wouldn't be until hours later when Callie woke up. When she did, Johnny was standing in the doorway of the balcony again, fully dressed: white shirt, gray pants, black shoes, and suspenders, with a cup of coffee in his hand and a .45 caliber pistol stuck down his pants at the small of his back.

"How long have you been up?" asked Callie, still under the sheets, turning to one side, stirring a bit.

"I guess about an hour," said Johnny, only then turning to smile, giving Callie a pleasant look.

"You have a wonderful home here," he then said, a little more seriously, "…and Emma's great…she made the coffee for me," he said, gesturing with the cup.

"Can't say the same about the husband, though…don't think he likes me."

"Why? What did he say?" Callie asked, suddenly fully

awake and concerned, becoming wide-eyed and stark still beneath the sheet.

"Is there something wrong?" she asked, on the verge of panic. William was known to be outspoken,

"At times, a little too outspoken," thought Callie. While Johnny was prone to react, the two for sure didn't make a good combination, especially not with Johnny carrying a gun.

"No…no…everything's fine," said Johnny, a wicked smile on his face, which, to Callie, meant trouble, "…we just said 'hello' to each other, nothing else."

"You sure?"

"Positive."

"Well, how do you know he doesn't like you?" asked Callie, at ease again.

"Because… he didn't smile or introduce himself, not like Emma. It's just the feelin' I got from seein' him."

"You're probably right," said Callie, balling herself up into a fetal position, sheets pulled up chin high, "…William hates it when I bring other people home with me."

"Wow…and here I am thinkin' of how we can have a

party out here. Been thinkin' 'bout it all night long."

"A party?"

"Yeah, a party. We'd keep it discreet, of course," said Johnny, coming over to sit beside Callie on the bed,

"…the kind'a' party that just anybody wouldn't be invited. Only the prettiest girls and the richest men.

"Why, we'll have the big wigs comin' all the way from New Orleans, Houston, and Dallas and from places as far away as Detroit and Chicago. And believe me, we'll make a lotta money."

"Oh yeah? How're we supposed to make money from havin' a party?" asked Callie, as if totally naïve.

"Well, darlin'…the prettiest girls won't be here for nothin'…and with all the bedrooms that are in this house..." said Johnny, giving Callie a wink and more of the same wicked smile.

"I'll watch the door and be in charge of security," he said, all business again,

"…you'll watch the girls and collect all the money. Other than that, all we gotta do is fix the place up a little," said Johnny, looking around at spots on the wall where the paint had started to crack and peel, and then on the floor where old carpeting and rugs needed to be replaced.

"I figure if we invest a couple grand in repairs and maybe some new furniture here and there, then the place might be up to par and ready for business.

"And if the first party turns into a success, then we'll have another, and then another, and keep right on going.

"We'll even keep the family name; call it The Devereaux House," which was how the brothel got started.

Callie agreed to almost everything Johnny had suggested and even paid for what he wanted to be replaced and repaired. It really didn't take much convincing; all she wanted was to have a good time. And as far as the house goes, she always thought it needed to be a little livelier anyway, regardless of how much money Johnny thought they would make. Besides, Callie was already rich, worth millions; she just never bothered to tell Johnny.

William and Emma didn't like the idea, but neither of them had a say in the matter and reluctantly agreed to stay on as butler and cook. Callie thanked them and even gave them both a substantial raise in pay, something she'd planned to do anyway.

"So, let the good times roll," said Callie, all excited, remembering how her father, Ted, used to say it,

"Laissez Le bon temps rouler."

But that was then...things had changed a lot in twelve years.

## Chapter 20

At seventy-eight years old, not only had William's role been reduced to doing simple things like taking and picking Dominique up from school every day, but also, when it came to groceries and other supplies the Devereaux House might've needed...he did that too, all the shopping. This had all been turned into a routine he'd gotten used to and enjoyed, actually. However, because Callie had already planned to go into town for a visit to the hairdresser that day, she decided that she would be the one to do whatever shopping that needed to be done,

"I'll be right there by all the stores anyway. So, I might as well do it," she said, as if it just made sense. And it did.

"I can stop and get Dominique, too."

Regardless, it wasn't often when Callie would visit the city of Lafayette, at least not during hours when bars and nightclubs weren't open, which was usually the only reason why she would go. Other than that, whenever she made an appearance during the daytime, it usually became a spectacle with people pointing, accusing Callie of flaunting herself, doing whatever she could to ruin marriages, something mostly the insecure, married women were saying.

The flamboyance of Callie's style was what mostly got their attention. For instance, since inheriting the Devereaux fortune, Callie vowed that from then on, every Devereaux and guest of a Devereaux would either drive or be driven around in a Cadillac, and she'd just bought two, brand new, both in the year of 1972. One was triple white, a four-door sedan that she decided William would drive as a chauffeur. The one she bought for herself was a two-door coupe, candy apple red, with a white convertible top and soft, white leather seats.

"The only one like it in these parts," the salesman told Callie the day she bought it.

Earlier, before leaving that morning, she told William, "It won't be until at least a couple more hours when I'll be ready to head out. Pick two of our guys and have them wash and wax the car for me."

Kidding around, William asked,

"You sure you want two to wash it and not three?" It was a sarcastic comment, of course, from feeling so left out, remembering the times when it was just him and him alone they would ask and depend on to wash and service all the cars.

"Actually, three's not a bad idea," said Callie, in a cheerful mood, responding quickly, kidding around.

"Yeah, pick three guys, but have the third one come up and help me decide what to wear," she said, standing at the foot of the staircase landing, looking back at William, smiling.

The witty response made William laugh. But not to be outdone, he told Callie,

"You want the third guy to come up and help you decide what to wear? What kind'a' shit is that? I thought it was just the car you wanted washed and waxed."

"Aw…you're funny," said Callie on her way back up the stairs. She couldn't help but laugh as well, though,

"Two guys, William. Pick two guys," she said afterward, disappearing behind the bedroom door.

* * * *

The red convertible Cadillac set the road on fire with Callie at times driving almost at full speed with the top down and radio turned up, blasting those working the fields away with Little Richard's "Good Golly Miss Molly." It was an "all eyes on me" time for Callie, and for just a moment or two, those she passed did stop and looked up.

It wasn't very long at all before she was there, driving the city limits. The Bank of Lafayette was the first planned stop.

"Well...Ms Devereaux...what a pleasant surprise," said Harold Bynes, the bank manager, a man in his late forties, tall and rail thin with an old, hand-me-down suit and eyeglasses. He really wasn't too happy about seeing Callie, not at all, and it showed.

Harold had visited the Devereaux House on numerous occasions and claimed to have fallen in love, not with Callie, but with one of the other girls, which was why it made him so nervous seeing Callie there in the bank, sitting across from him. Harold was married with three kids and seemed more afraid of Mrs. Bynes than he was of anything else.

"What can I do for you?" he asked, adjusting his tie over and over again as if suddenly being choked.

"Signs of nervousness," thought Callie.

She saved him the embarrassment of laughing but couldn't help thinking how funny it was.

"Harold, honey…relax. I'm runnin' a lil' short on cash, that's all…and thought that since I was here in the bank, the least I could do was come over and say hello. But don't worry; this ain't a shake-down or nothin'… I've got my own money," she said, handing him a withdrawal slip.

"Like I told you before, we don't kiss and tell, none of us. And if you don't want your wife to know what you've been doin', then that's fine…your secret's safe wit' me, I promise," she said, sharing with him the kind of smile that only an impish woman would share.

"Thanks…I appreciate it," said Harold, relieved but still showing signs of being extremely nervous, wishing Callie would hurry up and leave.

"I'll have one of the tellers get this for you," he said, rising from behind the desk where he'd been sitting, holding up and showing her the withdrawal slip first.

Fifteen minutes later, Callie had the Cadillac moving again, down Main Street, but this time with Fats Domino singing,

"I've found my thrill… on Blue Berry Hill."

The volume was still turned up, and people in the whole downtown area were watching, store clerks and customers alike, coming out to stand on the sidewalk just to see where the music was coming from.

* * * *

The only other thing Callie didn't do to attract more attention and stares was wear something too revealing or provocative. What she had on was a suit, actually, a cream-colored matching skirt and jacket, and a red silk blouse… an outfit that looked very businesslike. It was just that the further into the afternoon it got, the more the sun came out, warming things up, which made it too hot for a jacket. So, with the way Callie had started to sweat, she decided to skip shopping,

"I'll have William come back and do it later," she said, feeling as if she was about to burn up.

With that, the next stop she made was at the hairdresser, where the air conditioner was usually turned up high.

The Devereaux House had been updated and well equipped with all the latest gadgets and inventions: radio, telephones, television, etc. Hence, regardless of what time it was, having already called and made an appointment for Callie, Beth Ellen, the hairdresser, had a chair ready and waiting.

"Here… let me get that for you," said Beth Ellen, helping Callie peel off the jacket she'd been wearing,

"You must me be burnin' up with all this on."

"Believe me, I am," said Callie, ignoring the snobbish looks and mean stares and whispers of all the other women she'd walked past in the waiting area.

"It wasn't so bad this mornin' when I left the house, but the further it gets into the day, the warmer it gets."

"Typical for the kind'a' weather we be havin' down here in Southern Louisiana."

Beth Ellen, a true blond with blue eyes, wasn't quite as tall as Callie but, surprisingly, had a lot more curves and sex appeal than an average white girl. She was the girl Harold Bynes had supposedly fallen in love with, a girl from the Devereaux House who was also Callie's best friend.

"Harold's wife was here earlier," said Beth, throwing the beauty cape over the clothes Callie had on, fastening it around the neck,

"…sat right in the chair where you're at now."

"That must've been fun."

"Can you believe it? The woman went on and on like her and I were friends, tellin' me about the oldest daughter who's only just now gettin' a period at fourteen and about the youngest just gettin' over a bout with the measles."

"I can believe it," said Callie, enjoying it while Beth Ellen began the hair treatment. "She's probably dense."

The place was packed, especially in the waiting area, as it was with all the booths, where the twelve other hairdressers were busy washing, drying, and styling the hair of other patrons who were mostly either fast asleep or deep in conversation, telling stories about their sons and daughters as well.

Every once in a while, Callie would look up and catch one or two of them still staring. Even so, regardless of how they might've felt about her, being around them didn't bother Callie one bit. But still, she couldn't help but think,

"White women with their big hairdos and plastered makeup facials aren't any better than me, no matter what they think. So, fuck 'em." Nevertheless, it wasn't a thought that she would dwell on for very long,

"I bet she hadn't a clue that you're the one ole' Harold's been pourin' his heart and soul out to.

"You and him still foolin' around?" asked Callie, eyes closed while Beth Ellen ran a comb and then a brush through Callie's long hair.

"Whenever he gets the time and extra money. From what he tells me, nowadays, the wife's got him on a tight budget. And now that I'm no longer at the Devereaux House, he not only has to pay for spending time with me, he's also gotta get a room for us somewhere too, that is if he wants a lil' nookie," said Beth Ellen, laughing about it. "…which can get to be quite expensive when you're tryin' to be discreet and do it in another town." She thought that was funny, too.

* * * *

It wasn't until an hour later that Beth Ellen finished, just as Dominique was about to be let out of school.

Other parents who were there to pick up their sons and daughters mostly drove family cars, sedans, and station wagons, which made the red convertible coupe that Callie was driving stand out even more, especially with Elvis Presley sounding out loudly over the Cadillac's custom speakers, inviting everybody, in song, to do the "Jail House Rock."

Callie saw nothing wrong with it, even with how everybody there was staring as well.

* * * *

Because of all the spoiled, troublesome brats who were there in attendance, it should've been called the hard knock school for rich white kids and others who could afford it, but instead, it was called The Napoleon Learning Center.

They had another whole different set of segregation and discrimination rules in Southeast Louisiana back then, especially when it came to schools. One was that there was no prejudice against the all-mighty dollar. And two…if your money was long enough to pay the ridiculous tuition fees, then your child was also welcomed and isolated against the rest of the populated school kids.

However, in the case of Dominique Devereaux being accepted, not only did her mother have the necessary funds to pay whatever tuition she might've been charged, but acceptance was approved mainly because it was where Callie, Ted, George, and all the other Devereaux family members before she had attended classes. And so did others through generations as far back as 1812, the year Louisiana first became a state, and when the school was founded in part by a Devereaux, a French man, Jean Claude Devereaux. It's just that back then, nobody ever thought a Devereaux child would be black.

* * * *

While Callie sat in the car and waited, entertained by Elvis, one of the more jovial parents walked by with his two daughters and son. Having a good time, the eldest daughter and he stopped there right beside Callie's car and rocked just as Elvis had been asking. Of course, the daughter was a much better dancer than her dad, but that didn't stop him from trying.

Callie couldn't help but laugh and smile, having finally found somebody in good spirits just as she was.

They all laughed and waved at each other when the song and dance was over. A minute or two later, Dominique, being escorted by a classmate, a boy about the same age and as dark as she was, walked up, said goodbye to him, and then got in the car, too.

"Who's the boy?" Callie asked.

"Seth Evans," said Dominique, "…him and I have a class together."

"Oh yeah? Is that why he walked you out?"

"He walked me out because it was on the way," said Dominique.

"His mom's parked back there," she added, turning to look.

At the same time, Callie looked in the rear-view mirror just in time to see Seth get in and close the door of a black Cadillac sedan parked a few cars behind them.

A moment or two later, it took off and drove by. Callie looked over in time to see who was driving and recognized

Seth's mom right away. She was the daughter of John and Betty Evans, owners of Evan's Mortuary, the same people who handled Bessie's funeral arrangements.

"Small world," said Callie, waiting for other cars to go by so that she and Dominique could leave, too.

Just then, a station wagon pulled beside them. The driver was the same man she saw dancing. He smiled at Callie, head and shoulders be-bopping away, and turned up the station wagon's radio just in time to catch the tail end of a Beach Boy song, "Surfing U.S.A."

After the song and bebop was over, he turned the sound down and said to Callie,

"Hi… I'm Bob Macklin. My daughter here is Nora," he said of the eldest daughter sitting in the front seat beside him, "…Todd and Samantha are in the back."

The whole time, the only thing Callie was thinking was,

"*Wow, he's got a killer smile,*" and it showed with the way she smiled back and looked at him.

"Hi, Bob, Nora, Todd, Samantha… nice ta' meet 'cha. I'm Callie Devereaux, and this is my daughter, Dominique," said Callie, still with a cordial smile.

The sound of a horn blowing behind them broke up what

little eye contact she and Bob seemed to be having.

"Well… it's nice meeting you, too. Hope to see you again soon," said Bob, waving goodbye to both Callie and Dominique.

No other words were spoken before Bob pulled off, but by then, he'd already given a good impression; Callie still wore a smile on her face to prove it.

"Can we go now? I gotta pee," said Dominique to bring Callie out of the reverie of abstract musing…she was definitely in a world all of her own, thinking about Bob.

## Chapter 21

"Lord… please let me live to see eighty," said William in silent prayer, something he'd been doing a lot lately, praying…hoping to live a lot longer while at the same time getting a lot closer to God.

Old age was finally starting to set in and get the best of him. It made him aware of things that once upon a time he took for granted, like being able to walk without pain, not to mention being able to run like he used to and jump over things. Now, in the mornings, and sometimes twice a day, he took medication to help fight inflammation that, from a buildup in the joint of his knees, had made it, whereas, at times, he could hardly walk. On some days, he hurt so bad that not even the medication helped. It definitely made him walk a little differently and move a lot slower.

"At least I haven't lost my mind yet," he said jokingly but just as quickly wishing he hadn't.

"Funny," he thought, "Who else but a person insane would question their own sanity?"

It also bothered him that Callie, the wayward child he cared so much about, had been relieving him of so many things to do.

"Sparing him the trouble" was what she called it when she and Emma talked amongst themselves. But to him, it was like she was being too sympathetic, which in this case was pretty much the borderline of being pitied.

"I still haven't died yet, you know," he once told her as a reminder, hoping she would understand and have a little more faith.

Even Emma had been treating him differently, questioning him at every turn and juncture and lying when she thought it might make him feel better. For example, Callie had been gone for hours but was expected back at any moment. Nevertheless, on one of those rare occasions when nature permitted a sudden rise in stamina that brought on an urge for sex that, for an old man like him, couldn't or wouldn't be put off or ignored… they ended up in bed for all of fifteen minutes, which nearly took William's breath away.

But when he said to his wife,

"Baby…tell the truth. I still got it, don't I?" he asked,

just to see what she would say.

She told him,

"Yeah, baby…for a while there I was in heaven." He knew, then and there, that life had passed him by…there was a time when he would spend more than fifteen minutes just on foreplay alone.

Yet, on that particular day, by the time he finished, sweat was pouring, and he was all but out of breath, barely able to talk and breathe at the same time.

But not Emma; she lay in bed beside him, breathing normally, hair and makeup still intact, without an ounce of sweat dripping from anywhere. Once again, he said it out loud,

"I still haven't died yet," a reminder to himself and a thankful quote for the little bit that he was still able to do.

Hearing car doors slam, one after another, made them both jump up to get dressed; William, quickly in boxer shorts, socks, a T-shirt, overalls, and boots. It took a little longer for Emma,

*"I ain't the only one gettin' old,"* he thought, watching her slowly maneuver underwear, including granny panties and a big bra, and then all the other clothes and things she

had to put on; being over seventy didn't help her move any faster either.

Emma wasn't skinny, nor was she a very large woman, but short and stout with big breasts, hips, and thighs,

*"The same way she was fifty years ago when I decided she was the woman I wanted to marry,"* thought William, reflecting back on blissful years.

* * * *

"What's wrong wit' her?" asked William, coming down the hall to meet Dominique and Callie at the staircase landing. Dominique didn't say anything, just headed straight upstairs wearing a sad face.

"She mad 'cause I told her she couldn't go to a party."

"Whose party?" William asked.

"A boy at school."

"She's twelve years old… why can't she go?"

"'Cause I said she couldn't," said Callie, ready to turn the wrath on William.

"Because you said she couldn't," William said, anyway. William had developed a bad habit of repeating things.

"Didn't you go to parties and eat cake and ice cream when you was little?" he asked, although he knew the answer already…most of the time, he was the one who took her.

"Yeah, you did."

"But it usually wasn't just cake and ice cream I was there for."

"And you think Dominique's gon' be like you?"

"I doubt it… she got way more sense than that."

"Well, thanks," said Callie, taking offense at William's comparison and assumption.

William realized then that talking to Callie about the subject they were on was a lost cause,

"...and a vast waste of time."

Unconsciously, he wiped his brow. He hadn't realized it, but sweat was still pouring.

"What's wrong wit' you?" asked Callie, "Why you sweatin' like that?" but when she looked down the hall and saw Emma coming out of the back bedroom, tying on an apron, then right away, Callie knew why William was sweating…plus his T-shirt was on backward, a dead giveaway.

She laughed a little and giggled and then smiled.

William saw it when she looked down the hall at Emma,

"What's so funny?" he asked, chest stuck out, taking offense, "You think I'm too old for everything else... what, you think I'm too old for that, too?"

"Did you hear me say anything?" Callie asked, taking off up the stairs.

"I just don't want you to die tryin'," she said, looking back down the staircase at William, laughing at him again.

"The tombstone on your grave'll read, 'Here he lies after one last try.'" This time, when she laughed, Callie hurried inside the bedroom and slammed the door behind her to keep from hearing what else William had to say.

"One last try?" he said, repeating her again anyway as if he couldn't believe that she'd said it,

"For your information, I still got it. Ain't no 'one last try' shit here, my dear. Maybe 'one last try' for somebody else, but not for me," he said, walking out the door on his way to sit on the front porch, mumbling as he went,

"I know what I can do. Hell… I still got it."

# Chapter 22

Dominique was thinking of only one thing.

*"Gettin' the hell outta this house."* She'd learned such language and phrases from her mother, who was still in the room next door,

"...with the radio turned up, absorbed in more of the same decade-old, depressin' ass songs that she had playin' in the car earlier," thought Dominique.

At twelve years old, Dominique had been forced to grow up fast, living in a house with the likes of a woman like Callie Devereaux.

"Surely spirits have overtaken her by now," thought Dominique since the only other stop that they made on the way home was at a liquor store.

"She's probably dancin' too…with no one in particular, just wit' a glass in one hand and the whole bottle of gin in the other."

As fast as she could, Dominique changed clothes, finished what little homework there was to do, and was on her way down the stairs. William was still on the front porch, fanning gnats and flies, dozing off now and then, oblivious to everything else around him.

"Hey," said Dominique when she got in the kitchen, allowing herself to fall softly, face first inside the comfort of Emma's opened arms and big bosomy breast…Emma had been at the kitchen table watching the last episode of soap operas on the little ten-inch portable black and white TV Callie had bought for her. And since Mary had been deported back to Jamaica, Emma was the only other person in the house that Dominique felt close to.

"Awwwwww… hey baby," said Emma, taking a gentle hold of her, "What's wrong?" she asked, noticing Dominique's unhappy face and sad demeanor.

"Momma's bein' mean again."

"How? What's she done this time?"

"A boy at school's havin' a birthday party, and momma said I can't go."

"Typical," thought Emma, as usual, disappointed in

Callie's poor decision-making.

"Everybody's goin' 'cept me," said Dominique, letting it all pour out, the hurt and pain in how discontent it made her feel.

"Seth Evan's the one havin' the party, and supposedly his mom's orderin' cake and ice cream. Too bad there won't be any for me."

"Yes, there will," said Emma. Normally, she wouldn't intervene, and she wouldn't this time either, but the solution was simple and within the boundaries of her being the cook.

"Tell you what," she said, turning squarely to face Dominique head-on with a gentle hold of Dominique by both shoulders.

"I'll make a cake just for you…one with chocolate icing on it. And ice cream and chocolate as well. And if you want, when it's ready, I'll have some too.

"I know William'll want some, as much as he like's eatin' chocolate cake.

"We'll have our own lil' party," Emma said, making it sound oh-so-good.

"Okay," said Dominique, already anticipating the taste of it, especially with how good she knew Emma could cook.

"The cake I'm gon' make gon' be way better than they ole' store-bought cake anyway…just wait, you'll see," said Emma, expressing it with great excitement, enticing the mind of a child.

"Okay," Dominique said again, but this time with a big smile on her face.

"Now you go on outside and play, and I'll get started."

By then, Dominique had started giggling,

"Okay," she said one last time, overcome by good humor.

"Good job…thank you, Lord," said Emma, watching while a joyful Dominique skipped part of the way and then ran the rest of the way out of the house.

Emma had always been good with children. She was just unable to have any of her own.

"*John Henry ruined me*," she thought, remembering the first man she married, "*…beat me so bad 'till I couldn't have no kids at all.*"

Although married at the time, Emma was just a fifteen-year-old girl, a child who had more or less been forced into marriage... it definitely wasn't done of her own choosing.

"*Yeah, I was just a kid myself, actually*," she thought, going back in time,

"*Big John Henry Salmon, he was thirty-somethin'. He knew how old I was too, but didn't care...back then, nobody seemed to care how old a girl was who got married, especially not if the parents didn't say anything. And mine were dead.*

"Yes, sir. Big John Henry Salmon, Luke Devereaux's right-hand man. He was just too mean and cruel to people...a big ole' bully," said Emma, in thought, going about making a cake.

"*The last time he beat me, though, Luke Devereaux wouldn't stand for it anymore...took me outta the fields. Told me, 'You gon' cook in the kitchen from now on so's I can keep an eye on you.'*

"*I remember John Henry came to the house that day thinkin' he was just gon' make me leave and go wit' him. Luke Devereaux stopped him in the front yard and gave him a fair warnin', 'Alright, John...go on back to work now, or find yourself somethin' else to do...Emma stayin' here.' But John Henry wouldn't listen... I guess he thought Luke Devereaux was playin' or wasn't gon' do nothin' to him. And as soon as he stepped his big behind on the porch, Luke emptied his lil' derringer pistol in the center of John's chest. He was dead before he hit the ground, and here I been cookin' ever since."*

## Chapter 23

Conditions on the front porch became a lot more tolerable and then quite pleasant when a cool breeze blew in that not only cooled things off a little but kept flies and gnats at bay too, allowing William a chance to sleep sound and peacefully, that is until he heard one of the screen doors slam shut…

*"Dominique, whenever she goes out the back, she always lets the door slam shut."*

It was definitely her. When William jumped up and walked through the house, he saw that Emma, the only other person there on the first floor, was still in the kitchen, busy doing what she usually would do: cook. Callie was still upstairs. Dominique, however, was outside, walking with a purpose as if in cadence, away from the house.

"Where she goin'?" he asked, more to himself than to anybody else, wondering first if what he thought she was about to do was safe. But then also became extremely curious the more he saw her walk toward the tree line of the wooded bayou…so far, nobody but Dominique had seen the inexplicable Ms. Ladeaux, which William thought was strange, a woman in the swamp that nobody but a child had seen.

"I better go see what she up to," he said, again more so to himself than to anybody else. But Emma piped in any way.

"Alright now… you be careful out there," she told him as if William might be more prone to getting hurt than Dominique, a twelve-year-old.

Once again, he felt insulted.

"Emma… you just worry 'bout cookin', and I'll worry 'bout takin' care of me," he said on his way out the back door, too. It slammed shut again, just not as hard as it had done before when Dominique had walked through it.

It wasn't until then, after he'd gotten outside that William noticed how Dominique had dressed, in not only an old pair of overalls but in long sleeves too,

"The best repellent against mosquitoes that I can think of," said William, watching as the vision of Dominique began to slowly disappear behind trees, foliage, and the growth of dense shrubbery.

"If I'm not mistaken, she had on boots, too," he said, recollecting all that he remembered seeing.

"Smart girl," he thought, realizing that maybe, after all, he might've underestimated Dominique's intelligence and ability to survive in the woods.

"She just like her grandma used to be," he said, sounding very much impressed.

* * * *

Ms. Ladeaux was in the usual place and was busy catching one fish after another,

"Well, hello there… 'bout time you got here," she said, turning to look just as Dominique took a step out on the old wooden pier, which was more of a platform actually, a platform that extended slightly over the water.

"The fish bitin' good today."

"I see," said Dominique after getting closer, noticing that the bucket sitting beside Ms. Ladeaux was nearly filled. She watched Ms. Ladeaux throw in another fish, put more bait on a hook, and then throw the line back out in the water.

"I would'a' been here sooner, but momma picked me up

today and made me mad again."

Ms. Ladeaux chuckled and laughed.

"Yo' momma stay makin' you mad. You alright?" she asked, momentarily diverting her attention from the cork connected to the line in the water to Dominique's solemn face.

"Yeah, I'm alright…me and Emma talked… and guess what," said Dominique, becoming cheerful in an instant, "Emma's makin' me a chocolate cake and ice cream too. They're both my favorites."

"Well, good for you…that ought'a' make you happy."

"I'm tellin' you, it does," said Dominique, giggling a little from already being happy.

\* \* \* \*

Dominique's tiny footprints weren't hard to follow, nor was the sound of when she started talking and giggling.

"*She's definitely not alone,*" William thought, making sure each step he took was taken carefully so as to not make a sound.

And then, finally, he was able to see them… from a distance, of course, but close enough to see Dominique and a gray-haired old woman on the same pier that he and Bessie used to fish from.

*"The last time I came out here, it was all grown over,"* he thought, remembering back when he shot and killed the hog.

It was a wonder how the land around the pier had suddenly gotten so clear and accessible. But what was more amazing was that the woman did, in fact, look a little like Bessie.

*"If it is, she's aged quite a bit. I doubt it's her, though,"* he thought, but looking especially at the woman's gray hair and the hat the woman was wearing…it looked a lot like the hat Bessie said she'd gotten from Billie Holiday.

His eyes weren't as good as they used to be, and from where he stood, the distance was too far to be sure of anything he thought he'd seen. But then, while Dominique fixed another pole and line to throw out in the water, the woman began to make a joyful sound that brought back a lot of memories.

*"Oh God,"* thought William, amazed. He wouldn't have believed it if he wasn't standing there to hear it himself. The woman was humming the sound of a sweet melody, a melody of the same song Bessie used to sing all the time;

"Good mornin' heartache, you old gloomy sight.

"Good mornin' heartache thought we said goodbye last night…"

"No…it can't be," thought William, but in words that came out aloud.

"Bessie's dead…I saw it wit' my own eyes when she died."

He was becoming overwhelmed, which brought on a faint feeling. The faint feeling made him stumble and take a couple of steps backward in an attempt to regain his composure and footing. That's when he stepped on what he thought was a tree root or maybe even a branch fallen from a tree. But what it turned out to be was a rather large snake, a very poisonous large snake…a cotton mouth.

The snake curled up and was initially aiming to bite William's hanging right hand. When he looked down, the snake was already in motion and struck William like a bolt of lightning, which was also how it must've felt.

\* \* \* \*

When William yelled, "AHHHHHHH!!!"

Dominique and Ms. Ladeaux both looked at each other and then in the direction of where the yell came from. And there was William, struggling to get himself free from the venomous grip of fangs the huge snake had sunk into him.

Like a flash, Dominique took off running toward him, but not before William broke free of the snake and started running, too, straight toward the house.

"I'll go tell momma," said a much quicker Dominique, passing him to go get help.

"Smart girl," said William again about Dominique, but in a lot of pain already from where the snake had bitten him and from trying to run on two bad knees. The pressure on his lungs was more than he could take; he was almost out of breath.

He saw it when Dominique broke across the tree line and ran into the opening, not far from the back door of the house, but that was just moments before William passed out and fell to the ground.

# Chapter 24

As if with clairvoyant powers, William, while unconscious and with both eyes closed, could still see the sky. But it's a dark sky, darkened by gloom and fright, with fast-moving black clouds, ominous, like time in a life that had been terribly altered and fast-forwarded.

There was also the woman's face, Bessie's face, that was actually looking down at him with the darkened sky and clouds looming. But it was an aged old Bessie who was still wearing the same old clothes and hat she was wearing the day she was killed. She was also wearing a look of concern that worried him...seeing how concerned she was made him feel that maybe, by this time, he should be even more afraid and frightened than ever.

"Lord, am I gonna die?" he asked.

And then suddenly things changed, and he saw his mother, who died in a house fire long ago when he was just a little boy…and his father, who died trying to save her. Both of them were looking even more worried and concerned than Bessie as if William too might be doomed just as they already were.

They were telling him,

"Get up…get up, son, and go back. Live again," which is what Bessie had been trying to say all along,

"Don't die like this."

So, with all the will-power and strength that he could possibly muster, William forced both eyes back open, and almost immediately, the pain hit where the snake bit him, except this time, it was as if the whole side of his hand was on fire, but burning from the inside out, and slowly spreading, penetrating, working its way upward.

He could hear it clearly when Callie yelled.

"Oh, my God… WILLIAM!!!" she was running, jumping over things, breaking the tree line in a hurry with Dominique and Emma right behind her.

Bessie, or Ms. Ladeaux, or whoever she was, was standing off to one side, away in the distance, desperately urging him to get up, too. Even so, it was all he could do to just lay there and look around.

However, when she got there, Callie got him up and moving,

"Come on, William…don't die on me. Let's go," she said, not taking no for an answer. And somehow, she got him up, back across the tree line, across the yard, and in the back seat of the car.

Emma sat beside him, crying while Dominique, in the passenger side of the front seat with Callie, looked on from front to back and back up front again, keeping a close eye, watching both the road up ahead as well as William's deteriorating condition.

William was in a lot of pain, and it showed, but Callie was driving so fast until, at times, it felt as if all four wheels were coming off the ground and that they all might die in a car wreck.

But then, William blacked out again, except this time he stayed out, and there was nothing, just the quiet and total darkness.

# Chapter 25

**Lafayette Memorial Hospital**

"It's a good thing you got him here when you did, or else we probably wouldn't've been able to save him. Not saying that he's outta the woods yet because he's not... but he's responding well.

"What I mean is, we've given him the antidote, and we've gotten him stable, but we're still waiting for the fever to break, which, in time, I'm sure it will. But let's keep our fingers crossed until then," said the acting physician, explaining things a little nervously, which was understandable, being that the physician was none other than Bob Macklin, the man Callie met and saw dancing at Dominique's school.

"Awwww...thank you so very much," said Callie, holding Bob's hand in a friendly gesture, showing gratitude but standing there just as nervous as he was.

# Buckets, Shovels, Ghost and Worms

"We appreciate what you've done."

"You're welcome… and I'm sure he'll appreciate what you've done too, once he wakes up," said Bob, smiling a little to lighten the mood.

Callie laughed.

"I sure hope so," she said, finally letting go of Bob's hand after getting used to it, warming to the feel of his touch.

"Girl, get a grip...get a hold of yourself," said a thought from within, from places in a woman no one else should know about.

She laughed again and was quite giddy actually.

"I had no idea you were a doctor," she said, in an attempt at regaining some kind of composure,

"I sure couldn't tell by those dance moves," she said to lighten the mood even more.

"Yeah, well…you have to have a keen eye to recognize the kind'a' moves I be makin'," said Bob, still smiling, wishing Callie hadn't let go, his hand feeling lonely now that she had.

"I'm filling in, actually; Doc Marlowe hasn't gotten here yet…he's off, delivering a baby somewhere."

"You guys have coffee here?" Callie asked, wanting to steer the rest of their conversation away from within earshot of Emma and Dominique, thinking and hoping that whatever else she and Bob might say would get more personal.

\* \* \* \*

In the cafeteria, after they'd both gotten a filled cup of coffee, steaming from the brim, and had taken seats at a table across from one another, Callie stated the obvious,

"I don't see a ring on your finger, mister."

"You don't have one on your finger either, Ms. Callie Devereaux," said Bob, being friendly and facetious at the same time but with a more serious look on his face.

"Come on, Bob…you know what I'm sayin'. I've never been married. What about you?"

"Of course, I have… I've got three kids to prove it."

"Oh, brother… you're definitely not from around here. People in Louisiana don't necessarily get married because they've had children, and I've got one to prove it, too."

"I guess you got me there," said Bob, smiling, having fun with Callie,

"I'm from California, actually, San Diego. My wife, she

was from here. And after years of baby deliveries, I have indeed learned that holy matrimony isn't quite a requirement when it comes to having sex in Louisiana. It isn't in San Diego either. It's just somethin' I was brought up to believe in."

"Oh yeah?" said Callie, thinking that Bob might be a little naïve, old-fashioned, simple, or whatever,

"…but he's cute," she thought, holding full eye contact.

"Ok, so where's the Mrs. at now, Mr. Macklin?" she asked, still gazing closely at Bob from across the table, considering Bob's innocence a virtue and finding him quite interesting.

"Whoever she is, she shouldn't let you just wander around alone so much," said Callie, using a foot of hers to find Bob's feet under the table.

"Believe me, if she could help it, she would," said Bob, rearranging both feet, the serious look back on his face again.

"Unfortunately, my wife, Tammy, died a few months after we moved here," he said, forcing himself to smile again anyway.

"Awwwwww…" said Callie, embarrassed and feeling bad for him, wishing she hadn't asked or tried to touch his foot. "Sorry… hope I didn't offend you."

"No, you're alright. I'm long past being hurt anymore. I get lonely at times, though," said Bob, showing that he could flirt a little too,

"…especially after meeting someone like you," he said, feet back in place, touching Callie's again.

That's when the intercom came alive just before Callie could respond or say what it was she wanted to say,

"Doctor Macklin…room 104, stat," which meant his presence was needed in a hurry.

"Is that William's room?" Callie asked, on the verge of panic.

"I'm afraid it is," said Bob, taking off in a sprint with Callie right behind him.

# Chapter 26

"William… calm down and relax," said Callie once she and Bob Macklin had gotten there in William's room.

Nurses, along with Emma and Dominique, were already there, but William, wide-eyed and terribly frightened, had been in a fearful rage, fighting them all off while trying his best to remove the I.V. and get out of bed.

"You're in a hospital for a reason, and these people are here to help you," Callie told him, making it plain and clear, hoping he would lay there and do what the nurses wanted him to do.

But William's response was plain and clear,

"I wanna go home, Callie…this ain't the place where I wanna be."

Not a day in his life had William been sick, nor had he ever had a reason to be in a hospital, which was what frightened him, especially after having had a supernatural experience involving loved ones urging him to go on and live. As far as he knew, hospitals were one of the last places people were brought just before they were going to die.

Callie, who knew William well enough to know what he was thinking, took a gentle hold of him and started a gentle rub down of William's forehead and hair, lightly and with all tenderness.

Regardless of how much the two of them argued, fussed, and fought with each other, the love and bond they shared was strong and unbreakable.

"Oh, William," Callie began, speaking softly, a smile on her face and a look in her eyes that expressed more compassion and kindness than she was usually willing to show,

"You're not gonna die, not now you're not...I promise," she said before looking over at Bob Macklin, who had, by then, taken up the space on the other side, holding William's arm to not only keep him from harming himself, trying to get up, but also to keep him from snatching out the IV.

"See that handsome fella standing there beside you?" she asked, forcing William to look too. Bob had put on a smile for him as well.

"He's Doctor Bob Macklin, a friend of mine. He's not gonna let you die, and neither am I."

It took a while longer for the persuasive part of what Callie said to register, but slowly, William's tense body began to relax a little, and as it did, Bob let go. But not Callie… she was crying and holding on to him even more.

"You know I'm mad at you, right?" she said, with tears streaming down.

"For what? What I do?" William asked, his voice hoarse and barely audible, but he was back to his old self, more worried and concerned about Callie than he was about anything else, including his own welfare.

"Because you almost got yourself killed, that's why," said Callie, sounding like a little girl again, balling over, crying as if, for once, she was finally able to release some old, store up the hurt and pain...pain that was still bottled up from when Bessie died, and pain from when Doc Elliott told her that Ted had died.

"I couldn't take losing you too," she said, all choked up.

At that point, William had shed a few tears and had his arms draped around Callie as well, and everybody else in the room had started crying. Afterward, as a precautionary measure, Bob had a nurse add a sedative to William's IV bag so that it would be administered intravenously without William knowing it, thinking that maybe William would sleep for a while instead of trying to get up and leave. At least while he slept, they wouldn't have to monitor and keep such a close eye on him.

"I hope he's able to get over this," said Callie after everybody else had left the room and William was asleep.

"How about you? It seems as though you've got a few things to get over as well. You wanna tell me about what brought on all the tears?" Bob asked.

Callie looked at Bob and smiled before she gave him a kiss on the lips as if to say, Thank you for what he'd done for William. But then, with a twinkle in her eye, she looked at him and said,

"Another time, another place."

She walked away after that and left Bob standing there, wondering.

In the lobby, he saw her leading Dominique and Emma away, headed toward the doors that lead to the parking lot. She looked back once and said over a shoulder,

"We'll see you in the morning."

But Bob couldn't seem to take his eyes off her and stood

there watching until she was gone, well out of sight. Even then, it took a nurse to come along and remind him of other patients that needed to be seen and that he needed to get moving.

He walked away with a smile on his face.

# Chapter 27

After having been sheltered most of her life and kept away from harsh or severe situations, Dominique was stunned to see the way William was carrying on at the hospital, cursing and giving nurses such a hard time. He was in a hospital gown and had an IV in his arm, but he was still trying to fight them, demanding that he be let out of bed and allowed to go home. Things got a lot better once the acting physician and Callie got there to explain things. Otherwise, with the way it seemed, William might not have ever calmed down.

However, she got worried again when Callie cried; she'd never seen her mother so upset to cry and shed tears either...

*"Ok... maybe once, when Doc Elliott died,"* thought Dominique, but it uncharacteristically made Callie seem weak and vulnerable, unlike the Callie Devereaux that Dominique had ever known.

Dominique's inquiring mind was also curious to know why Ms. Ladeaux hadn't come to the hospital and wondered,

*"Doesn't she care if William lives or dies?"*

She asked Emma about it, but all she would say was,

"Hush up, child... I thought I told you never to talk about that," and she wouldn't, ever again, especially not if it made Emma mad; there was still a matter of whether Emma would make the chocolate cake and ice cream or not,

*"...something she obviously won't do,"* Dominique thought, "...not if Emma gets too upset or pissed off."

And Callie, after being assured that William would be alright, could think of nothing else besides Mr. Bob Macklin, the doctor. It was quite embarrassing, though, how she broke down and cried in front of him,

*"It's too soon to let the cat outta the bag,"* she thought, planning to be a lot more reserved in the way she presented herself. She was thinking this, basically, from being so ashamed of ever having had a nervous breakdown,

"Nope... don't want him knowin' nothin' 'bout that yet. I'm sure he'll find out about it sooner or later, though, just as I'll find out things about him too," she said so no one else could hear, envisioning her and Bob being married already,

"He is the marrying kind," she thought, driving along happily after reaching out to turn up the sound on the radio just in case what she was thinking came out aloud in actual words,

*"...words no one else is supposed to hear,"* she thought, and then said, "With the music turned up, I can always pretend to be singing."

The whole time, Dominique and Emma had both been looking, first at Callie and then at each other after hearing all that Callie had said.

## Chapter 28

William spent a total of five days there in the hospital. He'd lost a little weight, which was insignificant to how he'd lost the use of his right-hand ring and pinky fingers… a terrible blow for somebody who used their hands a lot, especially if the person happened to be like William, right-handed. Nevertheless, no matter how great a misfortune, it was something he would just have to get used to.

Other than that, he was still alive and doing just fine. In fact, considering what he'd gone through and lost, William was in quite good spirits. Even the nurses thought so, the ones that he'd fought with included.

Upon his discharge, they were all there, wishing him well. One of them spoke kindly when she told William,

"Alright, Mr. Burns…take care of yourself. Don't do nothin' I wouldn't do."

But then, one of the other nurses, knowing how afraid

William was of hospitals, couldn't resist and found it an opportune time to joke and tease him about it,

"Yeah…and we'll save a bed just for you so that anytime you're ready to come back, you'll feel welcomed and right at home."

"I'll be damned. If I do, Popeye's a sissy," said William, on his way out in a wheelchair with another nurse pushing him.

"So, don't hold your breath, Sista. Ain't no way in thee hell I'll ever be ready to come back to this place again. Not so y'all can keep on usin' me as a damn pin cushion.

"No thanks," he said, telling her this over a shoulder after they'd gotten further down the hall, almost out the door.

It was all said in good humor; they laughed, and William laughed. He was dead serious, though. When he got in the car, the first thing he did was look upward, toward the sky, to tell God,

"Thank you, Lord…thank you for sendin' me home one more time."

\* \* \* \*

After saying goodbye and thanking all the nurses, Callie got in, too, and let the top down. And when she did, she took off going, as the term goes, like a bat outta hell, and with the music turned up...turned up too loud, actually.

William asked her,

"It's kind'a' loud, don't you think?" But all Callie did was smile and kept on driving...she obviously didn't hear him.

William gave up after a while, smiling back at her, and sat back in the seat.

He figured,

*"With the way she drivin', it wouldn't be long before they we home. And I won't have to deal with it anymore,"* at least that's what he hoped.

The radio station that Callie liked was one of the ones that played songs from the sixties, ten years prior, part of an era that she'd missed from being stricken with mental illness.

The Beatles were singing,

"I wanna hold your hand," a song that rocked the nation and inspired much of what went on during Beatle-mania, a time when so many of America's young, up-and-coming hopefuls seemed to go insane as well. Thinking back on it, the youth of America might've been worse off than Callie.

The song made Callie's head swim just as it had done to millions of others when the song first came out. It was bad enough that she was driving, trying to rock and sing along. Nevertheless, there's no doubt that the excitement would've been a lot greater had she not been driving.

Every once in a while, she'd look over at William. She patted him on the leg a few times and wore a big smile, happier than William had seen her in quite a while. Even so, the whole time, he was thinking,

"Poor child…her mind still ain't quite right…and'll probably never get no better. That's alright, though, she still my girl," he thought, looking over and smiling back at her.

"I would'a' been dead if it hadn't'a been for you," he said, not loud enough so Callie could hear him, but in something more like a private thought, thanking her just the same.

William hadn't bothered to volunteer and tell Emma about the affair he'd had with Bessie or about how he'd gotten her pregnant. He was sure that Bessie hadn't said anything about it either. Nevertheless, the way he felt about Callie was about the same as if he and Bessie were Callie's parents. It would probably be the closest he would ever come to having a child of his own. He loved her as much, that's for sure.

# Buckets, Shovels, Ghost and Worms

\* \* \* \*

Moods became somber once Callie was forced to slow down while going past a roadside work detail from nearby Angola State Prison…at least for William, it did. The last he remembered of seeing his two older brothers was when deputies from the sheriff's department came and put handcuffs and shackles on them.

The charge was theft; they'd supposedly stolen two live chickens from a nearby white landowner. William remembered it well, a night when they surprisingly had enough food to feed everybody, him and all seven of his other brothers and sisters.

Chicken and rice with beans and cornbread was what they all had. But he didn't think the crime his two older brothers had committed fit the bill of how they were punished. They were both given a stiff sentence of ten years of hard labor in the Angola State Prison, which was virtually like a life sentence. Angola's reputation for not only being one of the oldest, but also being one of the toughest-prison institutions in the United States was proven to be true over and over again. Very few men were expected to survive a year in its confinement, not to mention ten years.

As Callie drove by, the men on the detail in sweat-stained, grimy black and white striped uniforms all looked tired and terribly worn and beat as if the expression on their mostly dark faces had come from a surrender deep down inside their souls. It would've made the average person tearful and consider pardoning them all with the way they were watching while Callie drove by, especially after realizing there was nothing you could do to help. Men on horseback with harsh blue eyes, poked mouths stuffed full with chewing tobacco, wearing Stetson hats, and holding big guns made sure of it.

But regardless, it was just in Callie's nature to rebel and be mischievous. Once she'd gotten past the men on horseback, well out of range of their short-barreled shotguns, Callie stopped the car and started shouting lewd obscenities, blowing the horn along with blowing the men big wet simulated kisses, and waving at them, hoping to cheer all the sad faces. What she did even made William laugh and smile.

He never heard from either of his two older brothers again or from any of the other seven siblings. The next morning, after having had a last meal together, they all left, going their own separate ways in search of the next evening's meal.

The sad feeling didn't last for very long, though, and when William looked up, The Devereaux House, which by then had come into view, was a welcomed sight for sore eyes. Suddenly, by the time Callie turned into the driveway, all was well again.

There was already another car parked in the driveway, a car William didn't recognize…a station wagon. And Bob Macklin was standing there on the front porch, holding what looked to be an iced cold beer.

"Now I know why she so happy," William thought about Callie's sudden gratified demeanor, "…she got herself a new man, and a good one, as far as I can tell.

"It's about time," he thought, smiling to himself.

## Chapter 29

"Well, well…look what the cat drug in," said William once he'd climbed out of the car and gone toward the front porch, close enough so that Bob could hear him.

*"And hello to you too,"* thought Bob, not only in response to William's witful yet derogatory way of approaching and greeting him but also in lieu of the travesty William had made of an old cliché.

It should've been,

*"Look what the cat dragged in,"* thought Bob, not that William cared about the proper or improper use of metaphors the English language provided. Just getting his point across was what mattered.

"…and I ain't talkin' 'bout the stray cat we got runnin' 'round the back yard. I'm talkin' 'bout this pussy cat over here," said William, continuing with both; his speech as well as the steps he took along the way up the few porch stairs, giving Bob a wink as he did and then smiling after gesturing toward Callie who'd gotten out of the car to catch up and walk along beside him.

Bob smiled too but was taken aback and didn't quite know what to say to either correct William's poor choice of words, or defend Callie's honor. Either would've been a waste of time.

Callie, on the other hand, tuned right in, smiling, but told William, "Be nice, will you?" she seemed just as startled and embarrassed as Bob on both accounts, especially with William being so candid.

"I am bein' nice," he told her, pressing on, "…maybe not as nice as you, but nice."

Bob seemed like a pleasant enough guy, well-rounded and all.

"…*with a career in medicine*," William added in more of his own private thoughts.

However, if he had any worries, it wouldn't be about Bob. It would be about Callie and how much more he thought she might ruin a reputation already damaged and tarnished by a few too many indiscriminate sexual relationships.

But, in giving the benefit of the doubt, William asked himself,

*"What will people think if, instead of just fooling around, Callie and Bob do happen to get together and become a serious couple? Better yet, how will Dr. Macklin himself handle it, being the talk of the town?"* which William knew would surely happen with whoever Callie got involved with, especially with it being one of the town's newest physicians.

On the way inside the house, after the two of them shook hands, William leaned over and whispered in Bob's ear, "She's not a pussy cat at all. From my understanding, she's more of a tiger, if you know what I mean."

Bob laughed, but William kept a straight face and walked on by, thinking,

*"He'll learn...when he gets his heart broken. He'll learn for sure."*

The problem with having a relationship with Callie was that when and if they ever broke up, for whatever reason, people who knew her would automatically blame the breakup on her. Rightfully so in most cases, with how Callie was inclined to get out of hand and misbehave at times. However, too much blame might send Callie's mindset reeling into another declining tailspin, one from which she might not ever recover. This was something William worried about when it came to Callie meeting and dating new men.

Before Doc Elliott died, that's the one thing he warned them about. He said,

"Depression was what set it off the first time and could possibly set it off again."

Even if nobody else understood what Doc Elliott was saying, William sure did.

\* \* \* \*

*"Home sweet home,"* thought William once he'd gotten inside the house with a hand up on the screen door, allowing it to close slowly and silently behind him. He'd only been gone a week but had already missed being there something terribly. The first chance he got, he planned to oil both screen doors so neither would ever squeak again.

"Well…everything looks about the same," he said, standing there, taking it all in, enjoying the moment, overtaken by an overwhelming power of pure satisfaction.

It took a while longer before he decided to relinquish and start down the main hallway toward the kitchen, where next he expected to see and find Emma, which he did along with Dominique and three other small children: Nora, Todd, and Samantha, all of whom shared a striking resemblance of their father, Bob Macklin, with the same cuteness and California long blond hair.

Emma was busy serving them the last bit of chocolate cake and ice cream, which Dominique thought was better than whatever Santa might bring for Christmas. In other words, there was nothing better.

It took a while for any of them to look up and notice that he'd come in, but when they did, Emma, the first to speak, gasped and then smiled before telling him,

"My God, William… you scared me."

Dominique, who was just as surprised and happy about seeing him, did a quick evaluation, prioritizing before jumping up, leaving the cake and ice cream to run and give William a big hug around the neck. It felt good and made his day being so well received.

She told him,

"There isn't any more cake and ice cream, so I guess you're gonna have to get Emma to make some more."

"Get Emma to make some more for who?" William asked, using a finger to jab at Dominique's midsection, which made not only Dominique giggle and laugh but Nora and Samantha do too.

Todd, however, seemed too preoccupied and engrossed to notice; there was a spot on the floor that he seemed completely zoomed in on. At one point, Emma even had to lift his chin in order to feed him a spoon filled with ice cream just so he'd know what they were having.

At their home in San Diego, Todd had wandered out in the backyard and got in the pool by himself one night. After realizing he was gone, Bob and Jenny, Bob's wife, searched frantically and eventually found Todd lying at the bottom of the pool, unconscious. Applying CPR saved his life, but a lack of oxygen to the brain for so long had left him, for the most part, mentally incapacitated, much in the same way that Callie had been. Unfortunately for Todd, however, he hasn't been able to recover so far.

Nevertheless, although Todd, at nine years old, might've been disabled, his two sisters, Nora, ten years old, and Samantha, seven, who were both pretty little girls, toothy with wide smiles, weren't disabled at all and had remarkable aptitudes and high hopes for the future. Nora, for instance, had already mentioned wanting to be like her dad and become a doctor. Samantha was following in the same footsteps.

\* \* \* \*

"William's not an easy guy to figure out," said Bob, "...but if I had to guess, I'd say that he's not too happy about me being here."

"Oh, I think he likes you," said Callie. She and Bob were on the front porch, rocking chairs active, wine glasses in their hands, filled to the brim with white wine, while they talked and watched the sun go down. They'd been sharing evenings like this for almost a week.

"William doesn't usually say anything at all to men I bring home and can be quite rude, actually, especially if he doesn't want you here. But, the way he carried on with you, and now, with the kids...," the girls giggling in the kitchen hadn't stopped since he'd gotten there, "...I'd say that maybe you're the one from many whom he does like."

"Okay, well...do you think the fact that I saved his life might have something to do with it?"

"Yeah, it might," said Callie, responding to a question she thought was not only obvious but also a little funny. She took a sip of wine to hide it.

"There's no 'might' to it...you saving his life definitely has something to do with it, but not entirely," she said afterward, being more serious.

"He's dangerously honest. If he didn't like you, he'd let

you know either way, regardless.

"Why? Are you worried?" she asked. Sorry she'd laughed before at what Bob had asked.

"Of course not…but he was here first, and I wouldn't wanna be the cause of him being uncomfortable, especially not if things happen between you and me like how I'm hoping they might."

"Oh yeah? Things like what? What's supposed to happen?" Callie asked, turning toward Bob, becoming more and more interested in what he had to say.

"Didn't I tell you?" said Bob, feigning memory loss but also using an old Winston Churchill British accent to carry on.

"My dear…it seems that I've won you in an act of war, and now you're to become a sex slave for me."

"Oh, wow…I like it when you talk dirty."

"If that's true," he said, switching to a vaudeville voice of Groucho Marx, imitating the moving eyebrows and cigar smoking as well,

"…then wait'll we get upstairs, the show's just gettin' started."

"I can hardly wait," said Callie, totally entertained, enjoying the performance, but finishing the last bit of wine,

"I've got something a little stronger than this upstairs if you're up for it," she said, showing Bob the empty wine bottle.

"Oh, I'm up for it," he said, back to himself again, quite an original character, finishing what was left in his glass in one gulp.

"Well...what're we waitin' for? Lead the way, my lady," he said, tongue sticking out, overly exposed, wagging while he huffed and puffed as if he were a dog,

"Man's best friend," he said, "...or in this case, woman's best friend. I'm with you, honey."

Callie laughed, and then they were gone, disappearing up the main staircase, and behind Callie's opened and then closed bedroom door. It wouldn't be until the next morning before the two of them emerged again, a sexually motivated phenomenon neither of them would ever forget.

The lovemaking continued night after night, and then, a month later, they were married.

## Chapter 30

Rays of bright light from the sun shining down made everything glisten and sparkle on a day when not a cloud was seen to blemish the clear, blue sky. And across the dirt road, a field of hay, grown wild for so long, had been cut and left in round, fifteen hundred pound bales as far as the eye could see, in no sequential order, but in succession of how it was gathered and then spewed out of big Ford tractors and baling machines.

"William… how do you… like…this one?" asked Todd about a painting he'd done of the landscape in front of the house. He spoke with a speech impediment, in sort of a slow drawl, stuttering at times, which was still much better than him not speaking at all, which was how it was two years prior.

He had an easel set up with a canvas on it, and in one hand, a board with an array of paint colors on it while the other hand held a small paintbrush. He'd learned a lot in two years and was, in fact, especially for an eleven-year-old child, showing signs of being a natural, talented beyond the eleven years of his youth.

"I like it, but I think it needs a little more color," said William, twenty feet away, peering at it from a rocking chair on the front porch.

The bright red tail end of Callie's convertible Cadillac parked in the driveway, the only part of Callie's car on Todd's painting, was what William referred to.

"Okay...I'll...fix it," said Todd. And then, with strokes of magic, making only the little of what could be seen of the red car stand out and seem of some importance.

It was William who first took an interest and encouraged him once he realized Todd had talent. Talking for him was difficult and, at times, quite embarrassing and burdensome, whereas painting was just the opposite: easy and rudimentary.

Furthermore, William, without any kind of formal education or training himself, definitely without a doctor's or psychiatric degree, took what little he'd learned from when Doc Elliott was treating Callie and applied some of the same methods to helping Todd. That and the therapy treatments Todd had already been getting from actual doctors and psychiatrists helped the progress come along quicker than they thought it would. Although much of the results were accredited to William and what he'd done for Todd at home.

It started the same week that Bob Macklin and the kids moved in, right after he and Callie were married. It took some getting used to for William and Emma, suddenly having a house filled with children all in the way of almost everything they tried to do, especially in the kitchen.

On quick notice, Bob hired and brought along with them a nanny/housekeeper. But Bridgett, a thirty-something-year-old hippie type, liberal woman, rail thin.

"Too thin if you ask me," thought Emma, about the nanny whose long, auburn hair and pale white skin, as she thought"...in obvious need of a sun tan," was, at times, no help at all when it came to having control of, or disciplining the children.

"Probably 'cause she was high all the time. The woman smokes too much marijuana," another thought from Emma.

Mostly, during the weekends and at times when the kids weren't in school, Emma would have to be the one to keep them calm and in order, especially the girls, including Dominique, who was insisting more and more on becoming the next Ms. Betty Crocker.

One afternoon, Emma took them all out to pick berries for blueberry pies she wanted to make, which was how Todd's talents were discovered. Actually, Emma brought Todd along only so she could keep an eye on him, not so he could actually pick berries. And because of it, maybe out of boredom from not having anything else to do, Todd took it upon himself to find another use for blueberries.

So, back at the house, he took a hand and squeezed until the juice came out, which, along with a finger from the other hand, he used to make a wall drawing, an exceptional drawing at that, mostly of Emma with a head scarf and apron on, an Aunt Jemima look alike.

No amount of soap and water or scrubbing would get the stain completely out, though. The entire wall had to be painted over, which was what made William go out the next day and buy Todd an easel with paintbrushes and paper to do his drawings on instead. He eventually graduated to using canvasses and better quality paints and brushes, which furthered his learning and knowledge of painting, something he'd done quite well, actually.

It was a different story about how Todd had gotten his voice back. Not since the day of the near drowning incident that happened to him at their home in San Diego had anybody heard Todd utter a word or sound similar to him trying to speak, not until the day of the big storm.

## Chapter 31

Callie could hardly take the way that Bob, breathing harder and harder to keep up with the way his body was moving, kept penetrating, each time going deeper and deeper.

"I really don't think you know how much I love you. You don't do you?" he asked between breaths without missing a stroke, exerting himself wholeheartedly.

"Probably not enough," said Callie, uttering back, just on impulsive, blurting out what she thought was the truth.

However, pretending to be unimpressed was just a ploy and all she could do to keep from letting out a scream. The way Bob made love to her was so good that it was all she could do otherwise, blurt out the truth.

The clock said that it was after four in the morning. After a long twenty-four-hour shift, Bob had left the hospital and came straight home to find Callie lying in bed, wide awake and naked, waiting for him.

Shortly afterward, the rain had started, first as a light drizzle, barely even noticeable, which later turned into a torrential downpour, great weather for sex. And then the wind started blowing, in gusts, shifting now and then while the rain pelted the house and ground. Every once in a while, thunder would roar, and a momentary strike of lightning would brighten the nighttime sky.

By then, Bob had showered and gotten in bed naked, right beside Callie, their bodies almost immediately becoming intertwined, entangled, and sweaty from just the beginning of making love.

"Nothing's better than this," said Bob about the ambiance, "...hard rain in the morning while in bed with the one you love. Perfect," he thought, allowing his mind to unwind and go where Callie was trying to take it.

At a certain point, when Callie thought the friction from the way she was being penetrated might make her explode, she threw both arms around him and started whispering things in Bob's ear,

"Go ahead, baby…fuck me. It's all yours…as much as you want."

And Bob, doing his best to oblige, helped himself by

going harder and stronger, in constant rhythm.

"That's it…that's it, baby," said Callie, still whispering in Bob's ear but holding on a lot tighter.

"Uh huh… yes… just like that. Oh, my God!!!" With Bob moving at a steady rhythmic pace, first slow, and then fast and harder, Callie finally did climax and scream.

Bob followed suit and let out a loud noise as well, something indescribable yet filled with the passion of ecstasy.

"I'm never gonna get enough of you," he told Callie afterward with what little strength and breath he had left, "…never in a million years."

Callie, however, was speechless, at least until the feeling from the enormous sensation had died down a little. Then, finally, between breaths, and with both arms still around him, she held on and told Bob,

"You better not get enough, not ever. I'll probably die if you do."

* * * *

The same week that William bought Todd's first easel and paint set was the same week a Category 4 hurricane bound for Louisiana, off the Gulf of Mexico, plummeted the area with high winds and rain. It lingered over the ocean for two whole days before finally coming ashore, bringing with it not only dark clouds and more rain but also hail and wind gusts up to 120 mph.

New Orleans was hit the hardest, with Lake Pontchartrain spilling water over the man-made levees that protected half the city from floods. Those living elsewhere, near the bayou, were hit pretty hard as well, with the water from adjoining rivers, creeks, and waterways rising and flooding everything there, too.

On the very first day when the storm first brought bad weather, it was considered that, in all probability, they would more than likely have to evacuate the Devereaux House and leave in search of higher, drier ground.

When Callie insisted that everybody pack a bag,

"...just in case," she told them. Dominique thought of Ms. Ladeaux and wondered if she would be all alright. Usually, no rain or anything else would stop Ms. Ladeaux from fishing, and Dominique was thinking,

"She might not know about the storm that's coming and could very well be out in it now, fishing."

Nobody saw it when she put on rain gear and boots and ran out the back door...nobody but Nora.

"Dominique…where're you goin'?" she asked in a low voice so no one else would hear. Although the frightful, troubled look on her face told how she felt,

"I'm scared," she said, scared for Dominique if she went out the door and into the swamp.

"Don't be…I'll be right back," Dominique told her, "Just stay here. And don't tell nobody," said Dominique, insisting before taking off in a hurry.

But then, Todd saw Nora put on boots and run out anyway, which made him run out a few minutes later to find out where she might be going as well.

\* \* \* \*

The ground was soaked and saturated in more places than others after nearly a full day of downpours. From past experiences and from having walked through it so many other times, Dominique knew that with the ground being so wet, the swamp could be a very dangerous place. From the tree line on, each step was taken gently until she built up enough confidence and self-trust to go a little faster and a little further while trying to figure out, on the fly, which way to step and which way not to step.

It wasn't long before she was finally able to see the little wooden pier where she and Ms. Ladeaux usually fished.

Ms. Ladeaux wasn't there, "Thank God," thought Dominique.

However, strangely, the place looked overgrown with weeds, vines, and grass growing wildly. Not how it usually looked when they were there fishing, clear of everything growing wildly.

Dominique was just about to take a few more steps toward it when she heard a loud, piercing scream.

"Oh, my God…Nora," she thought, and took off running in the direction where she thought the scream might've come from.

When she got there, sure enough, Nora was stuck in muddy water, almost in the exact same spot where Dominique had once been stuck. Nevertheless, Nora was sinking fast; already, since the short time Dominique had gotten there, Nora had sunk another six inches or more.

"Hold on, Nora…I'm goin' to get help," she said and had taken a few steps toward the house when Nora screamed again,

"NO!!! Dominique, don't leave," she said, sinking even further, maybe another six inches or so.

Nora was clearly terrified, and rightfully so. Not too far

off in the distance, the girls both heard a splash and looked over just in time to see the tail of a large alligator slithering down in the water. Not only was Nora sinking by the minute, on the verge of drowning, but now an alligator was coming to make dinner out of her.

"Dominique…please…help me," said Nora, crying, pleading, asking that Dominique, a twelve-year-old girl, do the impossible and save the day.

Dominique looked toward the house once more and was even more surprised to see Todd standing there behind her. By then, Nora had sunk, and at the same time, the water had risen past where Nora's midsection should've been; the jeans that she was wearing were below the water, and Minnie Mouse, on the long-sleeved pink T-shirt she had on was starting to get wet.

There was a tree branch on the ground that Dominique picked up and used to reach out to Nora. But when Nora grabbed it, Dominique wasn't strong enough to pull Nora out, nor was Nora strong enough to hold on to be pulled out. After a few tries, the idea was abandoned.

Dominique looked toward the house again,

*"We're gonna need an adult for this,"* she thought, concluding what appeared to be obvious.

But if she ran for help, what would happen to Nora? What if the alligator got too close and nobody was there to fight it off?

"HELP ME, DOMINIQUE… PLEASE!!!" said Nora, crying out, clearly panic-stricken and overwhelmed with fear.

Finally, Dominique turned to Todd, who looked just as nervous and frightened as the girls, twisting and squeezing his hands in a wringing motion as if he didn't know what else to do with them.

"TODD!!! LOOK AT ME!!!" Dominique yelled and told him.

It surprised her when he turned his head and did as he was told. The two of them looked into each other's eyes for a moment before Dominique told him,

"You gotta go get help, Todd... NOW!!! PLEASE!!! We gotta save Nora."

She was even more surprised when he did that as well, turned on a dime, and took off running toward the house. She'd never heard him say a word, but the only hope they had was that he would somehow communicate to somebody in the house that Nora was in grave danger and needed help, FAST. Her life depended upon it.

# Chapter 32

The rain had started in a torrential downpour again. Emma was preparing a nice meal, maybe the last for a while.

Bob was still upstairs in bed, getting some much-needed rest, and Callie had started a fire in one of the living room's fireplaces. From a collection of 45s, she'd just put on a record when William walked in.

"I've got dreams…dreams to remember," an old, slow, heartfelt Otis Redding song.

"Are we in love again, or did somebody else die that I don't know about?" William asked, making fun of the kind of music Callie had put on.

"Don't know about you, my man, but I'm in love," Callie told him, swaying and dancing around the room with a make-believe partner.

"Listen to it…the song tells it all," she said, still dancing and swaying to keep up with the beat of the music.

"Yeah, I heard the two of you love birds up there this mornin'… you screamin', and Bob soundin' somethin' like a damn hog in heat.

"I just hope Bridgett and the kids didn't hear it. Maybe they did and just didn't say nothin', or didn't know what the hell was goin' on. Either way that would be a helluva thing for y'all to have to explain," said William, laughing a little, thinking what he said was funny.

"Dreams…dreams to remember," quite a song when Otis first recorded it.

Callie ignored William's last remark and remained hypnotized by both the lyrics and the song's melody while singing along softly and soulfully to anybody who wanted to hear, including the make-believe dance partner.

William was just about to make another laughable comment when Todd, soaked from the rain head to toe, ran in and stopped in front of him. It was just an instinct, but William knew something was terribly wrong the moment Todd came in, especially with the way he was breathing, as if on the verge of hyperventilating.

Callie felt the same thing and stopped dancing. William kneeled in front of him. Todd never made eye contact but found a spot on the floor to look at, still huffing and puffing and wringing both hands again as usual when something was bothering him.

William took a gentle hold of Todd's upper arms and shoulders,

"Okay… calm down," he told Todd, still unsure why Todd seemed so excited.

"Take a deep breath, and breathe slow," William told Todd, lifting his chin, forcing eye contact, and then taking a deep breath himself and exhaling, giving an example of what he wanted Todd to do.

It worked… Todd, following William's example, took one deep breath after another. After a few times, with the release of each breath, Todd made a guttural noise that sounded more like an attempted pronunciation.

"Na… Na…"

"Take your time," William told him, realizing Todd's dilemma; he wanted to say something but couldn't.

"Na… Na…"

Nevertheless, both Callie and William also realized that what Todd wanted to say was no doubt about something very important; the tears that welled in Todd's eyes and fell in big drops confirmed it.

"Okay, Todd…come here. Take it easy," said Callie, in a motherly gesture, coming forward, arms open, in an effort to comfort him. But Todd pulled himself back and tried speaking once again.

"Na… Na…"

Samantha, who had been in the kitchen with Emma the whole time, came in and stood beside him. She explained, "He's trying to say 'Nora'."

That's when Todd, with all his effort, was finally able to get it out,

"NORA!!! NORA!!! NORA!!!" he yelled, pointing toward the back of the house, "NORA!!!"

Samantha, at seven years old, knew exactly what it was that her brother was trying to say but didn't realize the importance of it… she didn't realize what Todd was trying to communicate was that Nora, their older sister, was in grave danger and needed help right away.

The noise must've awakened Bob, or maybe it was hearing his son speak for the first time in years. Whatever it was woke him from a dead sleep. He'd made it only halfway down the staircase when William and Callie, not knowing what else to do, looked to little Samantha for answers.

"Where's Nora?" William asked, with a hand now on one of Samantha's small shoulders as well.

"Nora and Dominique are both outside," she told him.

"They're back there...in the woods," she said, pointing the way Todd had done.

William, realizing the possible danger, couldn't stand up straight and run fast enough. Bob took off right behind him with just a pair of pants on, no shoes, boots, or anything else. On the way, William stopped and grabbed a loaded shotgun from a top shelf off the back porch. By then, Bob was already out the back door, running full speed toward the tree line. Nora was screaming at the top of her lungs and yelling,

"DADDY!!! HELP ME!!!"

The cry for help reverberated soundly throughout and touched the hearts of all those who heard it. She was definitely in trouble and may be in danger of losing her life.

*  *  *  *

The look on Nora's face showed how relieved she was to see her father when Bob got there and jumped in the water beside her.

"It's gonna be alright, honey. Daddy's here now," he told her. Hearing how Nora screamed and yelled in fear broke his heart, and he'd be damned if he'd let her worry any further.

Even so, she was still stuck. Bob had to somehow get Nora out of the mud, and not only that but when Dominique screamed, he became aware of another hidden danger, one that required his immediate attention. Fifteen feet or so away, he saw that the eyes of an alligator, skimming the water, were slowly coming toward them.

Dominique threw a stick at it and missed, and the alligator kept coming. Bob was about to risk life and limb and go after the alligator himself when William called out and yelled,

"BOB!!! GET BACK!!!" just before taking aim and firing a shot.

The alligator's forward momentum kept it coming, but after the smoke cleared, the animal had turned belly up and died.

"DADDY!!!" Nora called out to get everybody's attention again. The water had gotten just about up to Nora's mouth and nostrils, too far up for comfort.

With one threat already gone, Bob ducked underwater

and, feeling somewhat frenzied, used his bare hands to dig Nora out. When he came up, one pull and Nora came free in Bob's arms. Her naked feet were dangling. She'd lost the boots she had on, along with the worried look of possibly dying. She smiled instead and waved at Dominique, a way of thanking her.

Dominique smiled and waved back, totally relieved, but quickly looked away. Somewhere in the distance, she heard the faint sound of a different song from the one Callie had been playing, a song that gave the twelve-year-old girl goose-bumps;

"Good mornin' heartache, you old gloomy sight.

"Good mornin' heartache, thought we said goodbye last night…"

## Chapter 33

No two people could've been more right for each other than Bob and Callie, which proved to be true once they met. In no time at all, the two became inseparable and undeniable soul mates. At first, people weren't exactly happy or excited about the idea of them being together, but later, because of how they were envied, it made them the talk of the town and not for any of the wrong reasons that William had been worried about.

Both were at ease and very successful with their own chosen careers, which oftentimes called for long work hours: Bob at Lafayette Memorial and Callie on the Devereaux farm, where, after coming to her senses, she decided to take full control and run things again. Therefore, because leisure time was scarce, not much of it was spent out in public. Nonetheless, whenever they were out and about in town together, people knew just by seeing them how Bob and Callie always smiled and seemed so happy interacting with one another. And with the kids as well, that these two, Bob and Callie, really were meant to be, sharing the greatest passionate attraction of all…love.

* * * *

Finally, it was carnival time. Kids and adults alike had waited all year long, sacrificing and saving money, looking forward to when the traveling amusement park would come to their town. This is when it would be alright to eat red and caramel-coated candied apples and cotton candy of any color. When the time would be right to intermingle with everybody in town that you've ever known. A time when the expressed phrase of having fun wasn't overly exaggerated.

* * * *

The man serving as Emcee was loud, vociferous, fat, and no taller than the size of a midget, wearing a tuxedo jacket with a tail and a white shirt and bow tie with a tiny pair of shiny patent leather shoes. A top hat, along with the black cane he was carrying, finished the outfit.

But not everybody liked the man's style. Some, the do-gooders and Sunday-go-to-church folks, even thought him to be obnoxious and quite rude, especially with one particular announcement the man-made.

"Hurry, hurry, ladies and gentlemen, step right up. See the monkey climb up the pole.

"The further he climbs, the further you can see up his...hooold that man before he steps in that bucket of...ssshhhhut that door before I kick you up your...aaassskk that man does he have a ticket to the show. And if he don't, tell him to go to...hello folks, the show starts in five minutes."

Callie thought the man was funny and liked him. So did Bob and quite a few others.

\* \* \* \*

There was a strong man there in tights and a bathing suit, prancing around, and was, with bare hands, lifting dumbbells and bending steel bars.

A two-headed woman with two different personalities was there, along with a man who could dance on broken glass with bare feet before doing something even more amazing when he walked on beds of hot coals, all without getting injured or hurting himself.

Others, performing phenomenal feats, were there as well: a sword-swallower, a woman without a spine who could fold and close herself up inside a suitcase. Many of them were amazing and fun to watch, but the main attractions were the rides.

"Daddy..." said Samantha, holding Bob's hand and

pointing toward the merry-go-round. Nine years old was a bit over the hill for a kid still wanting to ride the merry-go-round, but the nostalgic affair or remembering how she and her mother used to ride it together made the merry-go-round Samantha's favorite. So, they all got on and picked a different replicated horse to ride on anyway, just for the sake of Samantha.

The Ferris wheel was next, which Dominique and Nora thought would be boring until Seth Evans and his good friend, Michael Jackson, showed up in jeans and flannel shirts.

"Good evening, ma'am, sir," the two young men both said to Bob and Callie after they'd gotten Dominique and Nora's attention, who suddenly couldn't stop smiling.

"Can Dominique and me ride together?" Seth asked, looking from Callie to Bob, who both had different opinions.

While Seth did all the talking, Michael kept quiet, anticipating and hoping that he would be given permission to ride with Nora as well. Not if it were up to Callie, though; she'd begun to frown immediately before Seth even finished asking for permission. But Bob, winning overall in the end, smiled and gave the go-ahead.

"Sure, if Michael'll dance and sing a song for us," Bob said, hoping to get a laugh.

"No, just kidding. Have fun," he said, watching proudly while his two little girls, both Dominique and Nora, went on what was virtually their first dates.

"It'll be your fault if they get pregnant," said Callie after the kids were locked in and the Ferris wheel began its initial climb upwards.

"It'll be a first if they or anybody else get pregnant in a Ferris wheel," said Bob, "…and if it happens to one of our girls, then we'll probably get rich."

"Ha ha…very funny," said Callie before Bob leaned over to get a kiss.

Seth and his friend smiled and said goodbye afterward when the ride was over. The Macklin/Devereaux clan continued on.

The bumper cars were Todd's favorite, even though he was never able to drive more than five feet before somebody else, driving another car, knocked him silly.

They'd all had their fair share of food and candy, and last but not least were the games. In the goldfish toss, Dominique and Nora both won a plastic bag of water with a goldfish in it.

And the shooting galleries; it took a whole roll of

quarters before Bob finally won Callie a huge stuffed animal.

Todd threw a thousand rings at bowling pins but never hooked any of them and shot a thousand baskets, too, without winning anything at all.

Samantha and Callie just watched and cheered everybody else on. However, Bob looked over and saw yet another ride for them to adventure upon, one of his favorites...the spinning tea cups.

"Wait," he said, smiling, grabbing Callie's hand and leading them all toward it.

"Honey..." said Callie, starting to protest from not really being a person who enjoyed the topsy-turvy turning effect of carnival rides.

"Bob, no...let's skip this one."

But Bob wasn't taking no for an answer. The kids were all for it, too, especially after they'd gotten closer and could hear how loud the laughter was from those already riding it.

So, there they were, all piling into one small but oversized teacup amongst many others, already loaded with families ready to share a laugh and joyous time together. And once it started twirling and spinning, none of them could stop giggling, not even Callie, who was still giggling and laughing on the way home until Bob started a song.

"Row, row, row your boat gently down the stream," one by one, they all joined in until everybody in the car was singing, "…merrily, merrily, merrily, merrily, life is but a dream."

Once they were home, Bob stopped the car in the driveway, and then it became a race to see who could get to use the bathrooms first: the one upstairs and the one at the back of the house.

The kids all ran upstairs, but Bob and Callie, heading toward the back of the house, were stopped dead in their tracks by what they saw in the kitchen. Emma was laid out cold on the kitchen floor, and William was sitting there on the floor beside her, holding Emma's hand.

He looked up when Bob and Callie came in,

"My baby…" he said, crying, his face filled with tears, "My baby done gon' and left me."

Bob went to work fast, first checking for a pulse and then performing CPR when he couldn't find one. But it was too late. For the last few years, Emma had been battling both high blood pressure and sugar diabetes, and because of one or the other, or maybe both, had had an epileptic seizure and died.

"My baby," cried William, all choked up. And then the kids came, and everybody cried.

## Chapter 34

The choir stood and began a soft but heartfelt chorus of Amazing Grace. While they did, the last few surviving family members and friends, of which there were many, made their way inside the church to pay homage and see Emma Burns one last time.

She lay as if to look peacefully asleep. It was the same scenario as when Bessie's services were held, and there at the same old Southern Baptist church, with the Evan's family as the same morticians.

People took their time filing by, not only to take one last look at Emma but also to express sympathy toward William, the man who loved and spent almost his entire adult life with her.

William, wearing the appropriate attire: a black suit, white shirt, black tie, black shoes, and an even darker disposition, sat stealthily still and quiet. He sat at the end of the first row in the aisle seat, right across from where the pallbearers had placed Emma's glistening mahogany casket.

Emma's brother and his wife sat beside William, and Emma's two sisters and their husbands, all from California, sat further down in the same row. However, William hadn't said more than two words to any of them or to anybody else, not since the night Emma died. He had everybody worried about him.

"Amazing grace…how sweet the sound…that saved a wrench like me.

"I once was lost, but now I'm found…was blind, but now I see."

Bob and Callie sat behind William in the second row, along with Nora, Dominique, Samantha, Todd, and a few more of Emma's relatives, nieces, and nephews.

"T'was grace that taught my heart to fear…and grace my fears relieved."

By the time the song was finished, everybody in the church had been seated.

"Amen," said the minister after coming to the pulpit. He wiped his brow and then straightened the microphone, adjusting it perfectly so that when he spoke, everybody in the church would be able to hear him,

"Mrs. Emma Burns," he began, taking a long look out amongst the crowded congregation, "...what a wonderful woman.

"I've known her practically all my life, and not once have I ever seen her too upset or deprived of confidence, hope, or faith...that's because she always believed in God wholeheartedly."

"Amen," said one of the deacons sitting behind the minister.

And from the congregation, another person shouted, "Take her home, Lord."

"...and if I had to guess, I'd say that Emma's smiling down on all of us right now from heaven. So fret not, my brother," the minister said, looking directly at William, "She'll be waitin' with a place saved for you too."

"Amen, amen," said the congregation, some of which were now standing, clapping hands and smiling joyously.

Dominique turned around to look, and at the very back of the church, amongst those sitting in the very last row, was Ms. Ladeaux. She smiled and waved at Dominique before some of the others stood and began clapping hands. The view was blocked momentarily. When the path was clear again, Dominique looked around and saw that Ms. Ladeaux was gone.

"The Bible says that 'God has a place for us all.' But, will we get there is the question," said the minister, purging forward, questioning faith and religious conviction,

"Emma, she believed…and guess what…so do I.

"Y'all don't hear me," he said, as if doubtful amongst a congregation now in full pledge, each of them promising earnestly, if to no one else other than to themselves, that they too will forever believe in God.

"Take us all home, Lord," someone else shouted.

At the end of the day, his job was done; he'd cleansed the house. It was common practice, a ploy used by most ministers; by creating doubt, he'd actually removed all doubt.

"He's right," thought William, who looked over at the casket with Emma in it and finally smiled inside,

"Thank you, Lord, to have ever brought her into my life."

After services were over, William tried having a conversation with everybody and apologized for being so rude beforehand.

"We understand…you've lost somebody you loved dearly," said one of Emma's sisters.

"God forbid, but if it was me, I probably wouldn't've held up any better," the woman's husband said.

They were all at the Devereaux House. Other women of the church congregation had brought fired chicken and greens, baked ham and field peas along with cornbread, macaroni and cheese, and enough food in general to feed everybody there. And in the end, it was a celebration.

Before leaving, one particular deacon of the church pulled William aside,

"You know…I was just in Shreveport a week or so ago, went to visit a sister of mine. While I was there, she took me to church with her, and I met this woman…Ms. Viola Ray…Viola Ray Stinson. And I swear, you and her look so much alike; the two of you could be twins. She even told me her maiden name was Burns. I just thought I'd mention it to see if you had relatives there."

"I'm not sure…maybe I do," said William, remembering that he did, in fact, have a sister named Viola Ray, named after their father, Raymond. He hadn't seen or heard from her in over fifty years,

"…but sure would like to see her again now if she's still alive," he thought, wondering.

"How many other 'Viola Ray's' could there have been in the world?"

"What's the name of the church where you met her?" he asked, "I might have to take a trip up there."

"Mt. Saint Olive. You can't miss it. It's the biggest church they've got in Shreveport."

* * * *

Bob, after making sure the kids were all tucked in and asleep, came back to bed and found Callie's face all wet with a steady flow of tears.

"Honey…what's wrong?" he asked, "Why are you crying?"

"Emma and William…they've been around all my life, longer than either of my parents," she said as if finally coming to terms with it.

"It's just so sad that Emma died.

"And now William…he's not alright either. I can tell by the look on his face he's hurtin' somethin' awful."

"Yeah, I know…and I'm so sorry," said Bob, climbing in bed beside Callie, taking hold of her so that she lay slightly on top of him,

"Maybe it'll help if this Ms. Viola Ray person does turn out to be William's sister. From what he's told us, everything about her sounds about right."

"Yeah, I hope so too. That would give him somethin' more to focus on other than just Emma bein' gone. I couldn't take losin' both of 'em right now."

"You won't, honey. But remember, regardless of anybody else, you've still got me…and I ain't goin' nowhere, no time soon."

"Awwwwww, honey. I'm sorry if that's the way I made it sound," said Callie, pulling herself up to give Bob a kiss,

"Our lives together mean more to me than anything."

"Me too," said Bob, using one hand to fondle Callie's breast and the other hand to turn off the light, "I couldn't imagine living life without you."

# Chapter 35

"At last…my love has come along," sang Etta James on the radio.

"A station for lovers, obviously," thought William, switching it as quickly as his fingers would turn the dial. Love songs weren't what he wanted to hear. They bought on too many memories…memories of a past life that suddenly seemed so long ago.

The next radio station he landed on was perfect,

"If you need…a little lovin'…call on me, that's all you gotta do.

"No more lonely nights…to endure alone. All you gotta do is …pick…up …the telephone and dial now… 6-3-4-5-7-8-9, that's my number," sang the man known as The Wicked, Wilson Pickett, a star recording artist back then.

On a bright, clear, sunny day, William was riding north

on Interstate 49 to Shreveport, Louisiana. The day was Sunday, and William was on his way to church.

He would've been fine driving his old Ford pickup truck, but Callie insisted he take the white Cadillac, which did make him feel a little better, riding with a suit on. And besides, the Cadillac rode a lot better,

"...like riding along in a cloud," William was thinking. "...a car well worth the ten thousand dollars Callie paid for it."

The whole time, a cruising speed of sixty miles an hour was maintained, five miles an hour less than what the actual speed limit was.

"Hell, I ain't in no rush," said William, something he said often, especially while driving. And anybody who knew him knew what he said was true...William never rushed to go anywhere.

Never in life had he ever even gotten a speeding ticket,

"...and ain't about to get one now," he thought, watching all the other cars and trucks pass by him in the left lane.

* * * *

"So, you're my Uncle William," said the woman standing in front of him, amazed.

"I can shol' tell…you and momma look just alike," she said, in regards to approval and high esteem, all while sharing a wide smile from ear to ear.

William had decided to wait until the following Sunday, a week after Emma's funeral, to drive up to Shreveport. Finding the church wasn't a problem, nor was finding somebody who knew Viola Ray…he'd gotten there just as the minister was finishing the sermon and was immediately ushered in and introduced to Tammy, Viola's daughter.

*"…in her fifties,"* thought William of Tammy.

"An average-sized woman with brown skin and graying hair that fell along the shoulders."

"Momma wasn't feelin' so good this mornin' and didn't come to church. I was thinkin' 'bout stayin' home too, but then she told me that somebody was supposed to come that I might wanna meet.

"I thought it might've been my knight in shining armor she was talkin' about. I had no idea it would be you," said Tammy, smiling, all excited about meeting William, who was a little confused; he hadn't called ahead and told anybody he was coming. So, how were they supposed to know about the plans he'd made to visit?

But then, Tammy explained,

"Doctors still don't know why, but a few years ago, for some reason, Momma lost her eyesight. And has ever since been havin' visions of things, sometimes even before they happen...like today. She didn't know, per se, that it was you I was supposed to meet here at the church, just that the person comin' was somebody very important."

"Well, I'm glad," said William, flattered and glad to finally be able to get a word in otherwise,

"It's been almost sixty years since me and Viola have seen each other. So when I heard a woman named Viola Ray was a member of this particular church… yeah, I had to come to find out if it was my sister."

"She's told me the story about what happened when y'all was kids. She talks about it a lot, wondering if you made it all right.

"Tell you what…instead of you and me standin' 'round talkin', why don't we get outta here so I can take you home to momma. I swear, it's gon' make her day," said Tammy, headed for the door with William right behind her.

"I'll follow you," he said, out in the parking lot when Tammy took out keys and stopped beside an old burgundy Pontiac Bonneville. The Cadillac was parked in the next aisle over.

# Buckets, Shovels, Ghost and Worms

\* \* \* \*

The drive to where Viola lived took about twenty minutes. She lived on the outskirts, clear across town, in an area densely populated by a forest of cedar, cypress, and oak trees.

There were two houses in what was considered an opening. They sat side by side, about fifty feet apart; one where Viola lived, and one where Tammy lived next door. Both were old homes that sat on block foundations and were no more elaborate than maybe what a renovated two-bedroom shack would've been.

William wondered if they even had bathrooms or running water. And with the front doors opened, it gave a view from the front porch that you could see straight through the house, from the front porch to all the way out the back, that is, if both doors were opened.

It didn't help the homely image when William saw chickens clucking and walking freely under and around both houses. For a moment, it made him wonder,

"Who actually owned the place, Viola Ray and Tammy, or the chickens?" Of course, what he thought was a joke.

"Uncle William," said Tammy, standing on the threshold of Viola's front door, beckoning towards him…she'd already gone inside to spread the news about who it was that she'd brought home. But William had just been standing there, outside amongst the chickens.

Tammy told William,

"Momma said, 'Come on in,'" and he did, tentatively, while still looking around at the outside of a house, a house that looked very much like the one he'd been born in.

However, once past the threshold, he immediately saw that the inside of the house was a totally different story. The place was immaculate, clean, and well-furnished, not what you might expect to see in a house so far out in the country.

"I feel like I've finally made it back home," he told the woman, waiting with open arms to give him a hug.

"And you have…you have," said Viola, shedding a few joyful tears while smiling,

"Aw, William…come here and let me put my arms around you," she said after becoming overwhelmed with joy.

Tammy, standing off to one side, was shedding tears as well, and before long, so was William.

"I thought I wasn't gon' ever see you again," he told Viola in a voice all choked up while embracing her as if he never wanted to let go.

"God made a way, baby," said Viola, holding on to him too. "He always does."

For the next two hours, Viola and William talked nonstop, catching up on things, explaining all that had happened to them since childhood, including Emma's funeral and how William had found out about Viola.

"I could tell somethin' was wrong," Viola told him, "…I just didn't know what exactly."

Viola knew a lot more about the rest of the family and told William about them,

"Our two oldest brothers, Frank and Joe, were both killed in prison; Joe, in a fight, and Frank, supposedly while trying to escape. Poor things… it hurt me to my heart the way they were treated."

"Yeah, me too. I still can't get past the harsh sentence them boys were given… all for stealin' chickens."

"That's why now I keep a whole yard full of 'em," said Viola, in spite of it all, "…and can eat one whenever I get ready."

Edward, another of their brothers, had died,

"He had kidney failure," and so had one of their other sisters, Althena.

"It ain't been that long since Althena died, about three months ago," said Viola,

"She was married to a guy in the Navy. They lived in San Diego."

William thought about Bob, "San Diego...that's where Bob's from."

"Sweety still livin' though," said Viola. Sweety was the youngest, just a baby, the last that William remembered.

"When we was all leavin', I took her with me, and a white woman right here in Shreveport took us in.

"Sweety eventually met Johnny, a man from Mississippi. He went to Detroit and got him a job at one of the big car factories, Ford Motor Company, if I'm not mistaken.

"They ended up gettin' married and had eight kids together."

"Wow… eight?" said William.

"Uh huh… there was a time when I'd catch Greyhound and go up there to see 'em. It's been a while now, though."

"Obviously, because she'd gone blind," thought William.

"We still call each other and talk on the phone now and then, just not as much as we used to."

"She probably don't remember me," said William, hoping for just the opposite.

"She does, actually…it's just been so long.

"Before you leave, I'm'a give you the number. Maybe y'all can talk and visit each other."

"I sure hope so."

The conversation went on and on until late in the evening. Tammy cooked and served dinner, and William spent the night. However, early the next morning, he was awakened by the pungent odor of marijuana. He knew because Bridgett, the housekeeper at home, smoked it. Bridgett got too bold and careless, though, and made the mistake of smoking it in the house,

"…that's how she got fired," thought William, remembering exactly how it happened. Bob smelled it first and was pissed. Later, he said, it more surprised him than anything that she would actually have the audacity and be so bold. That was the last day Bridgett worked at the Devereaux House.

William thought,

*"Viola probably smokes it for medical reasons;"* researchers had announced that smoking marijuana helped those with cataracts. In some states, laws have been passed to allow those suffering from cataract symptoms to smoke legally.

"I don't smoke, hopin' I can see again. I smoke to keep my nerves calm," Viola told him, "…ain't nothin' I can do about my eyes. Smokin' weed keeps me from worryin' about it," Viola said, sharing a big smile.

"I do understand," said William, thinking of Emma.

Before lunch, he'd made the bed he slept in and was saying goodbye.

"Let's not be strangers, William…it took too long for this to happen as it is. And don't worry so much about your wife. You might miss her, but believe me, she's in a much better place. Just be glad you had a chance to know her," said Viola, giving him the best advice she could think of.

"I am," said William, fighting back tears as he gave her and Tammy both big hugs,

"…but sometimes I just can't help it," he thought on his way out the door.

On the way back home, he was thinking,

"Maybe I should try smoking a little marijuana, anything to keep from worryin' so much."

* * * *

"Can I ask you a question?"

"Sure, baby...what is it?"

"Why do people die?" asked Dominique, quite a serious question for a fourteen-year-old. The water was low, and she and Ms. Ladeaux had taken a seat on the small wooden pier with their feet dangling and their lines taut out in the water, catching Brim, Crappie, and Catfish.

"People die because nobody was meant to live forever," Ms Ladeaux told her while sharing a smile.

"What about Emma? Do you think she died and went to heaven?"

Ms Ladeaux smiled again,

"Of course, she did...Emma was already an angel."

Dominique smiled as if she might agree but then asked,

"Ok, I agree that she was sweet, and I surely hope she went to heaven, but how do you know for sure she went to heaven?"

"Because I knew Emma and knew where she came from. You must not believe it when I said she was already an angel?" Ms Ladeaux asked after noticing a look on Dominique's face that showed she wasn't convinced.

"Listen...I can't explain everything now, but believe me, one day, you'll understand why I can be so sure about what I'm talking about. And again...yes, Emma did go to heaven...all good people do when they die."

\* \* \* \*

On this particular day, Dominique had brought a bucket with her, and all the fish they caught had filled it. She'd just crossed the tree line, heading home, when William pulled up in the driveway.

"Dinner," she said, holding the bucket up proudly so he could see it.

"Let me get changed, and I'll help you clean 'em," he said after coming around back to meet her.

He'd just said hello to everybody else in the house and was on his way to change clothes when the phone rang. It was Viola Ray calling for him.

"Hello," he said, wondering why she'd called so soon.

"William," she began, sounding a bit hysterical,

"...the house where you live. Get out...you're all in great danger."

## Chapter 36

What made the change of weather from fall to winter so different from any other year was that it came abruptly, all at once, instead of how it usually happened—gradually.

The very next day after William's return home from Shreveport, temperatures had dropped drastically, twenty degrees or more.

It was in December… Christmas carols and hymns were being sung, and decorations and ads were displayed on television and on billboards, and everywhere else imaginable to influence America to get in the spirit of spending money…and yes, it was indeed well overdue for cold weather, just not as it happened, all at once.

Todd woke with a fever and was kept home from school. A glass of juice and aspirin did the job of bringing it down, and by mid-afternoon, he was feeling fine and painting again. However, instead of having the canvas and easel outside as he usually did, he had it inside, set up in front of the living room window.

Everything was as usual, with him working on yet another boring view of the landscape. That is until seven heavily armed men on horseback rode into the yard and changed everything, an image Todd captured immediately and held on to it as the view that he saw was a Polaroid.

Later, this particular painting would become very famous and a highly sought-after piece of artwork as well for being a part of the Angola prison legend… it was said that even if an inmate did happen to make it past the gun line unscathed and elude officers, he would never survive the dangers of the swift-moving Mississippi River currents, or the twenty miles of murky swamp and darkened wooded area around it.

"Gentlemen… how can I help you?" asked Callie as one of the men came down off the horse he was riding.

Callie heard the commotion, came downstairs in a hurry, and ran quickly out of the house to find out what the hell was going on. She recognized one of the men as a guard over the roadside prison work detail and wasn't too happy about him being there at the house. Not only that, but she'd only been home a few minutes, taking a much-needed break from work...she didn't appreciate the disturbance either.

"Ma'am," the man on the horse said when he began, first by tipping his hat politely,

"I'm Officer Timothy Milton from Angola State Prison. Unfortunately, we've got three men attempting to escape. Where they've gotten off to, we're not sure, and as a precaution, we're checking all possibilities.

"Have you, by chance, seen them?"

"Well, hell no… and why would you think I might've seen them?"

"It's just that I noticed how sympathetic you were the other day when you saw some of them working on the side of the road," he said, looking over at Callie's car in the driveway, remembering the red convertible distinctively.

"Now wait just a goddamn minute, Officer Milton or whoever you are," said Callie, becoming flustered.

"Havin' sympathy is one thing, but helping a convict escape from prison custody is another. I really don't appreciate you insinuating that I'm involved at all.

"Now, if you'll excuse me, I think I'll get back to what I was doing. And maybe a call to the Governor might be in order.

"Good day, sir," said Callie before turning her heels and

storming back inside the house.

Mentioning that she might call the Governor had been a bluff. It might've been feasible or practical before Ted died; like his grandfather, Luke Devereaux, Ted was friends with probably every elected official and politician there was in the entire state of Louisiana. But the new Governor, David Dukes, as a publicly known and admitted Klan's man, it was doubtful that he would've been as concerned about Callie's complaints or problems or even her well-being.

In the end, Officer Milton's comments were overlooked. Nevertheless, as a precautionary measure, a high alert warning was sent out to everybody there that she had working for her.

*"It's better to be safe than sorry,"* she thought, all the while arming herself with a sidearm as well.

# Chapter 37

"I've got somebody I want you to meet," said William at the end of the day when Callie came home from work.

When she walked in, he was standing there at the door, smiling, and seemed in a very good mood,

*"A lot better than how he's been acting lately, moping around all sad and dejected,"* thought Callie, which, for the most part, was how he'd been since Emma died.

"Can't it wait until after I go upstairs and use the bathroom?" Callie asked with one hand on the stairway railing on her way up, thinking that if she didn't hurry, she might pee on herself.

"Come on… it won't take but a minute. She's right in here," said William, insisting.

*"She?"* thought Callie, raising a brow, now more curious than anything, wondering not only who the woman

was but also about the content of William's intentions in introducing her.

"Ok," said Callie, redirecting, for the moment putting off going upstairs to use the bathroom and instead going along, following as William led the way toward the kitchen.

The kids were already there at the kitchen table, and the woman that William wanted her to meet was serving them an after-school snack.

"Callie… meet Nikki."

The two women smiled, shook hands, and said "hello" to each other.

"Now, I know it's a bit soon," said William, continuing, standing between the two women, "…but Nikki's a friend and a damn good cook who happens to be in need of a job. I thought you should meet her and at least consider it."

"Ok," said Callie, still at a loss for words…the woman was a younger version of Emma at maybe forty years old; dark-skinned, short and stout, with big breasts and a big butt, which made Callie wonder if being the cook was all William had in mind for her.

In the meantime, the kids were ecstatic. They'd taken to Nikki and were enjoying the fact that someone else was finally in the house who could cook and serve them their meals on time and properly. Bob, Callie, and William had all given it a shot, taking turns filling in, and had made more of a disaster of it than anything else.

"I take it that you've done this kinda' work before," said Callie, watching while Nikki moved around at ease as if cooking and working in the kitchen was second nature.

"I actually haven't, but as the oldest of nine children, I learned how to cook almost before I learned how to walk."

And then William handed Callie a bowl filled with steaming hot gumbo and rice. Nikki passed her a spoon, which Callie used to dig right in.

"Um," she said before she could even swallow.

And when she did swallow, she said,

"Um," again, and while taking in another spoonful.

She asked,

"You made this?"

"Uh-huh," said Nikki, watching as Callie continued to eat as if famished. Gumbo was Callie's favorite, and up until then, she didn't think anybody alive could make it any better than Emma. But Nikki proved otherwise.

## Buckets, Shovels, Ghost and Worms

Again, the kids were ecstatic, laughing aloud, especially Nora and Samantha, both with missing teeth, watching Callie devour the bowl of gumbo.

"Okay, why don't you give me ten minutes and then meet me in the living room so that we can sit and talk and work everything out," said Callie, turning to walk away, taking the bowl with her.

"Yes, ma'am," said Nikki, smiling from ear to ear.

But then, as an afterthought, Callie turned back around,

"Excuse me for wanting to know, but… you don't smoke pot, do you?" she asked after another spoonful of gumbo had gone down.

"No, ma'am… I've never drank or smoked."

"Good… ten minutes," said Callie, turning to leave again after shoveling in yet another spoonful of the Gumbo she'd been missing so much.

"This is delicious," she said over a shoulder, holding up the spoon.

"Ten minutes."

* * * *

"…and you say that she's a friend of William's and was already here, working when you got home?" asked Bob.

"My God, honey… I don't think if we'd run a full-page ad in the paper, we would've found a better replacement for Emma.

"She's fantastic," Bob said after finishing the last of the meal Nikki had made for them: Cornish hen and stuffing, candied yams, and collard greens with smoked neck bones, a favorite southern meal for Bob, who was totally sold on Nikki.

"Did you notice William?" asked Callie from on her side of the bed, nightgown on, under the covers already, but leaning over on one elbow with an inquisitive yet inquiring look, exposing suspicion.

"He seems awfully happy all of a sudden."

"Why shouldn't he be?" said Bob, with no suspicion at all and glad that William had found her.

"And have you wondered how they might've met? Nikki's from all the way over in Lake Charles."

"Honey… I think you're jumping to conclusions."

"And maybe you haven't noticed… she looks an awful lot like Emma, don't you think?" Callie asked.

"Now that you mention it… yeah, she does sorta favor Emma."

"Sorta? Man, she's short and stout and got the same big butt and big breast."

Bob laughed a little before saying, "Callie, you really are jumping to conclusions."

"I'm just sayin'…"

"Just sayin' what?" Bob asked, with the smile gone now.

"If havin' another woman around who looks like Emma is what it takes to make the man happy, then so be it. Personally, I see nothin' wrong with it."

"You will if you start hearin' another woman in the house besides me screamin' in the middle of the night."

"Speaking of which," said Bob, turning the light off and sliding his nude body into bed beside Callie's.

"I've been wantin' to do this all day," he said, coming closer and falling over in Callie's opened arms.

"Ok… you better make it good then," she said, raising the nightgown and guiding Bob inside between opened legs.

"Yes, ma'am."

## Chapter 38

Early the next morning, before the sun had come up, the kids hadn't even been awakened for school yet, but William was up listening to what some might call Christmas carols of the adult version, one of which he liked more than the others,

"Merry Christmas, baby… you've sure been good to me," a classic Charles Brown song, recorded in 1947. Yet, the song was still an old-time holiday favorite, played quite often by disc jockeys of local Blues stations all over America. On this particular morning, it also happened to be a song that fits right in with the way William was feeling. Instead of singing along, though, William hummed and enjoyed it while the record played in its entirety.

William had also gone out that morning and cut down what was probably the best-looking Douglas Fir Christmas tree in the whole forest and had the tree placed perfectly, standing tall in front of the living room window. A string of colorful lights was added as a wrap-around, but further decorations wouldn't be done until the kids were home from school, a treat he'd save just for them.

In the meantime, the Christmas spirit was alive and in full effect. William even wore a red and white Santa hat to prove it and was sipping eggnog spiked with corn liquor.

Nikki, on the other hand, wearing a Santa hat as well, had been busy cooking breakfast and setting a table fit for a feast, smiling all the while as if maybe during the night, God had shined down on her too.

"Mornin'," said Bob to William, on his way in to do hospital rounds,

"Nice tree."

Callie came down the stairs right behind him, took notice of the Douglas Fir, and then, with a complacent smile, looked at William. Once they were close enough, she spoke in a low voice and told him,

"The tree doesn't get you off the hook… you still should be ashamed of yourself."

"Look who's talkin'," said William, responding quickly, "…the love child of Southern Louisiana."

Callie wanted to say something else, but William held up a hand, stopping her,

"Don't be comin' down here tryin' to rain on my parade," he said, with all seriousness, but then smiled when he said,

"Hell… I can't help 'cause I'm good lookin' and still got it."

Bob laughed and kept on walking, thinking of the vitamin E and D tablets he'd given William for energy and more stamina.

"Maybe the vitamins gave William a little more confidence, as well," thought Bob.

"Mornin'," he said in the kitchen when Nikki looked up at him, smiling.

"Mornin', sir.

"Coffee's already ready, and I'll be finished with breakfast in about ten minutes," she said, still in the midst of getting it all done.

"Wonderful. I think I'll stay and have some then," said Bob, filling mugs for both him and Callie before marching off toward the dining room table, staying clear of being in the way.

It was indeed turning out to be a very good morning: good music, good food, and very good company. The kids sure thought so, coming downstairs to find William in costume, standing beside a tree that he'd said they could decorate.

For breakfast, Nikki made pancakes, French toast, grits, eggs, bacon, sausage, biscuits, and fried ham, and had maple syrup, butter, and jam to go along with it. Everybody ate until they could eat no more, which was why they were all late for work and school, except Nikki and William, who both worked there at the Devereaux House.

\* \* \* \*

After saying goodbye to Tammy and Viola Ray, William had left Shreveport, drove straight down to Lake Charles, and used a key from his own key ring to open the door of a house where Nikki had been staying.

Since 1911, when he was still a teenager and had gotten his first pay of a dollar and a half a week, William had been saving his money, almost every dime. He didn't live extravagantly or needed to spend any of it on food or anything else, and over sixty years, had amassed a wealth of over three hundred thousand dollars. Therefore, he could very well afford to house and take care of a young woman he'd secretly fallen in love with.

Of course, now, since Emma had died and left him her money too, the wealth had doubled, and ultimately, there was no need to keep Nikki a secret anymore.

"Being an unfaithful husband was never a part of the plan. It's just somethin' that happened," said William, sincerely explaining it all to Callie later in the day while the two of them sat on the porch, relaxing, enjoying a glass of lemonade and each other's company. Nikki was in bed, asleep, taking a nap before the kids came home.

"Well… where and how did the two of you meet?" Callie asked, all ears and on the edge of her seat, eager to know.

"Out in the country, near Baton Rouge, in an area so thick that all you could see was trees and foliage, no houses or anything else. And it didn't help that it was late in the evening because out of nowhere, she just ran out in the middle of the road, crying, lookin' buck wild and scared half to death with not a stitch of clothes on. I had to jam on brakes just to keep from hittin' her."

"Yeah, sure you did," said Callie as if maybe she didn't believe him,

"You jammed on brakes when you saw a naked woman, period. She didn't have to be standin' in the middle of the road."

But it was true… William had driven to Baton Rouge to

get a much-needed part for a tractor, a part that they needed right away. It just so happened that the supply store in Baton Rouge was the only store that had it. And on the way back was when it all happened, just as William said it did, right before dark.

"I'll never forget the look of terror on Nikki's face, or all the welts she had over her body… it looked as if she'd been beaten with a damn extension cord or some kind of a thin leather strap."

Right after she got in the truck and William took off, a man with only a pair of pants on came running out in the road, yelling,

"GET BACK HERE, YOU BITCH!!!"

"I didn't know if he had a gun or not, so I sped up, puttin' more distance between us.

"Nikki was a nervous wreck. It took a long time before she finally calmed down and said anything I could understand. She kept cryin' and mumblin' words in what I thought was French, which was actually Cajun French.

"Merci…merci boucoup. Thanks…many thanks," and, "S'il vous plait…bin dieu avoir pitie. Please… good God, have mercy."

"I guess it didn't help either that she was still naked, sittin' there beside me."

William said he eventually found a general store that was still open where he was able to buy Nikki an outfit of clothing, some shoes, and some food,

"She said she was hungry and couldn't remember the last time she had somethin' to eat."

"My God," said Callie intensely, becoming more of a believer as William went on telling her the story.

Nikki's parents had been Haitian immigrants who'd moved to Louisiana after being granted United States work visas. However, like William's parents had both been killed, Nikki's parents had both been killed too, leaving behind nine small kids to fend for themselves, something William said the two of them had in common, which was what started a bond between them.

When William found Nikki, she'd already grown up and was a young woman of twenty-nine years old, but she didn't know much at all about life and was quite naïve. That's because, at twelve, she'd met a man, a Haitian, who'd taken her in and raised her as his own until she started growing breasts and having periods. Then he made Nikki his girlfriend and wouldn't let her out of the house anymore. He kept her isolated; no TV or phone either. It was the same man

William saw standing out in the middle of the road.

"Nikki said that for so long he kept lots of dolls around that seemed to keep her under a spell."

"Yeah, 'gris-gris,'" said Callie, which in Cajun dialogue meant spell or charm," as with voodoo, a nefarious act.

"Who knows… maybe he had other women under a spell as well. But anyway, one day, she said she took the dolls and threw them all in the fireplace. That's when the man became outraged. He tore off all of Nikki's clothes and started beatin' her with a cord that he'd ripped from a lamp pole.

"She said at one point, he started swinging it so hard that after a while, he slipped and fell and hurt himself. That's when she took off running straight out the door. She'd never been able to run before, not before the dolls were all burned; it was as if they were what kept her from doing so."

"Why didn't you bring her here then, in the first place?" asked Callie, as if she didn't already know. "We would've taken care of her."

"But that's the thing… I didn't want anybody to know about her, and neither did she, especially not Emma.

"We drove around for a while that night; I listened while

she did most of the talking. Finally, we ended up in Lake Charles.

"I saw a sign that said rooms for rent. Pay by the week. There was a store nearby and lots of restaurants where she could buy food if she wanted it. So, I rented one of the rooms, paid for a week, and gave Nikki some money. I promised I'd come back the next day, which I did.

"I eventually rented a house, though, bought some furniture and Nikki some more clothes. She and I have been seein' each other ever since, for over eleven years."

"Wow… eleven years," said Callie, feeling a bit disappointed and betrayed, "…and you're just now tellin' me about it?"

William looked over and smiled.

"Believe me… you'll get over it," he said, getting up to leave on his way to get the kids from school.

"Besides, you gotta understand… havin' a mistress isn't somethin' you want everybody else to know."

As William was leaving, the men on horseback rode by, and again, Officer Milton tipped his hat,

"Afternoon, ma'am," he said, all courteous and polite. But Callie said nothing and, as she did before, left the porch, storming back inside the house.

# Chapter 39

Nikki and William wanted to waste no more time getting married and wanted to do so right away, just not in churches.

"Why not?" asked Callie.

"Too much gossip," William told her,

"Even you had a brow raised when I mentioned there was another woman I wanted you to meet. You didn't know it was Nikki or that she and I were in any kind of relationship, but you raised a brow just the same."

"Yeah..." said Callie, realizing he did have a point. "But there are other churches where the people in it don't know who you are."

"They'll probably do the same thing, talk and worry about how old I am, gettin' married to a woman as young as Nikki, instead of talkin' about what matters most, that she and I both believe in God and seriously love each other.

Nikki had already agreed.

"…and if they ever find out about Emma, they'll talk about that too, about how soon after Emma's death was it when I decided to get married again," said William, making what he thought was another good point.

He and Nikki planned to get married on the following Friday at the courthouse in Lafayette. They'd already had the blood test done. Now, all they needed were the marriage license and then witnesses at the ceremony.

"Well…you know I'm gonna be there," said Callie as if there wasn't even a question of doubt.

"And so am I," said Bob, thinking.

"If Callie is gonna be there, then so am I."

"Oooo… I wanna go," said Dominique, who, at fourteen, couldn't wait to be grown and was yearning more and more for experiences of adult life, especially at an event as important as a wedding, whether it was at the courthouse or not. It made her think of Seth Evans and where the two of them might get married.

"So do I… I wanna go too," said Nora, who, at twelve, thought of herself as being almost a teenager. Therefore, anything Dominique wanted or was given permission to do, she wanted to do it, too.

"What about me?" asked Samantha, not wanting to be left out either, which was how she'd been feeling lately with Nora clinging more and more to Dominique, who was five years older and a teenager who had no time for a nine-year-old.

"Me… too… William," said Todd, who had actually become very good friends with William,

"I… wanna… be… the best man," he said, and meant every word he said.

Nikki laughed, feeling the love.

"That's everybody in the whole house," she said, holding on to William as if for dear life, a cozy setting.

"We're a family," said Callie afterward, speaking for everybody.

"Yeah… one for all, and all for one," said Bob.

"Alright, y'all, that's enough… and we're not the three Musketeers either, Bob," said William, making fun of him, "…soundin' like a broke-down ass comedian."

"I do appreciate the support, though, from all of you…

or I should say we appreciate the support," William said with a smile, looking down at Nikki, whose eyes were on him, too.

"What about a reception then?" asked Callie, thinking of how they could all celebrate.

"Nah... there won't be no reception either, not unless y'all wanna have one. Me and Nikki gonna go down to Galveston for a couple of days, have ourselves a little honeymoon in Texas, near the beach."

"Awwwwww... how romantic," said Dominique, as if she really knew what honeymoons were all about. It made them all wonder.

"Sounds like a plan to me," said Bob, "...and a very good one."

"Ok, well...at least let me be the one who pays for it all... it's the least I can do," said Callie, not wanting to take no for an answer.

"Alright, it's your money. I'm on a tight budget anyway," said William.

"Aw, nigga... you've been on a tight budget all your life. It's time to live a little," said Callie,

"Ain't that right?" she said, nudging Nikki, who was at

a loss for words; until recently, she'd never earned a dollar or had ever done anything extravagant either and still didn't know much about spending money. So, how would she know?

Callie, after noticing the bewildered look on Nikki's face and remembering the story that William told her, finally picked up on it and said,

"Girl, don't let William get you down there and be a cheapskate. Don't let him fool you…William's got plenty of money."

"Alright, Callie…now you really are gettin' carried away, tellin' everybody 'bout how much money I got," said William, who couldn't read or write very well, and entrusted Callie to handle almost all of his personal business that included banking. So, she knew exactly how much money he had.

Even so, he'd always been a miser and very serious about finances, especially when it came to his own bank account, which he insisted was nobody else's business.

"Don't you worry, we'll have a good time whether you chip in and help pay for anything or not…don't you worry," he told her.

## Chapter 40

Friday, the day of the wedding, the sun was hidden behind heavily darkened clouds.

Bob and William, both dressed in gray three-piece suits, white shirts, and black ties, stood on the front porch, looking up at what they knew would soon become a downpour.

"Rain, shine, sleet or snow, ain't nothin' gon' stop us from gettin' married," said William, determined. Although deep in his heart, he took the stormy weather as an omen, a sign of bad things to come.

"I don't blame you, William…I wouldn't let it stop me either," said Bob, being an optimistic voice in William's ear.

"It'll pass… If not, we'll go straight through it."

"Damn right we will," said William.

A moment later, Todd came out on the porch wearing a

# Buckets, Shovels, Ghost and Worms

gray three-piece suit as well,

"Aw… there's my best man," said William, smiling, extending a hand. Todd took it and shook William's hand proudly.

William asked him,

"You ready?"

"Uh-huh," said Todd.

"I am, too," William told him.

"Ok…we've got a stop to make at the flower shop first, and then one at the gas station. So, if you wanna make it to Galveston before dark, I suggest we go ahead and get goin'… the women'll catch up and meet us at the courthouse," said Bob, the coordinator.

"Ready when you are," said William, a gentle hand atop Todd's head.

It was Callie's idea, but as the tradition goes, William had been forbidden to sleep in the same bed or even see Nikki, in all, twenty-four hours before they were supposed to be married. So, he and Bob followed the tradition too and went out and got drunk that night, something neither of them had done in a while, which was quite refreshing… it gave them both a chance to unwind and really get to know one another.

And there they were the next day, the two of them, along with Todd, making their way off the front porch when Callie came running out.

"Wait!" she said, a new 35mm Canon with an attached close-up lens in hand. She'd bought the new camera for just this occasion, "Let me get a few shots of you handsome guys."

The first shot was of the three of them standing together on the ground, just off the porch, in a pose with William on one side, Bob on the other, and Todd in the middle, all smiling and feeling good about themselves.

In all, Callie took about ten different pictures before the first drops of rain broke up the photography session.

"We'll meet you all there," said Bob after Todd and William had already gotten in and started the car and gotten the windshield wipers going with the Cadillac engine humming like a well-oiled luxury machine.

"'K, babe," said Callie, kissing Bob goodbye and then throwing up a hand at Todd and William.

* * * *

Two other couples waiting to get married were there

ahead of William and Nikki. There were forms that both of them needed to fill out and then a show of identification, but surprisingly, after their names were called, the rest of the process took place, and things happened quickly. Before long, Nikki and William were both saying their "I do's" before the justice of the peace proclaimed,

"I now pronounce you man and wife."

And to William, said,

"You may kiss the bride."

Callie cried. And Dominique cried. At first, Samantha and Nora both thought something might've been wrong and wondered why Callie and Dominique weren't smiling when they should've both been happy.

With a big smile on his face, Bob said,

"Congratulations," and gave Nikki a hug and shook William's hand afterward. Only then did Nora and Samantha finally catch on and figure things out, that the tears they saw Callie and Dominique shed were tears of joy and not because something was wrong.

Todd had only one thought: how he could possibly capture the image and put the whole scene on a painted canvas.

After lining William's pockets with crisp one hundred dollar bills, Callie said goodbye, and so did Bob, wishing the newlywed couple well on their honeymoon. The kids did too, and they were off, William and Nikki, driving in the rain down one highway and another, then on I-10 heading west toward the Texas border.

"That was fun…why don't you and I get married again," said Callie, smiling on the way home. The rain hadn't let up yet and was coming down even harder.

"Right about now, I'd settle for just another honeymoon," said Bob, keeping his eyes on the road while trying to drive through a torrential downpour,

"Weather like this…you might even get pregnant again."

"Let's try it and see," said Callie, a hand on Bob's leg.

And they would have, except when they got home, the back door had been kicked in, and the Devereux House had been invaded by three men in dirty, soiled prison uniforms, the kind the convicts wore. And two of them had guns.

"Callie… Ma'tite ange. My little angel," said Johnny Le Fleur, a big smile on his face. He was one of the ones who had a gun in his hand and had it pointed right at them.

"I'm glad you've made it home. How nice of you to join us."

## Chapter 41

"NO!!! How dare you? GET OUT!!!" said Callie, adamantly and unyielding, yelling while storming across the floor in a rage toward Johnny,

"I want you outta my house, NOW!!!"

"Awwwwww CALLIEEE," said Johnny, French accent still intact, calling out Callie's name in lengthened, drawn-out vowels and syllables. The gun in his hand was a big Remington .38 caliber revolver.

*"My gun,"* thought Callie...the sidearm she'd armed herself with the day Officer Milton made her aware of inmates who had escaped from Angola State Prison.

*"They've obviously searched the house,"* she thought, which was probably true; one of the other men had William's shotgun.

Recognizing the danger made Callie come up short.

Deciding not to get too close.

Johnny continued,

"…and here I am thinking you might be glad to see me," this was something said in a way as if somehow his feelings were hurt.

"Hardly," said Callie, becoming a bit retentive as suddenly, Johnny had started toward her but with the barrel of the gun raised. Fourteen years and Callie remembered distinctively that Johnny wouldn't hesitate to kill, not even a woman, her either, especially if he'd gotten pissed off enough or felt his life was in danger.

"Ok…enough with the charade," said Johnny, stone-faced, no longer smiling.

"SIT!!!" he said, yelling at them with a finger pointed toward the living room, where there were two couches. The third escaped convict was stretched out on one of them already and appeared to be sleeping.

"It's not you I came to see at all," Johnny told Callie bitterly, "It's your husband, the doctor."

Immediately, Bob and Callie both started to wonder how it was that Johnny, an escaped convict, knew so much about them. Sure, Callie had already told Bob about Johnny, which was something that happened years ago.

*"But recently?"*

Then it came to both of their minds that, when they were married, a newspaper reporter had indeed done an interview and printed a story about the then newlyweds; a picture of them was even put in the paper. Johnny had, no doubt, read about them and knew where to go at a time like now when an inconspicuous medical treatment was needed.

"We have a man injured," he said, focusing his attention on Bob, "…snake bite."

Without being told anything further, Bob went over and went to work on the man, first checking for a pulse… the man actually looked dead already but wasn't.

"He will be soon, though, without the proper treatment," thought Bob.

"I have a bag in the car. You don't mind, do you?" he asked, hesitating but leaning toward the door.

"Stay where you are," said Johnny, "My friend, he'll get it for you."

Bob then told the other man which car it was in and where he should look to find it. In less than five minutes, the man was back, rain-soaked, but handing Bob the medical bag he'd asked for.

* * * *

Upon further inspection, Bob found that not only had the man on the couch been bitten once, but he'd actually been bitten three times. In the last few days, the escaped convicts had hidden themselves well within the swamp's crude boundaries, at times submerged in water amongst alligators and other dangerous reptiles. At other times, crawling around in mud with all the same dangers lurking. And sleeping wherever they could.

Bob was thinking,

*"He more than likely stumbled across a whole bed of snakes, which might explain why he ended up with three bites instead of just one."*

And then Bob told Johnny,

"I suggest we get him to a hospital."

"No can do, Doc," said Johnny, sensing what Bob was thinking:

*"...a trip to the hospital and the authorities would be called."*

"In your bag, was there the antivenin?" he asked instead.

"I've got antivenin, and I've got penicillin, but he's terribly dehydrated… an IV needs to be added."

"No, no, no…" said Johnny as if maybe he was starting to lose patience.

"Maybe you're not getting a clear picture of what's going on here. We're wanted fugitives, which means we can't go to a hospital or anywhere else a normal citizen might go for help. We came here because you're our only hope.

"Now...instead of making excuses, go ahead and treat him…and do it as if the survival of your family depends on it. Get my drift?" Johnny asked with a cold-blooded stare that he shifted from Bob over to where Callie and the kids were sitting and then back to Bob again.

*"I need to buy more time,"* Bob thought while he began to treat the man anyway. He was thinking that even if he did save the man's life, Johnny or maybe even the other convict might still decide to kill all of them.

It was no secret; ten years prior, Johnny had been sentenced to life in prison for the murder of a man and his entire family, including a wife and two small children, simply because the man agreed to testify in court against him concerning another reported assault. So, putting it past the idea that he wouldn't do it again was absurd.

However, after seeing Bob go to work, giving the man a few injections, and constantly checking on the man's blood pressure and pulse, Johnny's hardcore demeanor seemed to soften.

He asked Dominique,

"How old are you now? Twelve? Thirteen?"

"Fourteen," Dominique told him, speaking softly, afraid of the man who had the gun.

"What about you?" Johnny asked Nora, "...and you? ...and you?" They all told him their age. Samantha even added,

"I have to go to the bathroom."

"Alright... one at a time," said Johnny, allowing it.

If a person didn't know any better, they might've taken Johnny as a nice guy with a soft heart for children, which for him neither was true. Callie remembered the tantrum that Johnny displayed, destroying the bedroom upstairs the night Dominique was born. Added to that, the two children were killed in retaliation for the one man's willingness to testify against him. No...Johnny's sudden show of kindness wouldn't be misconstrued. He was a cold-blooded killer, nothing more.

"I'm afraid I've done all I can do," said Bob, the stethoscope hanging around his neck, a worn out, worried look on his face.

"His vitals are all stable. I guess all we can do now is wait," he announced, hoping that would do as a diagnosis,

"At least for now," he hoped.

"Ok...rejoin your family then," said Johnny with a patient tone, but all the while unmasking the cold-blooded stare again.

"We'll see what happens by morning... how effective your work has been," he said, which Bob took as a threat, cramming himself back on the couch between Callie and all four children, feeling very unsure about their survival.

## Chapter 42

By morning, the man was dead. Bob looked over at him and saw one of the man's arms hanging down off the couch. His mouth was open, somewhat exposing the man's tongue, and both eyes were slightly cracked, whereas the pupils were showing.

"*A dead man's stare, the telltale sign.*" As an emergency room doctor, Bob had seen enough of them to know.

The kids were all lying against one another, asleep, and so were Callie and the other convict, asleep in a chair across the room with the shotgun leaning close by against the wall. But not Johnny; he was still standing as if he'd been awake the entire time, alert to every movement and sound.

Bob had been dozing but was now fully awake as well, wondering,

"*What the hell should I do?*"

"Doctor," said Johnny when Bob moved, "...check the status of your patient."

When Bob moved to get up, the other convict sleeping in the chair awakened and grabbed the shotgun. It was an instinct, an instinct of constantly being afraid and on guard.

Just the touch of the man's dangling, cold arm confirmed what Bob had been thinking, that the man was lifeless, dead. He folded the arm across the rest of the man's body and used the stethoscope to check for a heartbeat anyway, though, as if he still didn't know. After a few seconds of listening and lifting the man's eyelids, Bob told the truth and announced,

"He's dead."

"Aw, hell!!!" said the other convict who, up until then, had been relatively quiet.

"What're we supposed to do now, smart guy?" he asked, coming apart, looking at Johnny, panic heard in every word he spoke.

"Charlie was our key to gettin' outta here. Who's gonna fly the plane now? Sure, as hell, not you or me.

"I know one thing... I'm not goin' back there in that damn swamp again."

## Buckets, Shovels, Ghost and Worms

The plan for them had been to make it to a nearby airfield where Charlie, the man lying dead on the couch, a former Air Force pilot turned drug smuggler, could steal a plane and fly them all to freedom in South America.

Johnny seemed to be in deep thought thinking about it, and when he didn't say anything right away, the convict continued,

"I suggest we consider takin' a car from here and maybe one or two of the hostages."

"No…take the car or anything else you want, but leave my family alone," said Callie, again speaking adamantly and unyielding, which made Johnny look up.

"I'd say you're in no position to give orders. So, if I were you, I'd be quiet and SHUT THE HELL UP!!!" he said, shouting the last few words, making it clear who was and who wasn't in charge.

"The first thing we need to do is find ourselves a change of clothes. And then, you're right, maybe we do need to take a few of them with us," said Johnny to the other convict. However, his attention was focused on the couch where Callie and the kids were all staring back at him with frightful eyes and scared faces.

The whole time, Bob had been using a hand to search

around inside the medical bag, pretending to replace all that he'd taken out of it when actually what he was doing was looking for something: a white, pearl-handled switchblade. Years ago, he'd bought the knife as a souvenir in Mexico and kept it in his bag to use as a cutting tool when plastic or other soft material items needed to be cut. But the pointed blade was four inches, long enough to do permanent and or fatal damage if needed to be used as a weapon in self-defense, or in this case, to protect himself and his family.

He'd just gotten a grip on the handle when Johnny asked,

"Doc…what size are you?"

"Thirty-six pants," said Bob, speaking quickly as if he'd been startled, yet hoping he hadn't been caught,

"…extra-large shirt," he said, which was about the size of the other convict. Johnny already knew that he and William were about the same size. So, he told Callie,

"Take my friend here with you, and go round up a couple of outfits for us… nothin' fancy… some from the butler's closet, and some from your husband's closet."

Callie was hesitant at first and didn't want to move and leave the kids, but then thought better of it, deciding that it might not be such a good idea to get Johnny pissed off any more than he was already.

The other convict was on his way over to insist when Callie stood and started toward the staircase. She'd gotten within a foot of passing Johnny when Bob lunged and stabbed the other convict three times before anybody else even knew what happened.

The convict dropped the shotgun, and that's when Callie and Johnny turned to notice the damage Bob had done.

It still took a moment to register before Johnny fired a shot at Bob, only to have Callie attack, fighting him tooth and nail. And then Bob stabbed Johnny too, just before blacking out and collapsing on the floor with a big hole in his chest from being shot.

The kids were yelling and screaming, frightened and panicking from seeing all that was going on, especially after seeing that Bob had been shot. But Callie was still in a fight for her life as well… the stab wound had hurt and weakened Johnny, but not enough to make him give up and stop trying to kill Callie.

"I'm gonna make you pay, bitch," he said, turning into a madman, sweating profusely and grunting with spit flying from every spoken word.

A couple more shots were fired, but wildly because

Callie hadn't given up either. Each time a shot was fired, the reverberating sound was deafening, but Callie, who'd gotten a tight grip on the gun, was able to keep the barrel at bay and away from the kids.

With the two of them in a heap, rolling around on the floor, Johnny was eventually able to get the best of her and had Callie pinned down. He'd just about gotten the barrel of the gun pointed at Callie's head when a set of dirty boots walked over. The man the boots belonged to put a gun to Johnny's head and told him, "I'd let her go if I were you."

The feel of cold steel against his head and then the clicking sound of the firing mechanism being cocked finally registered. That's when Johnny let go and gave up.

Officer Milton, who'd come in the back door, reached down, took the gun, and pulled Johnny aside so that Callie could get up.

"Ma'am," he said, tipping the hat yet again, which, this time, brought on a great sense of relief and elation. And, just for a moment, allowed Callie a chance to cry. But then Bob coughed, and the tragedy was brought back to reality.

When she got to him, Bob was gurgling blood, struggling to breathe. Callie held his head while the kids huddled around and cried; it was all any of them could do. Unfortunately, by the time the ambulance arrived, the other convict was dead, and so was Bob.

## Chapter 43

"Amazing grace... how sweet the sound... that saved a wretch like me.

I once was lost, but now I'm found...was blind, but now I see."

It was the second time within a month that the lyrics of Amazing Grace were sung in the context of it being for the sad occasion of a funeral due to yet another person either dying or being killed at the Devereaux House.

William couldn't help remembering the phone call he'd gotten from Viola Ray, warning him that they all might be in danger. It made him wish otherwise and wonder,

*"If I'd done things differently, would my friend Bob still be alive?"*

Callie, who was extremely overwhelmed, devastated, being a better word for it, was somehow holding it together, being more of a woman and mother than William ever thought she'd be, displaying courage and fortitude at a time when most would've caved in. Although saddened, it made William awfully proud of her.

At Bob's funeral, not once did she cry out or break down. Sure, a tear fell here and there, but nothing excessive, no kind of outburst or anything resembling a total breakdown, requiring medical attention or comforting from William or anybody else. Instead, along with Dominique, Callie was the one who did most of the comforting herself when Nora and Samantha needed her there for them.

Todd stayed closer to William, the male figure, and tried to be strong, displaying more tolerance to what turned out to be quite a bit of anguish for an eleven-year-old boy to have to endure.

It was extremely heartbreaking to know Bob had been killed. He would most definitely be missed, but everybody understood the sacrifice and courage Bob showed during the most adverse time in trying to protect his family. Therefore, Callie and the kids stood strong, too, determined to prevail and protect Bob's honor.

****

It was a day later, after Bob's murder when William and Nikki got home to find a sheriff's squad car still in the driveway along with a detective's unit, two vehicles belonging to the state's crime lab, and one from Angola State Prison.

Callie and the kids were all up in their rooms, but men were still walking through the house, taking pictures and fingerprint samples, and samples of blood from the stains still visibly lodged over the living room floor.

An officer explained to William all that had happened and then took a statement as to what William saw prior to leaving. It wasn't until about thirty minutes later that William was finally allowed to go up and see Callie.

"I'm sorry you had to go through this," said William when he knocked and then opened the bedroom door to find Callie's saddened face staring back at him.

"Bob was a good man and didn't deserve how he died."

"Yeah, well... tell that to Mr. Johnny Le Fleur," said Callie in a way that expressed lots of anger.

William just stood there for a moment, digesting the bad taste and terrible feeling he got from memories of the day that he and Johnny met,

*"The day I should'a killed the son of a bitch,"* thought William, but instead said, "I always knew he was no good."

"I knew it too but couldn't help from wantin' to live on the wild side," said Callie's shaky voice, followed by a constant flow of tears,

"Silly me, huh?"

"No, baby… it's not your fault. We've all been young and dumb at one time or another in our lives, even me, I was too… can you believe it?" William asked, which brought a smile to both their faces.

"It's all God's will. So, go wit' it, and don't beat yourself up about it. We're all destined to die in some kind'a way. Bob's time just came a little sooner than we would've hoped.

"But I'm glad for one thing."

"Glad?" asked Callie's tear-stained face that, over the last few minutes, had gone from sad to amused and now confused.

"What's there to be glad about?" she asked.

"I'm glad that I ever got to meet him. Aren't you? Your husband was a great man.

"He couldn't dance worth a damn…you shoulda' seen him, Callie; he got drunk and danced his ass off the night we went out, made us both look bad.

"But I enjoyed bein' around him just the same. My man, Bob."

The wisecrack about Bob's bad dancing brought on another smile. Callie remembered the day of first meeting Bob when, along with Nora, he tried dancing to an Elvis favorite, "Jail House Rock," In fact, everything else she remembered about him brought on a smile too, everything up until when Johnny Le Fleur showed up.

****

It took three years to the day for Johnny to be executed. Upon their escape from prison, another inmate and two prison guards were killed as well, a total of six people in all.

The governor took a hard stance on being tough on crime, and along with the other victims' families, including Callie, they all insisted that the state's prosecutor get the process started and over with as soon as possible, which was what happened. A trial date was set and brought forthwith, and Johnny, after being found guilty on every charge against him, was sentenced to die in the electric chair.

"You sure you don't want me to go with you?" asked William on the day of the execution.

"Yeah, I'm sure… this somethin' I gotta do by myself," said Callie, dressed in black as if for a funeral: black dress, black shoes, black hat, and a black purse.

She wouldn't be alone, though. Family members of all the other victims, along with a representative of the Governor's office, the prosecuting attorney, other state representatives, the warden and other prison officials, and the press, were all on hand to wish Johnny a safe trip to hell.

When they brought him out, Johnny's head had been shaved, and his prison attire had been cleaned and starched. Even the chair looked clean and polished as if just for this particular special occasion.

While the guards were strapping him in, Johnny looked around and snickered and then laughed out aloud as if the audience were all a part of a comedy show. However, the situation became a lot more serious when the executioner put the wet sponge on top of his head and covered it with the metal crown, which would be the device to deliver the lethal volts of electricity.

The laughter turned into sniffles; he'd begun to cry. But instead of breaking down, praying to God, and asking for forgiveness, Johnny, a known agnostic, began spewing obscenities,

"FUCK YOU!!! FUCK ALL OF YOU!!!" he yelled, just before the man, standing behind and just to one side of him, hit the switch. Then Johnny's body began to quiver and shake uncontrollably, trembling and vibrating almost as if to a fancy tune while the thousand or so watts of electricity fried his brain.

When the man deactivated the switch, a doctor quickly stepped forward, stethoscope in hand, to monitor Johnny's heartbeat. But there wasn't any, and Johnny was pronounced dead. The man known as Johnny Le Fleur lived no longer. It was over almost as quickly as it started.

Representatives from the Governor's office stood and shook hands with the district attorney and all the prison officials who were in attendance. The victims' families and waiting members of the press walked out feeling as though justice had been served; Callie had even heard a few of them say so themselves. However, deep down inside, Callie felt that no form of so-called justice would be good enough… none of it would ever bring Bob back. Therefore, in a sense, it was all a waste of time, time that Callie would've rather spent doing something more purposeful, like nurturing what she had left: three beautiful daughters and a very talented son.

# PART II

## Chapter 44

Each kiss became more engaging than the one before, and each breath became more hurried and intense. The car windows were overcome with steam and fogged while those parked in cars around them were suddenly nonexistent and oblivious.

The dress Dominique had on became a wrinkled mess with Seth Evan's hand all over and underneath it, touching in places never touched before. Nothing felt better than feeling all over Dominique's soft and extremely pretty body. He couldn't help himself, and neither could she, letting him. They were in love and had been since for as long as either of them could remember. Except now, at seventeen, their bodies were hormonally active and were of an age to express themselves more physically.

Seth was an average guy with average height and weight and wasn't too bad-looking. But he made up for what he didn't have in good looks with extreme intelligence, which was what most people liked about him.

However, Dominique had become quite a beauty in her own way, dark and lovely, with an almost perfect nose and mouth and hazel eyes capable of taking the average young man's breath away. Everything else about her was almost perfect, too, at five foot six, a hundred thirty pounds, with curves in all the right places. Not to mention how sweet and soft-spoken she was in talking and expressing herself.

"Wait," she whispered, panting in Seth Evan's ear with both arms around him, which was driving Seth crazy; he had a hand on one of Dominique's breasts and was just about ready to go down and kiss it.

Dominique liked the way he responded to her, but still, she was unwilling to throw caution to the wind or overlook the promise she'd made to Callie about having or not having sex before being sure that Seth was the one she wanted to spend the rest of her life with.

"Don't be like me and give it up too soon or to just anybody. No, baby, I made way too many mistakes with men when I was young.

"Yeah, at times, it'll throb like hell and get seriously hot and wet, but I'm tellin' you… you need to take your time and fall in love, and be sure that he's as much in love with you as you are with him.

"If I had it to do all over again, I'd actually wait until after we've both said 'I do'. You'll know for sure then if he loves you," Callie told her in one of the many heart-to-heart talks they'd been having lately.

"No… we can't," Dominique told Seth, who, with a hand now inside Dominique's panties, had all but undressed her.

"Why not?" he asked, on the verge of premature ejaculation, "I want you so bad, baby."

"I know… and I want you too, but we gotta wait until after we're married," Dominique told him, standing firm on the decision she'd made,

"Let's watch the movie." They were at a drive-in movie theater, and the movie was "Gordon's War." Actor Paul Warfield portrayed a black soldier, home from the Vietnam War, who'd waged his own war against crime and criminals who'd all but taken over the old neighborhood with drugs and violence.

Seth planned to become a soldier as well and felt impressed by Gordon's plight and courage. He also planned to be the best husband he could be, willing to do whatever it took to make his future wife happy.

"We've already missed half of it anyway, thanks to

you," he said, smiling and then flinching after he'd changed positions, putting an arm around Dominique, but not expecting the elbow she hit him with,

"That's for lying," she smiled and told him.

"Ouch… Ok, I'm sorry… I take it back," he said, in surrender, while still smiling, even laughing a little from having such a good time with her.

There was no doubt the two were destined to be happily married and would hopefully have a long life together. Unfortunately, future happiness wasn't as certain for Nora as it seemed to be for Dominique.

Twenty-two-year-old Billy Rankin, like "The Fonz," a character portrayed by actor Henry Winkler from the old, 1970s show "Happy Days." But this example of the character happened to be there in the city of Lafayette, Louisiana, complete with greased hair slicked and combed straight back. And always with a black leather jacket on, with jeans and a t-shirt, riding atop a big boss hog, Harley Davidson motorcycle,

"…a mean riding machine. The baddest thing on two wheels" was how the character would've described the bike.

Why the girls liked him wasn't because Billy was so handsome, not as much as how fearless and cool they thought he was.

"Your father would kill you and me both if he was here and knew that I allowed you to go out with this guy.

"Uh uh… no, ma'am… forget it. Not even in your wildest dreams will I allow this to happen."

"Why not? You let Dominique go out on a date."

"Yeah, but first of all, Dominique's seventeen, two years older than you. Second...the age limit I set for her to go out was sixteen, not to mention how much classier Seth Evans happens to be compared to Billy.

"So, like I said… no, ma'am… not even in your wildest dreams," said Callie, a drink in hand on the front porch sitting next to William...a drink in his hand as well.

The nighttime sky was star-studded, and after a long hot day, there was just enough of a breeze that blew to make the night both comforting and relaxed, that is,

"...if it wasn't for Nora...bein' agitatin' as hell," thought Callie after saying "no" to Nora, again and again, about going out with Bad-Ass Billy Rankin.

"Agh!!! I hate this.

"I still don't know why Daddy wanted to move us all

out here in the first place.

"I wanna go back to San Diego and live with Uncle Mike, amongst other civilized people," said Nora, storming off, leaving behind a whole slew of venomously spewed words.

"Kind'a high-strung, ain't she?" William asked afterward, sipping from a glass of scotch and water he'd been holding on to, nursing.

"Too high-strung if you ask me," said Callie, taking a sip of straight Seagram's Gin from the glass she'd been drinking from.

"Yeah… kind'a like somebody else I used to know," said William, smiling pretentiously.

"Uncle Mike," Michael Macklin, Bob's younger brother, was the only member of Bob's family who made it to the funeral. Both their parents were dead, but out of the other relatives, mostly elderly uncles and aunts and a few cousins, Mike was the only one who responded with any kind of sympathetic condolences. Nonetheless, Mike, the beach bum, was broke; Callie even had to buy the round-trip ticket that got him there.

He was awfully good-looking and had lots of charm and charisma, but he had what Callie thought was

*"...a lot of hot air and empty space where his brain was supposed to be."*

So, she thought that Nora's wish to live with him was very unlikely. The next morning, however, when Callie went in to wake the kids for school, Nora was gone. And, a month and a half later, Callie did, in fact, receive a phone call from Mike telling her that a guy on a motorcycle, whom Callie thought was,

**"Billy Rankin, more than likely,"** had brought Nora there and dropped her off, tired, broke, hungry, and crying because she thought she might be pregnant.

"If I didn't know any better, I'd think that you gave birth to that child yourself," said William, smiling and laughing a little after hearing about what happened,

"She's startin' to act just like you."

"Oh hush, William… and you're startin' to get on my damn nerves," said Callie, clearly agitated,

"…how 'bout that!"

## Chapter 45

Running away from home to be with Billy Rankin was the worst thing Nora could've ever done. This she knew after only being gone a day, which was mostly spent on the back of Billy's motorcycle, riding on one two-lane highway after another through what seemed to be all rural areas and small towns of Louisiana and then Texas.

Once they got where they were going and stopped, it took another day just to recoup.

Now, instead of being in love like she thought she might be, she felt homesick and already had a deep regret about ever meeting Billy Rankin.

"Bonjour… hot enough for you?" Billy asked, speaking kindly when Callie stopped to get a shopping cart at the grocery store with Dominique, Samantha, and Nora all behind her. Billy was waiting in line for one of the cashiers to become available.

## Alvin Bell

"Any hotter, and we'll probably cook," said Callie.

Nora was the last to see him,

"Bonjour, Jolie fille, pretty lady," he said after Callie had gone down the aisle far enough not to hear him.

"What's your name?" he asked. And it began from there. The last thing he wanted to know was, "Can I call you sometime?"

And Nora, knowing that Callie wouldn't approve, told Billy,

"It'll probably be best if I called you." And she did, every night up until the night when she packed a bag and left. Billy was waiting a half mile or so down the road. Otherwise, the Harley's loud muffler might've awakened the whole house.

****

They were in a place called Juarez, a town just south of the Mexican border, in an area straight out of the Wild-Wild-West. What Nora mostly saw were men, Mexican and white biker dudes, all of them with overgrown mustaches and scraggly beards on rough-looking faces. Almost all of them were wearing badly worn cowboy boots and jeans.

Some wore tight t-shirts as well, flexing muscle, while

some wore flannel shirts and Stetson hats...any relic of who or what organization they belonged to, like the biker dudes who all wore leather vests, with or without shirts or hats on.

And guns… every single one of them had a knife, or gun, or both, and wore them proudly, strapped on them in plain view.

After a full day's rest, they went out and partied, something Nora had never done before, especially not when it included the consumption of drugs and alcohol.

The first shot of Tequila almost made Nora sick. The second was no better. She quickly became attuned to it, though, when those all around her thought seeing her sick was funny just because she wasn't used to drinking.

"I'll show 'em," she thought, slurring words that weren't even spoken.

In the midst of getting drunk, Billy told her,

"Stick out your tongue," and when she did, he dropped a pill on it, a microdot. The pill was so small, Nora thought, "What the hell," and swallowed it, thinking something so tiny couldn't be very harmful. But boy, was she wrong.

The pill was a microdot dosage of mescaline, a highly hallucinative form of acid similar to LSD. An hour later,

Nora started laughing and couldn't stop, not even when Billy made her walk to one of the back rooms and took off everything she had on.

A man came in behind them and got naked too...a tall and slim man, with a manhood hanging eight inches or more.

He came so close to Nora's face with his manhood that the smell of it almost made Nora sick. He obviously hadn't bathed in a while.

*"...a couple of days, at least,"* thought Nora. She thought that was funny too and kept on laughing until the man gave up on getting oral sex and forced Nora down on the bed and then himself between her legs. The effect of the drug that made everything so funny quickly wore off with the man banging away inside of her.

And when he was finished, another man came in, and then another. After the third, Nora passed out and lost count.

\*\*\*\*

The night when poor, little innocent, young Nora Macklin, unaware of the dangers two-legged wolves imposed, called and told Billy, The Big Bad Wolf, about wanting to go live with Uncle Mike in San Diego.

"I'm sick and tired of being here... told all the time about

## Buckets, Shovels, Ghost and Worms

what I can and cannot do. I'm sick of it," she told him.

All it took then was for Billy to ask, "You wanna run away with me? We'll ride down to Texas for a while and have some fun before heading out to San Diego. I've gotta go that way anyway, meet some folks in Tijuana," which Nora knew was just south of San Diego, across the U.S./Mexican border. What she didn't know was that Billy's idea of fun was for him to become Nora's pimp.

Billy wanted and used Nora to get money to buy himself a large quantity of cocaine. Pablo Escobar and the Medellin Columbian Cartel had set up shop in Tijuana and were selling their product at rock-bottom prices.

\*\*\*\*

When Nora woke up, Billy quickly stuck another pill in her mouth. This particular pill was different, even more hallucinative, one that got Nora so high she thought she saw pink elephants. Everything else was a blur: all the different men who came in and paid Billy to take advantage of her. She didn't remember anything, drinking from the bottle of Tequila either or eating the worm at the bottom of it. She eventually passed out and slept for three days straight.

A total of two weeks were spent there in Juarez before moving on to Columbus, New Mexico, where another two weeks of doped manipulation and unprotected sex started.

And then it was Yuma, Arizona. They spent about two weeks there as well before Billy was finally satisfied that he'd made enough money and was ready to cross the California state line and take Nora home to Uncle Mike. He disappeared after that and was never seen or heard from again.

## Chapter 46

A week later, Callie was on a first-class flight to San Diego. After noticing how tight she held on every time the plane hit pockets of turbulence, the man sitting beside her asked,

"This your first time flyin'?"

"Yeah," she muttered, which came out almost mute amongst the effects of being in air-tight fuselage cabin pressure.

"You'll have to speak a little louder," the man said, making a gesture with a hand cupped behind an ear, letting Callie know he couldn't hear her.

"Would you like to have a drink with me?" the man asked.

"I find they're quite relaxing when you're flying," he said with a smile, hoping to lighten the mood. What he didn't know was that, before takeoff, Callie had had a glass of champagne already, but now, in mid-flight, she would've probably preferred having straight gin or the whole bottle of champagne.

Like Callie, at least one of the man's parents had been white; she could tell by the straight hair texture and the light color of the man's skin. Thirty minutes later, drink in hand, and in deep conversation, Callie had also learned that the man was from Detroit and was visiting his daughter, who'd married a sailor stationed onboard one of the Coronado-based aircraft carriers...the USS Constellation. He thought the daughter's husband was a good man, just a little on the wild side. The whole purpose of visiting them was to make sure everything was copacetic.

By the time the plane landed, Callie knew everything about the man's wife, his kids, and the man's whole life story.

"Well, Mr. Hatton...I must say, you're quite interesting… and it was indeed very nice meeting you," she said once they were off the plane, making their way down the Jet-way.

"Please… call me Ollie," the man said, offering a hand to shake.

Callie shook it and told him, "You've been wonderful…

you definitely helped pass the time."

"Good… I'm glad. It seems you were a little nervous at first."

"Who you tryin'a' kid? I was a nervous wreck," Callie told him, which made them both laugh.

"Well, again…it was nice meeting you."

"Same here," said Ollie.

Just inside the terminal, Callie saw a lovely young woman with a light-skinned complexion, like Ollie's, standing beside a dark-skinned young man about the same age in navy garb. They had a small child with them, too, a little boy. As soon as Ollie got close, the three of them shared big smiles and wrapped joyful arms around him.

Callie's welcoming reunion wasn't as great, but at least Mike was there, standing to one side along the wall,

"How was your flight?" he asked, reaching for Callie's one piece of carry-on luggage.

"Long as hell… and there I was in Louisiana thinkin' I should've driven my car here."

"If you had, I wouldn't've expected you here for at least another day or so," he said, smiling.

"I've got two more bags," said Callie, giving Mike a quick kiss and pecking him on the cheek.

"Ok, we'll get 'em," he said, receiving Callie's short embrace kindly.

"By the way," Mike began before leading the way toward the baggage claim area, "…you look very nice."

"Why thank you," said Callie, "…so do you…you look nice as well."

And he did. Mike, instead of how he usually dressed in simple shorts and a t-shirt, had put on a pair of khaki pants, a decent button-down shirt, and moccasins, albeit still without socks. Nevertheless, he did look rather nice. But when Callie looked around, it seemed as if the entire terminal was filled with good-looking men, all tanned and buff,

"…and the women too, as far as that goes." Everybody she saw seemed to look comfortable and content, happy to be alive, living in a place some would consider paradise.

San Diego, the quietly kept secret jewel of America. A Southern California city with beaches of pure white sand and clear blue water outside the city streets with almost always perfect weather, with the ever-present lush hills and mountains in the background, something the entire state was famous for. And the attractions, like Sea World, where killer whales performed and put on acts of entertainment, dazzling enlightened crowds of thousands almost every day.

Upon approaching the runway, how and where the plane landed made Callie feel as if they were landing on one of the downtown San Diego city streets. Actually, the plane really had flown over the downtown area and landed just a few miles away, which was how close the airport was to San Diego's largest and tallest buildings.

Imperial Beach, a small community of mostly sailors and others on low budgets who wanted to live near the water, was where Mike lived in a small two-bedroom apartment. He could've gotten there a lot quicker if he'd taken the interstate I-5, which ran north and south through the entirety of the United States' west coast borders from Tijuana, Mexico, to the Canadian border. But Mike decided to give Callie the scenic tour instead, driving his little red convertible Volkswagen Beetle across the Coronado Bridge above the San Diego Bay.

"It's not a Cadillac convertible," he told Callie over the strain and roar of the loud engine. "…but she gets me where I gotta go," he said, his hand patting the dashboard as if the automobile actually had feelings.

"I hear ya'," said Callie, more interested in all she saw around her.

The downtown San Diego Embarcadero area was on one side, and NAS Naval Air Station, North Island was on the other side where the aircraft carriers USS Kitty Hawk, USS Ranger, and The USS Constellation were based…all of them happened to be in port. The sight of the huge ships made Callie think of Ollie and his family again.

Only a few minutes of driving took them through Coronado, and then they were on a stretch of highway that had the ocean on the right, but on the left was the legendary Hotel Coronado, a huge structure built in the early 1900's, known worldwide for its vast variety of in house luxuries and elegant amenities and style that's forever been second to none.

Later, they passed a building on the right, barracks for Navy seal personnel, some of whom were out running and swimming, involved in different types of endurance training while Mike and Callie rode by.

By the time Callie had relaxed and absorbed it all, they were there at Mike's apartment.

"So, how is she?" Callie asked before either of them had gotten out of Mike's car. Up until then, they'd been having only small talk while Mike was driving. But having concern for Nora was the whole reason why Callie had flown over a thousand miles to be there.

"She's ok...tryin' to come out of it. Being on a constant diet of hallucinatory drugs and Tequila can take quite a toll on you; believe me, I would know," said Mike, making it clear that he'd had some of the same experiences.

"She's still a little tired, though, and conscious about what it was she's gone through. Some days, she'll take five or six baths, one after another, I guess, to rid herself of some of the filth, which I think is mostly psychological, embedded from knowing what happened."

"Well, of course, Mike… she's a fifteen-year-old girl who's had a time with one helluva experience...more than what she expected, I'm sure.

"But we can't let her get caught up in self-pity either… she's gotta get over it and move on."

"Ok...so, what'a' you suggest we do?"

"I need to have a talk with her first, find out what state of mind she's in. Find out if havin' a baby's really what she wants."

"It's a little late for that, don't you think?"

"No… not really. She's still got options."

"Yeah, one of them being an abortion."

"That and others."

"I'm sure," said Mike, as a pro-life liberal, not liking the sound of where the conversation was going.

"Tell you what... I'll leave that part up to you and her to discuss. I want no part in deciding whether a child or a relative of mine lives or dies.

"Shall we?" he asked, reaching for the handle of the car door to let himself out.

"What kind'a neighborhood is this?" Callie asked after she'd gotten out too and was standing on the sidewalk, taking in the fresh smell of the ocean.

"The reason why I ask is because I might wanna take Nora for a walk, go down by the beach for a while."

"It's safe... nobody'll hurt you," said Mike after he'd gathered Callie's luggage and started for the door of his apartment.

"I've lived around here for over five years and have yet to hear about anybody gettin' mugged or raped," which made Callie feel a little better. Nevertheless, she wished she hadn't asked... he didn't come right out and say it, but it showed that Mike might've been a little offended,

"...or is it still the idea of Nora possibly having an

## Buckets, Shovels, Ghost and Worms

abortion that bothered him?" Callie wondered.

"Whatever," thought Callie... Mike being a little oversensitive would be the last thing she would worry about. Nora's well-being was the priority. Besides, it was Nora's sixteenth birthday.

## Chapter 47

Fishing was good, as usual; Brim and Crappie, and even Catfish were constantly biting, and Dominique and Ms. Ladeaux were constantly pulling them in, which was what bothered Dominique, the distinct repetitive occurrence of the way things always happened with them. And because of it, there were a few things Dominique wanted to know,

"For as long as you and I have been comin' out here, fishin', I've never asked about your family. Where are they?" she asked.

"I haven't got a family anymore," Ms. Ladeaux told her as if maybe they were all dead.

"Do you have a house somewhere nearby?" Dominique asked, on a roll, ready to ask one question after another.

*"Something that was bound to happen sooner or later,"* thought Ms. Ladeaux about Dominique suddenly becoming so inquisitive.

She was thinking, *"It's been eleven years, and only now has she begun askin' questions."*

"What if I told you I don't have a home anymore either?" asked Ms. Ladeaux with a bit of reluctance in what she planned to do next… it was time Dominique knew the truth.

"Then I'd think it's terrible, not havin' a home," said Dominique.

And she was about to ask,

"Where do you live then?" when all of a sudden, Ms. Ladeaux vanished. One minute, she was there sitting beside Dominique, and then the next, she was gone.

At first, as a child, Dominique thought,

*"Wow…Quite amazing,"* thinking that it was a feat so astounding that a person could actually disappear.

*"But how could that be?"* she wondered afterward, giving it further thought… it wasn't humanly possible.

The realization of it then became frightening, especially a few seconds later when Ms. Ladeaux reappeared again, but standing behind Dominique…it frightened and startled Dominique so much that she almost fell into the water.

Gasping, Dominique got up and took off running, leaving behind the bucket of fish they'd already caught and everything else, including the shoes she'd been wearing.

"Wait… don't go. I won't hurt you," said Ms. Ladeaux, calling behind her as tears began to fall, watching Dominique run away.

Later, bringing trash out the back, William found Dominique's shoes and a bucket of fish placed neatly at the bottom of the stairs. He figured Dominique had simply forgotten that she'd left them there. He took the shoes in the house and cleaned the fish himself.

After Nikki fried them all, William wondered why Dominique wouldn't eat any but didn't press the issue. Over a period of time, he also noticed that Dominique wouldn't go back in the swamp again, but didn't press that issue either, and felt relieved, thinking he wouldn't ever have to worry about going in behind her anymore.

****

Instead of them taking a walk together, Callie borrowed Mike's car keys and drove her and Nora to a nearby Black Angus restaurant where the two of them ordered steaks, medium rare, had salads and baked potatoes, and ate until they were stuffed. Nora even had dessert: chocolate cake.

Callie made sure the waitress knew that it was Nora's birthday, and when the cake was brought out, the waitress had a candle stuck in it and while the candle burned, other waitresses joined in singing Happy Birthday. The waitress's effort earned her an extra twenty-dollar tip.

Outside, on the sidewalk, Nora told Callie, "I haven't had a good meal like that since the night I left home."

"Did you enjoy it?"

"Yeah, I did."

"Ok, well… that's the way you gotta keep eatin' to make sure the baby's born healthy and strong," Callie told her, one mother to another.

It was decided that Nora would indeed have the baby after all and keep it.

"No abortion, and no giving it up for adoption." She said she couldn't stand the idea of either, regardless of not knowing who the father was. Knowing that she was the mother was enough. There was a long conversation about it between Callie and Nora, about all the lifelong responsibilities that came along with being a mother, about all the joy and the hurt and pain as well.

Nora, instead of flying back with Callie the next day,

also insisted on staying in Southern California.

"It's where we're from," she told Callie, who understood completely...for her, living anywhere else than in Louisiana, where she was from, wouldn't seem right either.

Mike would allow her to continue living with him until the baby was born. After that, Callie would fly back out, and Nora would get a car, and an apartment of her own.

# Chapter 48

Dominique looked at herself in the mirror.

"Uh uh uh. Damn, girl," she said, in a mood to be naughty and misbehave. She'd just gotten out of the shower and was standing there completely naked.

*"Eighteen, and how luscious you are,"* she thought, grabbing both nipples on size 38D breasts, pinching them even, feeling the moisture grow between her legs.

"Momma said there'd be days like this," she said with a mischievous smile, speaking to herself in the mirror, remembering when Callie said,

"At times, it'll throb like hell and get seriously hot and wet," which was how it was now.

"Oui," "Yes," she said, finding herself horny as hell.

Then, unconsciously, she began humming a tune, a

Betty Wright song.

"Tonight is the night... that you... make me a woman."

Prom night... she'd gotten some money from Callie and had already rented a limo and a room.

"You said you'd be gentle with me, and I... I hope you will." The words in the lyrics that Betty Wright sang were perfect,

"I'm nervous... and I'm tremblin'... waitin' for you to come on in."

Dominique had the most beautiful body and knew it, watching herself dance around in the mirror. Not an ounce of fat was anywhere to be seen, and all the right bumps and curves had evolved.

"Five feet, seven inches tall, and a hundred and thirty-five pounds," which she thought was even the right height and weight... everything was right: hair, skin complexion, and texture, even the hazel green eyes that, the older she got, became more hypnotizing.

"...and I'm all yours, honey," she said, the picture of Seth Evans stuck in a corner of the mirror with him staring back at her.

Nora had taken the plunge and wasn't a virgin anymore

and was, by then, five months pregnant to prove it.

*"And it's about time I did it too,"* thought Dominique, "…minus me gettin' pregnant, of course," she added in thought. Besides, Seth had already joined the army; he was to leave in two weeks, the day after graduation. Dominique was thinking,

*"After that, anything might happen. Who knows, we might never see each other again."*

So, like the song said when Betty Wright sang it, "Tonight is the night."

*"At least then we'll have something to remember each other by,"* she thought, "…a very special moment in time."

\* \* \* \*

Dominique spent the entire day pampering herself, first at the beauty salon, where she got a new hairdo and her nails polished pink. Next, she went shopping and bought what she thought was just the right burgundy dress and pink underwear. She spent an hour trying to decide what kind of perfume she should wear, finally deciding on Chanel No.5, a soft but popular fragrance.

A fifty-dollar tip plus cost had even persuaded a hotel clerk to have a bottle of Dom Perigon put on ice for them that evening that would be waiting to be opened when she and Seth were expected to be at the room. Last but not least, the limo driver was then given proper instructions.

Everything was set and planned perfectly—all except the outcome. At the end of the day, Seth's eighty-nine-year-old grandmother passed away, and all the plans that Dominique made were canceled.

Seth called and told her,

"Sorry, babe, but I won't be able to make it tonight… Grandma Ethel just died."

"Awwwwww… no," said Dominique with sincere compassion, feeling sorry for him.

"Yeah, the whole family's here. There's no way I'm gonna be able to get away… sorry."

"No, babe… it's quite alright, I understand. Sorry to hear about Grandma Ethel… I really liked her a lot," said Dominique, and she did. Seth's grandmother was always extremely nice and treated Dominique kindly and with the utmost respect.

* * * *

In the next two weeks, Grandma Ethel was laid to rest, Seth and Dominique both graduated high school, and the army had shipped Seth off to Fort Dix, New Jersey, for basic training.

"I promise, no matter what, I'll be back to get you," Seth told Dominique before leaving.

"So don't give up on us."

"I won't," Dominique told him, eyes glossy, on the verge of crying, "I promise."

"I'm gonna miss you," Seth told her.

"I'm'a miss you too," said Dominique, and after one last kiss, Seth was gone.

## Chapter 49

Another first-class flight,

*"...and another time for me to be nervous as hell,"* thought Callie, who, on this particular occasion, was accompanied by the whole crew: Dominique, Samantha, and Todd. Nikki and William, who both refused to fly, stayed behind and held things down at home.

Just before take-off, the intercom came to life,

"Good afternoon, ladies and gentlemen. Welcome on board flight 364, nonstop to San Diego," said the lovely young Continental Airlines employee standing in the aisle at the front of the plane, microphone in hand, making the announcement.

Callie noticed the girl had long, dark hair, hardly any makeup on, a gray and white striped shirt, burgundy tie and pants, and black shoes. After the girl had finished the announcement, Callie watched the girl walk by and thought,

"Wow… nice outfit, whether it's what she wears to work every day or not."

\* \* \* \*

Nora was in the ninth month of pregnancy and doing well, but the family was flying out to give the teenage expectant mother moral support. And it was a good thing because later, not long after the family arrived, Nora started having labor pains and then contractions.

It wouldn't be until twelve hours later, but when it was over, Nora had given birth to a healthy baby boy, Charlie Macklin.

"He looks a lot like Daddy and Uncle Mike," said Samantha, holding him the next day after Nora and Charlie had come home from the hospital.

And he did… he looked a lot like all of the Macklins, actually.

"Thank God," thought Callie, realizing, from experience, what a catastrophe it could've been otherwise.

"I'm only forty… too young to be called somebody's grandmother," she said, kidding but making a fuss over Charlie too.

After taking him from Samantha, Callie smiled proudly

and told Charlie,

"Grandma loves her lil' baby boy." It made everybody laugh the way she sat there cooing and contradicted herself.

They were all happy and excited about it, even Mike.

"Callie... Cindy and I are going out for drinks later. You're welcome to come along. We can make it sort of a celebration," he told her. Cindy was Mike's twenty-two-year-old bi-sexual girlfriend, tall with long, strawberry blond hair and gorgeous in ways that drove men wild - and women too.

At first, Callie was hesitant.

"Mike... I can't just leave the kids," she said as if the idea of going out and leaving them was absurd.

But then Mike told her, "Kids? What kids? All I see are grown-ass women and a grown-ass man," which made everybody laugh.

"Besides," he said, on a roll, "...you can't come to Cali without going out to party at least once, Callie," he said and smiled, thinking what he'd said was funny, although what really got Callie's attention was when Mike whispered and told her,

"Cindy's got the hots for you."

Callie had never been with a woman before but felt she might've had the urge since noticing and then becoming attracted to the flight attendant onboard the aircraft that flew them in.

"Yeah? You're kidding, right?" said Callie, somewhat embarrassed by the thought of even considering it.

"She's got the hots for me?" she asked, pretending to be more surprised than embarrassed. She'd met Mike's girlfriend and couldn't deny being attracted to her as well.

"Uh-huh," said Mike, smiling again, giving the impression that he might've even encouraged it, "…and she's bringing a friend.

"C'mon… it'll be fun," he said, which was all the encouragement it took.

"Ok… is fifteen minutes too long to wait for me to get dressed?" Callie asked, ready for a new adventure.

"No… not at all," said Mike. And twenty minutes later, Mike and Callie were riding down the street with the top down on Mike's convertible Volkswagen.

* * * *

Cindy's friend, Angie, was tall and blonde too, and just as gorgeous. Mike and Callie met them in the parking lot of

Flanagan's, a popular nightclub there in the Balboa Park area of San Diego.

When Mike pulled into the parking lot and parked next to Cindy's silver Toyota, Angie was just getting out of the back seat of a shiny new black Volvo sedan with chromed rims. The Volvo pulled off... two young black guys were in it, driving away.

Angie got back in with Cindy and waited until Mike had let the Volkswagen top up before she and Cindy got out again.

Cindy gave Mike a quick kiss before saying to Callie,

"Hey, girl... I'm glad you could make it," and proceeded to give Callie a kiss, too, except on the cheek.

"Mike would've never been forgiven if he had'a' shown up here without you," she said, smiling before changing the subject.

"Angie... meet Callie... she's the one I told you was from Louisiana," said Cindy, turning from one to the other and then back toward Callie, giving her another big smile.

"Hi... it's nice meeting you," Angie told Callie, giving her a big smile as well, while the four of them bounced toward the front entrance.

"Who were the two guys?" Mike asked.

"Al and Damon," Cindy told him.

"Damon's the Blow Master," Angie blurted, which was true. It wouldn't be until later that Callie figured out what "Blow Master" really meant.

Once inside, Callie found that the place was packed with a fascinating mixed crowd of Blacks, Whites, Hispanics, and Asians, and they were all there enjoying themselves, partying as if there wouldn't be a tomorrow.

Big, huge speakers were thumping and pumping out the sound of Junior's new song, "…take your time, young man. And momma used to say… live your life… live your life."

"What are you drinking?" Cindy asked once Mike was at the bar with the bartender's attention…Cindy was crowded in right behind him.

"Gin and tonic," said Callie, "…a double," she said loud enough to be heard over the crowd.

Cindy then looked and pointed at Angie,

"Tequila sunrise," Angie told her. And in just a few minutes, Cindy was passing back to them what they'd ordered.

There were no empty seats, so next they found a cozy corner, and wrapped inside a dollar bill was a white powdery substance that Angie referred to as blow, which was actually high-quality cocaine. Callie, in forty years, had never indulged in any type of heavy narcotics but was always curious to know why so many other people were in love with and addicted to cocaine. So, she tried it to find out why.

* * * *

The dollar bill was handled with care, very delicately when Angie pulled it out along with what was probably the smallest spoon ever made, thin and about the size of her middle fingers, which, along with Angie's hands, were like a surgeon's, long and steady. And with them, Angie did the honors, shoveling spoon full after spoon full of coke, one for each nostril, until all of them were sniffing and snorting infectiously.

A numbing sensation took effect almost immediately. It was as if part of Callie's face was no longer there. And then it began to drain down the back of her throat, a medicinal taste and a numbing sensation.

Suddenly, everything seemed to speed up a little and then a lot. Mike had gone to get more drinks without Callie even realizing it, and Angie, with the miniature spoon, was offering more coke. Before she knew it, they'd had four drinks, and Angie had pulled out a second folded dollar bill.

## Buckets, Shovels, Ghost and Worms

The music was blasting, but Callie couldn't tell what was playing anymore, only that it sounded awfully good... so good that they were suddenly all dancing, all except Mike, who was spending more time at the bar than he was there in the corner with them.

And then they were on the dance floor, the three of them: Cindy and Angie with Callie in between them, and dancing close, so close, that every once in a while, Cindy would lean in and kiss Callie with both lips and tongue. All the while, Angie had hands around Callie's waist, grinding her from behind. The dance floor was so packed that nobody else paid any attention.

After about three songs, Cindy grabbed Callie by the hand and said, "Follow me," which ended up being a trip to the nearest lady's room and a private stall where Angie produced yet more coke in another folded dollar bill.

Angie got busy shoveling it out again. Afterward, Cindy dropped down to both knees and lifted one of Callie's feet on the commode so that her legs were open. Angie kissed Callie's lips and fondled the top and bra she had on until both breasts were out and exposed, sitting pretty, nipples sticking out and getting harder and harder every time Angie touched or bent over to taste one of them. In the meantime, Cindy had pulled Callie's panties over to one side and was licking Callie in ways she'd only dreamed about.

In no time at all, she was exploding and experiencing pleasure never imagined. She'd just been seduced silently by two twenty-two-year-old girls and loved every moment of it.

It was all Callie could think about on the return flight home… that and how she wished she'd gone along with them afterward to meet Damon, the Blow Master, who had invited them all over for a little ménage à trois.

## Chapter 50

Being faithful and maintaining a sense of fidelity was becoming the hardest thing to do in Dominique's young, short-lived life. She kept thinking,

*"All this time, and I'm still a virgin."* The thought usually came after she'd taken a bath and was left standing in front of the mirror, naked, or at night when it was time to go to bed alone again.

It didn't help that Seth wasn't there to give her the love and affection she needed. Nor did being hit on constantly by men she thought were cute. However, on behalf of the men, a simple "hello" in the morning might be misconstrued by a young woman whose hormones had been ignited.

"Well… can't I just come there then and stay for like a weekend?" she asked Seth the last time he called, giving yet another excuse for why he couldn't be there. He'd been gone for over eight months and had put off coming home twice already.

"It's starting to drive me crazy bein' here without you," she told him, meaning it quite seriously. Whether Seth understood or not was a different story.

* * * *

For an eighteenth birthday present, Callie bought Dominique a new car, a Chevrolet Camaro, silver with chromed rims and black leather bucket seats. The car quickly became Dominique's pride and joy.

Since where they lived was on a dirt road, the car was usually dirty, which was what gave Dominique the excuse to go to Lafayette occasionally to get it washed.

Coincidentally, at a traffic light one day, a car pulled up beside her, a new, much faster, gold Camaro Iroc Z28, and Seth's friend, Michael Jackson, was the one who was driving it.

"Wanna race?" he asked, smiling at her with the engine revving,

"The loser buys lunch."

Dominique smiled back and said,

"Nah… no thanks. It wouldn't be fair. I'd make you

look bad, and then you might not wanna pay."

Michael laughed,

"You're probably right," he said, smiling afterward,

"Tell you what… to save me the embarrassment, forget about the race. Can a friend just buy a friend a meal then?" he asked, a warm look on his face.

"Sure… why not," said Dominique, feeling good about seeing Michael again.

"Alright, then… follow me," he said, and when the light turned green, he and Dominique both burned rubber peeling off as if they were having a race after all.

\* \* \* \*

It seemed innocent enough at first… Michael asked about Seth but quickly explained about how the two of them hadn't seen each other since before the end of the school year.

Michael didn't graduate; a fight got him expelled weeks before the actual graduation was supposed to take place. Dominique remembered that a white kid had been seriously hurt in the fight and that, later, a small caliber handgun had been found on campus as well, presumably belonging to Michael. No charges were ever filed, but school administrators at the Napoleon Learning Center quickly blamed it all on Michael, who was then labeled a bad boy and kicked out.

Word was that things turned for the worse when Michael moved to New Orleans and joined a gang of notorious drug dealers.

"You don't seem to be doin' too bad to me," said Dominique, staring across the table at him over the glass of Sprite she'd just taken a sip from.

"Why shouldn't I be?" Michael asked, flexing his bad-boy bravado.

"The kid I beat up called me a nigger and got exactly what he deserved."

"Yeah, but look at what all it cost you," said Dominique, reminding him.

"A scholarship, more than likely," said Michael… graduates of the Napoleon Learning Center were almost guaranteed a free ride at any college of their choice. Michael had planned to go on to one of the historically black colleges like Xavier or Grambling.

"Instead, here I am in the school of Hard Knocks, huh?" he said as if he knew what Dominique was thinking.

"That don't make me no dummy, though," he began, ready to explain himself.

"The whole purpose of gettin' an education was so that later in life, I'd be able to get a good job and work, makin' a good livin'. Well," said Michael, pausing long enough to sip beer from a green Heineken beer bottle,

"The way I see it, a hundred grand a year is a hundred grand a year, no matter how you make it."

"Yeah, you're right," said Dominique, shifting in the chair a bit.

"If you've made that much profit, then I agree with the money aspect of it as long as you realize that sellin' drugs isn't a career that you should glamorize. Because if you do, you'll end up broke and in jail or in Angola State Prison. Or maybe even worse."

"I'm well aware of that, too. And yes, a hundred grand is exactly how much I've made. As a matter of fact, I've been using some of it to make a few investments… in real estate and in a record label. I even plan to start makin' movies one day soon, too."

"Ok… wow… I'm impressed," said Dominique, smiling at him and giving him a look of approval.

"I'm glad to see that you've got it all so well planned out."

"I wouldn't say that I've got everything so well planned out," said Michael, leaning in a little as if to make the rest of their conversation more personal.

"There's a Stevie Wonder concert in New Orleans tomorrow night. I've got tickets, but no one to take with me. Would you like to go?" he asked. And that's when things became a lot more complicated.

"Michael… you're askin' me out on a date?"

"Yeah, why not? We're still friends, aren't we?" he asked.

"Yeah, we are, but Michael… Seth and I are engaged to be married."

"What does that have to do with us goin' to a concert together?" Michael asked,

"Seth doesn't expect you to just be bored half to death, sittin' 'round the house, doin' nothin', does he?"

"No…" said Dominique, realizing for the first time that that was exactly what she'd been doing, sitting around the house doing absolutely nothing. She'd even put off going to college for a year until after she and Seth had moved and settled down at whatever army base and city Seth would be stationed.

"And you don't think all he's been doin' is trainin' somewhere, tryin' to become the next Rambo, do you? That ain't all them army boys be doin'. I've got a cousin in the army. He's got a baby in three different countries."

"Who says I've been bored to death?" Dominique asked, pretending she didn't hear the rest of what Michael said about the possibility of Seth cheating.

"Dominique… c'mon. I'm not tryin' to hurt your feelins' or anything, but I know you all too well. You're a good girl. You've probably done nothin' else but sit at home, bored to death, waitin' on Seth."

"No, I haven't… I've taken a trip to San Diego," she said just to prove a point. She went on to explain about flying for the first time to see Nora, who'd had a baby recently.

"Ok, that's Nora… but what about you? When was the last time that you've gone out and had a good time?"

"Not since the last time Seth and I were at the movies, which was almost a year ago," thought Dominique without saying a word at first, but with an intense gaze fixed on Michael's alluring light brown eyes.

"What if?" she asked herself about the possibilities of what might happen.

"You're safe with me, I promise," Michael told her as if maybe he might've been able to read Dominique's mind.

"We'll have a good time, that's all."

"And that's what I'm afraid of," said Dominique, letting the cat out of the bag about the way she might be feeling. Michael was good-looking and had an athlete's physique at six foot one, two hundred and ten pounds, all muscle as far as Dominique could see, which she thought was sexy as hell.

"Aw, Michael…" she said as if deciding was tearing her apart. At the same time, it was quite a turn-on, too, imagining what might happen when the two of them were alone together. And then again, asked herself,

"What if?"

"What if what Michael said was true and Seth really was somewhere else enjoying himself with another woman?"

"I won't let you take advantage of me," she said with the decision being made already.

"I won't, I promise," said Michael.

"And if I tell you I'm ready to go home, I expect you to

take me home right then and there, you hear?" she said, pointing a finger at him.

"Alright, I will… just say the word."

"And I don't plan on stayin' out late either."

"Alright, okay," said Michael, laughing a little, finding all the restrictions Dominique was imposing funny.

"Should I have you home by twelve, then?"

"No… just when I say so," said Dominique, laughing a little too.

"Alright… I'll pick you up around six."

"Alright," said Dominique, and the date was set.

# Chapter 51

**Twenty-four hours later**

"Michael and I are just friends," she said, reminding herself that nothing was supposed to happen between them, least of all nothing that involved sex. Yet sex was all Dominique was able to think about.

*"Is that why I'm starting to feel so guilty?"* she wondered, only vaguely aware of what was going on, a conscientious battle like tug of war, the promise she made to Seth about marriage and being faithful versus the craving she had for having sex. Overall, the sexual craving was winning hands down.

* * * *

Rarely did Dominique wear makeup as she really didn't need any. She had the kind of natural beauty that made everything about her stand out without it. Nevertheless, while looking closely in the mirror, an inch or so from it,

Dominique added a few soft brush strokes of rouge anyway and then carefully penciled in eyeliner around both eyes. Wearing lipstick was what she decided against.

*"A little lip gloss'll do,"* she thought, puckering a few times after applying a smooth thin coat.

She'd already showered and slipped on a bra and black laced panties, but squeezing into a new, tight-fitting pair of straight-leg jeans was the hard part. Adding to that, a pair of black leather pumps and a thick red turtle-neck sweater completed the outfit.

Late in October, the fall season had set in, and meteorologists had warned that a breeze coming off the gulf might make the nighttime air in New Orleans cool and crisp. Even so, Dominique figured a jacket wouldn't be needed, and with the sweater she was wearing, she'd be ready for whatever kind of weather in Louisiana.

She'd gotten a new hairdo as well, a perm and tight curls that were, for the most part, kept intact except in the back, where the hair was combed straight down and left hanging longer than the rest.

*"I must say, I look damn good,"* she thought afterward, standing in front of the mirror, turning from side to side, inspecting how she looked from each and every angle.

"Not bad," she said just before she heard the front door open and close.

"MA... IS THAT YOU!?!" she asked, yelling from upstairs down to whoever it was that came in.

"NAH... IT'S ME," said William, yelling back at her,

"I GUESS YOUR MOM HASN'T GOT IN FROM WORK YET," but by then, Dominique had made it halfway down the staircase and could see for herself who it was.

"Oh, I thought you were her comin' in the door," she said, seeing Samantha and Todd standing there, too, with books in their hands. William had obviously just picked them up from school.

"Where're you goin' wit' all that makeup on?" William asked, in a way as if it was meant to criticize.

"It looks good to me," said Samantha in Dominique's defense.

"I like it too," said Todd.

"I didn't say it didn't look good," said William, finding it necessary to defend himself as well.

"It's just that I've never seen you with any on before."

Dominique laughed a little, taking all of what they said as a compliment.

"Guys… relax," she said, smiling. "I've got a date. One of Seth's friends is takin' me to a Stevie Wonder concert tonight at the Dome in New Orleans."

"Does Seth know about this?" William asked, feeling somewhat doubtful and making no effort to hide it.

"No… I haven't actually told Seth anything about it yet."

"Uh huh… like I thought," said William, showing his disapproval,

"Alright now… be careful, baby girl… you playin' wit' fire. Guys will go from bein' best friends to enemies tryin' to kill each other in a heartbeat 'bout money or a woman."

"William… Michael and I are just friends," said Dominique, responding with the same lame excuse she'd told herself earlier.

"Uh huh… that's what they all say," said William, not buying it, thinking Seth wouldn't be buying it either.

"Don't say I didn't warn you," he said before walking off, headed towards the kitchen.

\* \* \* \*

Nikki had fried fish, made gumbo, baked a hen, and had field peas and snap beans, whole kernel corn, and stewed okra and tomatoes with crackling bread on the side. She even had homemade ice cream and peach cobbler on the menu, but Dominique refused to eat any of it.

"I'm just not hungry," she said from her place at the dining room table, watching while the rest of the family dug in, eating everything heartily.

"You need to eat somethin' too," said Callie, a spoon in one hand, a big bowl of gumbo and rice in front of her. "You might get hungry later and wish you had."

"I'll be alright," Dominique told her and sipped from a tall glass of sweet iced tea.

"What time is Michael supposed to come get you?" asked Callie before taking a mouthful of gumbo.

"At six," said Dominique.

"It should be around six now, shouldn't it?" Callie asked. And then, as if on cue, William came in with a worried look on his face,

"Dominique… you got people here to see you," he said and stood there for a moment.

"William… who's out there?" Callie asked, knowing when something was bothering him.

"I'm not sure about who the other guy is, but Seth's out there too, and he doesn't look too happy."

"Oh dear," said Callie, getting up from the table and walking out right behind William and Dominique.

* * * *

A lot had happened in eight months: twelve weeks of basic training in New Jersey, eight weeks of MIT training in Kentucky, and the last thirteen weeks had been spent at Fort Lewis in Tacoma, Washington, where Seth was now stationed.

It was also where Seth met Denise Davidson, a fellow soldier from Miami. Turns out, Denise was engaged to be married as well and just as committed to another relationship as Seth. The long months of training had made them both lonely and in desperate need of love. However, neither of them had planned to be unfaithful and were left feeling bad about what they had done. Therefore, the affair had been brief. Afterward, Denise had even submitted a request to be transferred.

She'd been gone two weeks, and Seth had had plenty of time to think. And he found that it wasn't Denise whom he missed and longed for, but Dominique, the woman he still planned to marry and spend the rest of his life with.

\* \* \* \*

Seth had flown out of the Sea-Tac, Tacoma-Seattle International Airport that morning...a two hour and forty-minute flight to Denver, and then a two hour and thirty five minute flight to New Orleans.

From there, he rented a car and drove straight to get Dominique. Halfway there, though, he fell in behind another car, a car that seemed to be making all the same turns, even the same turn in Dominique's driveway.

Yet still, the real surprise didn't come until the door of the car in front of him opened, and he saw Michael get out. And even then, it didn't register why Michael was there, not until he saw Michael with the bouquet of roses.

"Who are those for?" Seth asked the moment he'd gotten out and started walking toward Michael. Who the roses were for was obvious, and for it, Seth wanted to punch Michael in the face.

"Seth… my man," said Michael, caught off guard and looking guilty like a kid whose hand had been caught in the cookie jar. But he quickly recovered and regained all composure.

"Dominique and I were gonna go to a Stevie Wonder concert tonight… and I bought roses for her because that's the kinda man I am."

Michael was bold, had a quick temper, and was also the kind man who wouldn't back down from a physical confrontation. Not only that, but Michael was about thirty pounds heavier than Seth and known for carrying a gun, a gun Seth knew Michael wouldn't hesitate to use. And even if he didn't have it on him, he would most definitely have one stashed inside the car somewhere.

Seth, although fresh out of combat training and with his best-dressed army uniform on, thought it was best to defuse the situation before things escalated into an all-out brawl, one that Seth might not win.

*"Besides,"* he thought, *"I really can't blame Michael."* Dominique was indeed extraordinarily beautiful and had gotten to be even more beautiful and sexy than Seth remembered.

*"…and probably lonely as hell by now,"* he thought, thinking back to how things had happened with him and Denise.

*"Michael surely hasn't forced himself on her and didn't have to… that's what I get for leavin' her,"* Seth thought, deciding to handle things differently but also wondering how

far things had gotten between them: Dominique and Michael.

He wouldn't have to wonder for very long, not as long as Michael was still standing there.

"Look, Seth," Michael said, beginning with an honest explanation, "...nothin's happened between us. It wasn't even until yesterday that we saw each other.

"Yeah, we had lunch together, but that's all. And yeah, I did ask her out, but not until after she told me how long you'd been gone. As far as I knew, you weren't ever comin' back. So here I am," he said, giving Seth a "what else can I say" expression.

"And here I am," Seth told Michael.

There was an awkward moment of silence while the two of them stood there in the driveway, looking at each other. Finally, after Dominique, Callie, and William came out and stood on the front porch, Michael told Seth,

"It's clear to me that I'm in the wrong place, and you're not. So why don't you take these," he said, passing Seth the bouquet of roses, "...and these too," he said, digging in one hip pocket, coming out with the concert tickets,

"Please... take your girl out and have a good time on

me."

Seth, looking at Michael, didn't say anything right away, not until Dominique came and stood right beside him,

"I think that might be a good idea... one that's well overdue," he said, looking from Michael down to Dominique, the woman he loved.

Michael, knowing when it was time to leave, got in and backed the car out of the driveway with them still standing there as if hypnotized, eyes locked on each other.

It wouldn't be until two days later, in a New Orleans hotel room, when hypnosis finally wore off. And two days after that, Seth and Dominique were married.

"Guess what," Dominique, smiling from ear to ear, told Seth on the return flight back to Sea-Tac International Airport.

"I'm not a virgin anymore."

"No shit, Sherlock," Seth said, smiling back,

"You're not a virgin anymore, and guess what else... you're mine, all mine." The two laughed, kissed, and then shared a very lustful but loving embrace.

# Chapter 52

*"Silence is golden… or is it?"* Callie wondered after being home alone for a few days, feeling disheartened.

The kids were missed, that's for sure, but they'd all grown up and were on their own.

*"…and probably never comin' back,"* said Callie, the thought of it making things seem even worse.

*"Can't say that I blame them,"* she thought, taking a good long look around, eyes landing a few feet away on the exact spot where Bob died.

"Too many bad memories in this house, even for me," she said, eyes shifting and landing on a view toward the back door, remembering how Bessie had been killed there, right outside of it, as well.

\* \* \* \*

## Buckets, Shovels, Ghost and Worms

After marrying Seth and moving to Tacoma, Dominique had only gone back home to Louisiana once, and that was to get the Camaro. Before then, she'd been commuting sixty miles a day to go to both work and to attend classes at the University of Washington in Seattle.

A year and a half later, Nora was married and pregnant again... she'd gotten comfortable and content being a housewife, and the wish that she'd once had to attend medical school had faded away.

The guy she married was in the Navy, a supply officer who, by chance, also happened to be stationed onboard the aircraft carrier USS Constellation.

The Constellation, on the verge of being decommissioned, was scheduled for dry dock and a much-needed overhaul in a last attempt at saving it. When the time came, the crew, along with the ship, were all transferred to Bremerton, Washington, only thirty miles away from Tacoma, where Dominique and Seth were living.

Samantha, the last of the Devereux household children to finally graduate from the Napoleon Learning Center, had started as a freshman at USC in Southern California. The real surprise, though, was Todd, the one with all the hidden talent. He was eventually awarded a scholarship in France, of all places, and started classes at a very prestigious art school in Paris. Todd's success made them all very proud.

So, with the kids gone, Callie didn't bother buying another car for the house but did buy one for William, a brand new 1983 navy blue Cadillac Coupe De Ville. It was an 85th birthday present.

The day he got the car, he and Nikki went to Shreveport to spend a few days with Viola, Ray, and Tammy. Supposedly, Sweetie and her husband were coming down from Detroit to also help celebrate William's birthday.

In the meantime, with everybody gone, Callie was left at home all alone. Nobody knew it, but at the last scheduled doctor's appointment, Callie had been diagnosed with leukemia, the same rare form of cancer that killed Connie, Callie's grandmother. Callie didn't bother saying anything about it so that no one would worry or make a fuss, but she was sure as hell worried, and with good reason... doctors had come a long way in advanced treatment since Connie had it in 1945, but there was still no cure, and very rarely did somebody diagnosed with cancer live for very long.

"Oh God... why me?" she asked after submitting and breaking down in tears while every sound echoed in an empty house.

"I'm so afraid. I just don't wanna die... not now, Lord," she said, hoping a prayer would be answered, but the only answer came in the form of more silence and pain... pain she'd been having more and more of, it seemed, since being diagnosed unfavorably.

****

"Now this is what I call havin' a good time," said Sweetie, looking around, sharing a smile with everybody at the table.

"…bein' here with all my family, especially with my big brother," she said, taking a gentle hold of William's arm while sitting there beside him… it was the first time they'd actually had a chance to visit.

"Lord knows, it's good seein' you."

"You too, sis'," said William, smiling back,

"It's been a long time… too long."

All of them were there: Viola Ray, Tammy, Nikki, William, Sweetie, and Bo, Sweetie's husband. They'd just come from church to Viola's house, where Tammy and Nikki had the table set with a big family meal waiting.

"Yeah… and you, my man," said Bo, taking a turn at getting a word in, "…you oughta' have a birthday more often if it means we get ta' eat like this."

"Alright, Bo… slow ya' role," said William, "Birthdays are comin' 'round fast enough as it is without you rushin' 'em.

"Wait until you get to be eighty-five; maybe then you'll see what I'm talkin' 'bout."

Everybody laughed.

But for the most part, Viola Ray, sitting at the head of the table with Tammy on one side and William on the other, had been quiet pretty much the whole time until Tammy leaned over and asked,

"Momma... what's wrong? The family's all here, and all this food we've cooked, yet you've hardly said a word or eaten anything."

"Baby, I'm fine," Viola Ray assured her before leaning over on the other side to tell William,

"Speakin' of family... William, did you know the woman you work for is sick?"

"What'a you mean, sick?" William asked, caught off guard and alarmed. "Callie?"

"Is that her name?"

"Yeah, it is," said William, a concerned look on his face. Viola Ray had obviously had another vision, and if the vision was about Callie, then William wanted to know.

"Ok, well… she don't want nobody to worry, but she's got cancer. I hate to be the one to tell you, but she don't have much longer to live."

Alvin Bell

# Chapter 53

Over a year had passed since Mount Saint Helens had blown its top and spewed mile after mile of molten ash. Evidence of Mount Saint Helens' violent eruption was found as far away as in places two states over. Yet, to Washingtonians, the sight of it in the distance remained astounding and beautiful as it was with a nearby much calmer Mount Rainier, both beautifully snow-top-covered mountains marking two different directions and perceptions.

\* \* \* \*

In Louisiana, while Callie was home, soaking in the misery of how she might die soon, William was in Shreveport having a good time with both his long-lost sisters.

Dominique and Nora were in Washington, having a family day themselves.

"Auntie Dom... look... there's another one," said

Charlie's excited voice, eyes wide, looking from one portside window to another, pointing out other ferries identical to the one they were on chugging along across the frigid waters of Puget Sound.

Charlie, at five years old with stubby little fingers and cute smiles, loved his mother and Grandma Callie and all his other aunties and uncles, but Dominique, whose name he still couldn't quite pronounce, was clearly the favorite.

\* \* \* \*

To live in the state of Washington around the waterways of Puget Sound meant getting a heavy dose of rain, nine out of twelve months of it in most cases, something that Seth discovered early on from being out in the field, combat training in it half the time.

When Dominique got there, the weather wore on her quickly, too, as it did with Nora and Tommy, a tall, handsome white guy from Grand Rapids, Michigan, who also happened to be Nora's new husband.

The USS Constellation, a conventional aircraft carrier, which was two and a half football fields long, was small compared to all the newer nuclear carriers. Even so, on the trip from San Diego, the Constellation was still large enough to accommodate its five thousand crew members and their families, with enough storage space left over so that each family could bring onboard two personal vehicles, the furniture that they owned, and all their pets and other personal belongings.

After the ship got them there, Nora and Tommy experienced a constant downpour of light rain for a month straight. The rain stopped for about a day and then poured another month straight.

"Is it always like this?" Nora asked after several pairs of shoes she'd brought with her had been water-logged, soaked, and ruined.

"Pretty much," Seth told her while Dominique and Charlie continued pointing out other passing boats and ships.

"The only time it really lets up is during the summer months. Then the weather is like it is in any other part of the country."

"Somethin' we'll just have to get used to," said Tommy, a navy man used to all kinds of changes in weather.

"It rained a lot when I was stationed in Maine and even at certain times in the Philippines."

"Yeah, well… I suggest we go out and buy some rain gear with how much it's been comin' down around here."

"That's fine… whatever you wanna do, honey," said

Tommy, knowing good and well that Nora's favorite thing in the world to do was spend money, shopping,

"We can go out and buy whatever you want," he told her, "…anything for you, baby."

For Tommy, money wasn't important, at least not as important as it was to having Nora, a beautiful woman twenty years younger than him. All it took was one time in bed together. From that point on, Tommy was whipped and in love, willing to do whatever it took to keep Nora happy.

"Anything, baby."

\* \* \* \*

It was Dominique's idea to take the ferry into Seattle to show Tommy and Nora around the city. It took an hour to get there either way from Bremerton, whether on the ferry, across Puget Sound, or if they decided to drive all the way around it. Dominique figured riding the ferry would be more of a treat for Charlie, and it was something that made the little boy's eyes shine bright the whole hour long.

Three ferries pulled in and docked all at the same time, and as passengers disembarked, both on foot and in passenger automobiles, Dominique drove them away and merged in traffic, all the while pointing out landmarks. So far, she'd been the only one of them who'd actually had a chance to venture out and learn the place.

"Okay… I'm not sure if any of you've ever heard of it or not, but that's the famous Pike Place Market overlooking the Elliott Bay waterfront here in Seattle," she said, passing just to the right of it.

"It's one of the oldest farmers' markets in the country."

"Isn't that where the guys toss fish to one another, like in the movie Sleepless in Seattle?" Nora asked, not sure but trying to remember it.

"Yeah, that's it. I forgot...it was in the movie Sleepless in Seattle.

"On the way back, we'll stop and get a better look at it."

A couple of blocks later, stealing a peek at Tommy in the rear-view mirror, Dominique asked,

"Tommy… are you a sports fan?"

"You're kidding, right?" Nora asked, responding before Tommy had a chance to say anything.

"When he's not workin' or at home tryin' to get some, that's all else he wants to do, watch whatever game that's on TV.

"Girl, he'll even watch golf," said Nora, which made them all laugh.

"What's wrong with that? I like golf," said Tommy in a halfhearted attempt at defending himself.

"Ok, well… that's the stadium where the Seattle Seahawks play," said Dominique, pointing out Century Link Field,

"The Seattle Mariners baseball team plays there too with my man Ichiro out in center field," Dominique told them, naming one of the Mariners star baseball players, hinting how she might've already become a fan.

"What about the Super Sonics? Where do they play?" asked Tommy, imagining being at one of the games, courtside.

"The stadium's just a few blocks away. The Sonics have made the playoffs every year so far with Gary Payton and Sean Kemp."

"Of course...Gary Payton, the Glove, and Sean Kemp, the Rain Man, are two of the best players in the league," said Tommy.

"I wonder who the genius was who compared Sean Kemp's dunks to Seattle's weather when it came to choosing a nickname for him?" said Nora, commenting to let everybody know how informative she was on sports as well.

Seth piped in and answered,

"Probably the same people who drafted him. Great PR work, if you ask me."

Seth and Tommy both wanted steaks. So, for lunch, Dominique drove them to a Black Angus restaurant on Stewart Avenue.

After a drive through Seward Park, and then down a few roads to get a good look at the famous Evergreen Point Bridge, the floating bridge from Seattle to Bellevue and other Eastside cities and communities. The bridge crossed Lake Washington, where once a year, high-powered boats were brought from all over the country to race, including the all-famous Budweiser boats.

Then they were back at Pike Place Market.

"I wanna pick up some fresh red snapper for dinner tonight," Dominique mentioned, sure that after having a chance to actually see it, they would all be glad they came.

* * * *

Sightseeing took a little longer than expected, and less than an hour was left, just enough time for a quick walk through the market before the next ferry was scheduled to leave going back to Bremerton.

Pike Place Fish Market was without walls but under shelter. Along the aisles on both sides, vendors had displayed, on beds of ice, the fresh catch of the day, whatever it was, lined up in plentiful stacks: flounder, grouper, red snapper, crab or shrimp, and any other kind of seafood or fish imaginable. All you had to do was see it and point it out, and someone was there to either de-vein, scale or clean in whatever way necessary to complete and wrap what you ordered neatly in paper. In the end, most customers found it a pleasure to pay for such good service.

The vendors all wore coats or heavy jackets, gloves, sweaters, long rubber aprons, and galosh boots to combat the force of a cold and wet working environment. Customers generally weren't as well prepared and usually didn't stay for as long as it was with Dominique's intentions.

After buying the fish she wanted, they were just about to leave when, from a peripheral view, Dominique made a shocking discovery. There was someone watching them, someone Dominique didn't think she would ever see again, especially not at Pike Place Market in Seattle.

Childhood memories came to mind: memories of being six years old and stuck in the mud again... memories of being comforted in times of need, and memories of being back in, of all places, the swamps of Louisiana.

And there she was, an older Ms. Ladeaux wearing the same dark skirt and thick, gray sweater with the old 1940s Billie Holiday party hat still on. She smiled and waved when Dominique looked and saw her. Dominique looked around, hoping somebody else had seen Ms. Ladeaux standing there too. Nobody did, though. And when Dominique turned away and then looked back again, Ms. Ladeaux wasn't even there anymore; it seemed that she'd vanished again.

# Chapter 54

Dark afternoon clouds made the moving image of two people engaging seem diabolical and look more like two entangled silhouettes standing. However, strikes of lightning lit up the sky, and each number of images in strobe successions showed clearly the blatant look of anger on the face of one tall, masculine figure and the blindsided look of fear and terror on the other, more feminine-shaped outline.

Their lips were moving too, but like in a silent movie, only an imaginary sound of what they might be saying was comprehended.

"NO!!! PLEASE DON'T!!!," was thought to have come from the more feminine outline-shaped figure.

And then,

"Bitch, I'll kill you," came from the other, him, the aggressor.

A knifed hand drew back and plunged forward, finding its mark in the torso of the woman begging to be spared the pain and torment.

Yet, the man, being the tormentor, showed no mercy and found satisfaction in what he'd done.

"Die, bitch," he said in only a whisper, plunging the knife again and again, and then one last time, assuring himself that life would no longer exist where it once was in her.

"Momma, NO!!!" Callie screamed, remembering it for more than what was thought to have been a dream; it was instead something that actually happened.

It was William's hand that touched Callie's shoulder to awaken her.

"Here… take a drink of this," he said, handing her a small glass half filled with gin.

"Whatever it was, you were dreamin' 'bout must'a' been awfully bad."

"It was," said Callie, taking a quick sip from the glass William was offering,

"I was dreamin' about that terrible man killin' momma again," she said, gasping.

## Buckets, Shovels, Ghost and Worms

It was Sunday evening, and the sun was doing a disappearing act of its own a few hours early, just as Nikki and William were arriving back from Shreveport. William saw Callie's new Mercedes parked in the driveway before realizing the front door of the house had been left wide open.

The house was dark and quiet, which was suspicious enough without actually knowing for sure that something was wrong.

Once inside, William's first reaction was to hurry and get the shotgun. Then he heard movement, and there on the couch was Callie. She was asleep but tossing and turning and finally yelling out loud.

"You know there's an actual story behind why your mother was killed, right?" William asked, taking a seat on the couch beside her and then pouring himself a small glass of gin as well.

"Ole' Jack Le Roux," he said, bringing the glass up to take a sip.

"The Ole' muthafucka," he said afterward.

"Wow… is that part of the story, him bein' a muthafucka?" Callie asked, gulping instead of sipping from the glass this time and frowning as the gin went down.

"If I'm not mistaken, and if I remember correctly, weren't you the one who shot his ass?"

"I was," said William, turning to look Callie dead in the eye, "...and I'd do it again if he was still alive."

"Who was he, this Jack Le Roux?" Callie asked. "All this time, and nobody's ever told me the whole story."

William looked down at the glass he was holding and seemed to lose himself in thought. After a while, he made a sound,

"Huh.

"Are you sure you wanna know?" he asked, looking up, fixing a gaze on Callie again.

"I promise, me tellin' you won't make things any better."

"Try me," said Callie, turning halfway around on the couch, folding and tucking a leg up underneath her to get more comfortable, facing William head-on.

"I'm all ears," she said, taking another sip from the glass and then fixing a stare, watching and waiting.

"Ok...well, first, I think I'd better tell you about me and your mother."

"You and my mother? What about you and my mother?" asked Callie, taken aback.

"We were in love," William told her, "This was way before her and Ted ever met. As a matter of fact, your father wasn't even born yet."

From there, William went on and told Callie everything, the whole story, explaining it all in detail as he went along, up to the point when Bessie was killed.

"I hated Jack with a passion but almost couldn't pull the trigger to kill him, not after hearin' him say that he'd given Bessie's baby away… our baby. I wanted to know who he'd given it to.

"Wit' that shotgun in my hands, I must'a' lost it, though, when he called me a boy and started comin' towards me. The next thing I knew, he was dead."

"Wow," said Callie, stunned.

"So, you mean to tell me that somewhere out in the world, I've got an older brother or sister?"

"Yeah… accordin' to what Jack told Bessie. And accordin' to her, after havin' it. All she remembers was not ever hearin' the baby cry and watchin' while they took it away, which left her thinkin' she'd had a miscarriage after all, especially after Jack tellin' her that that was what happened.

"But later, he changed his story and told Bessie that the child was actually born healthy. So yeah, accordin' to him, you've either got a brother or a sister out there somewhere...my son or daughter," William added sadly.

"But enough about that," he said, changing the subject before tears began to fall from him, thinking about a child he'd never seen.

"What's this I hear about you bein' sick?"

"What'a' you mean?" asked Callie, ready to deny the truth. "I'm not…"

"C'mon now…" said William, speaking and holding up a hand to interrupt the lie Callie was about to tell.

"Don't try to play dumb or lie to me 'cause it won't work."

"Damn…" said Callie. "I should'a' known you'd find out."

"Yeah, you should'a' known. But my problem is this…," said William, with a look of hurt and concern in his eyes, "Why was it that I had to find out about this from somebody else?

"This serious, Callie...somethin' I need to know about."

"Oh, William," said Callie, now with tears streaming down.

## Chapter 55

"Seth… you do still love me, don't you?" Dominique asked, calling out to Seth from on the bed in their bedroom. They'd spent most of the day together with Tommy, Nora, and Charlie in Seattle, and it hadn't been long since they'd gotten home. Everybody raved about the meal that Dominique made for them: grilled red snapper with sautéed onions and carrots along with red beans and rice, a specialty that Mary, the housekeeper from Jamaica, had taught Dominique how to make a long time ago.

Seth was in the bathroom, standing in front of the sink and mirror, brushing his teeth and gurgling. Dominique had already gotten undressed and under the covers, lying in bed, waiting for Seth to come to bed, too.

"Why would you ask somethin' like that? I love you with all my heart and soul," Seth said, still unsure of why the question had been asked.

"I saw an old friend today," said Dominique, snuggling close to Seth once he'd joined her in bed and gotten beside her, "…an old woman.

"One minute, she was there, smiling and waving at me, and the next minute she was gone.

"I turned around to see if maybe you had seen her too, but you hadn't; you and Tommy were busy asking a vendor about the price of lobster.

"I swear my head was only turned for maybe a split second, but when I looked back again, she was gone. I looked all around and didn't see her anywhere.

"You don't think I'm crazy, do you?" Dominique asked, unable to read the expression on Seth's face to tell whether he believed her or not.

"Honey… not at all. If I thought you were crazy, I wouldn't be here with you," said Seth, kidding while hoping to lighten the conversation.

However, he was beginning to understand the dilemma and purpose for why Dominique was questioning him and wanted to make things right with her.

"But, if you say she was there, then yes, I believe you," he added, sounding a lot more serious.

"Yeah, but you don't know the whole story behind this 'friend of mine' and me.

"We met a long time ago in the swamp, of all places. I was just a six-year-old little girl. I got stuck in the mud and was about to get bit by a couple of snakes.

"Well, anyway…" said Dominique, seeing the look on Seth's face, showing that he might've been getting a little impatient and bored with the story, more interested in having sex.

"…she killed the snakes," said Dominique, intent on finishing the story, "…and pulled me out of the mud, saved the day.

"We've been friends ever since, meetin' in the swamp every other day or so to talk and go fishin'."

"Ok… so, what do you think happened to her today?" Seth asked, still unsure of what to believe.

"Maybe you don't understand what it is I'm tryin' to say," said Dominique, turning on one side, looking up at Seth, forcing him to make an eye to eye contact with her,

"I think she's a ghost."

"A ghost?" asked Seth, perplexed and at a loss for words.

"Yeah… the last time we were in the swamp together, I asked Ms. Ladeaux, that's the woman's name…I asked her if she had family or a house nearby or anything; I'd never seen her with anybody other than me or at any place else other than near or in the swamp.

"She said no, that she had no other family or a house, which I thought was strange.

"I asked more personal questions, and eventually, I guess, to put it all in the right perspective, she disappeared… vanished and then reappeared standing behind me a few moments later.

"I was stunned at first and then terribly frightened. I remember bein' so startled I almost fell in the water.

"Then I took off, runnin' home as fast as I could afterward. I've never been back in the swamp again, nor had I seen her again either, not until today at Pike Place Market."

"And you think she's a ghost?" Seth asked with some skepticism but having compassion for the woman he loved. Nevertheless, he kept listening.

"I do… not only have I seen it when she disappeared, but she's also always wearin' the exact same ole' hand-me-down outfit of clothes that look like somethin' from back in the 1940s, especially the funky lookin' ole hat she wears.

"Don't get me wrong, though; as weird as it may sound, her and I were friends...best friends, actually," said Dominique, saddened by some of the old memories.

"Back then, momma used to be so mean. She'd say anything, whatever came to mind, which, in most cases, were some of the meanest things she could think of to say. She was miserable and seemed to take it all out on me.

"There were times when I just couldn't take it anymore. I'd take off runnin' out the back door and straight for the swamp. And there would be Ms. Ladeaux to comfort me and say all the things to me to make everything all right again. I really don't know how I would'a' made it back then without her," said Dominique, showing somewhat of a smile.

That's when Seth, who had been listening and waiting patiently, made his move.

"Well, I'm here for you now, babe," he said, taking hold of Dominique, holding her gently with both arms, kissing her on top of the head, and then kissing and working his way down until both lips were touching and kissing Dominique's lips.

Dominique became excited almost instantly, opening up to Seth, and then their tongues were touching and exploring each other's mouths. Before long, the room was hot and misty with an air of steamy hot sex.

## Chapter 56

"You tryin' to make me cum, huh, Seth? Huh?" asked Dominique, crying out from the biggest of passionate burning feelings...this, from how well she was being seduced.

"Oh God… YES!!!" she said after exploding for about the third time.

Seth became overpowered with passionate feelings inside of him, too. Wanting to share made him pour it on, more and more, the love and affection.

Dominique was soaking wet, panting, and breathing hard, holding on to Seth as if for dear life.

"You're makin' me feel so good," she said, voice barely audible and trembling until, all at once, like an explosion, a pleasure storm blew through every part of Dominique's body again, and in a way that left her feeling somewhat paralyzed.

"Oh, God," was all she could barely say.

The sun hadn't shown itself yet, and it was the third time during the night that Seth had kissed Dominique's neck and back, awakening her to make love again. Each time, the touch of his lips and skin against hers, and just the anticipation, and then the actual way that he entered and moved inside of her was enough to make Dominique scream. She was thinking how much she truly loved and appreciated the hunger and desire that Seth kept alive and distilled in her.

"You're gonna be late for work," she told him afterward, recovering quickly after hearing the clock sound when the alarm went off; both lay sweaty and spent, drained from all the orgasms.

Dominique went to use the bathroom. On the way back, Seth yelled out,

"I DON'T WANNA GO!!!" He was half joking, mimicking the early morning cry of a boy who'd stayed up too late and didn't want to get up and go to school the next morning.

But then, Seth was thinking seriously about not going anywhere for real.

"Why don't we both call in sick?" he said, hoping the idea would sound good and be tempting enough and that

Dominique would agree to do it too.

"We could stay right here in bed and make love all day long."

Dominique stood there and smiled, looking down at Seth, wondering what it would be like to be so fortunate as to be able to relive just half of the wonderful night they'd spent together. An awkward moment passed before Dominique got over the naughty temptation, and she finally told Seth,

"Honey... no... we can't. I've got class and two important lectures to attend, and you've got work... aren't y'all supposed to be gettin' ready for some kind of a big inspection or somethin'?"

"Yeah... a company inspection, one that's gonna include the entire battalion."

"Yeah, you're right," said Seth, being snapped back to the responsible world of reality.

"The company commander would probably have a damn fit if I or anybody else called in sick on one of the days before an inspection.

"Ok, I'm gettin' up," he said, announcing it while throwing both legs over the side of the bed.

"You want coffee?" Dominique asked a moment later, watching Seth, still groggy, march off toward the bathroom.

"Yeah, please," she heard him say, responding over a shoulder. "Hot and strong, no sugar."

A moment later, the shower came on, and then the bathroom door closed. When it opened again, a steaming hot cup of coffee was waiting there on the dresser, and Dominique was in the kitchen making breakfast.

It wasn't until Seth had finished eating and walked out the door in uniform that Dominique finally took a shower and got dressed as well: hair naturally in Shirley Temple curls, dark brown turtle neck sweater, tight brown tweed pants, too tight actually, and brown leather boots and jacket. A brown leather book bag filled with books completed the outfit.

"…ask me how I know, and I'll tell you so… she used to be my girl," sang Walter Williams and Eddie Le Vert of the O'Jays on the radio while Dominique drove to work feeling good and in the best of moods.

And then Marvin Gaye started the next song,

"I know a man ain't supposed to cry, but these tears I can't hold inside.

"Losin' you would end my life, you see, 'cause you mean that much to me.

"You could have told...me yourself that you loved someone else. Instead, I heard it through the grapevine."

By the time Dominique got to Seattle, the good mood and feelings had increased tenfold.

A parking space close to where she needed to go seemed to be available and waiting as if just for her. And standing outside the car, she found that, although the forecast had called for rain, the sun was shining.

The icing on the cake was that once inside the building, a seat up front where she liked to sit near the professor was available as well. All smiles, Dominique sat, unpacked a pen and notepad, and began taking notes.

All was fine until about halfway through the second lecture when a rather young female staff member came in looking for Dominique. At the onset, Dominique could tell something was terribly wrong; the girl wasn't smiling and was instead looking quite frightened and upset.

Before the girl could say anything, Dominique asked,

"What is it? What's wrong?" she asked, becoming alarmed.

It still took a moment for the staff member to actually say or share anything other than the terrifying look on her face. And then, from the girl's eyes, tears started to fall.

"You gotta come quick," she said, finally, though barely allowing the words to escape,

"I'm afraid there's been a terrible accident. Your husband…"

"My husband? What about my husband?" Dominique asked, becoming panic-stricken, especially with how long the girl was taking to explain things.

"He was run over by a truck, and I apologize," said the girl, startled when Dominique took steps toward her.

"As far as I know, he's alive, but barely," the girl said, totally in tears.

"I'm so sorry," she said, going on and on with more apologies as Dominique gathered all her things and started out the door.

"Do you know where they've taken him?" Dominique asked on the way out.

"As far as I know, he's still on base at the infirmary."

"Ok, thanks… Professor?" said Dominique on the way

out, acknowledging him as the authority, asking to be excused, although it was obvious with the situation she was leaving anyway.

"By all means… of course," the professor said, excusing Dominique.

Out in the hallway, trying to keep up with how fast Dominique was walking, the staff member grabbed Dominique by the arm.

"And again, I'd like to apologize," she said while even more tears were falling.

Finally, becoming suspicious, Dominique asked,

"Is there something else you wanna tell me?"

"Yeah," the girl said, her eyes glued to the floor for a while before finally looking up to face Dominique.

"My husband is also a soldier stationed at Fort Lewis. Unfortunately, he was the one who hit your husband. I'm so sorry," she said again, still in tears but falling apart this time.

Dominique broke down in tears and started crying, too, but then became angry and decided that it was best if she kept walking. She did and left the girl standing there in tears.

## Chapter 57

Dawn, just after the first light of morning, the sky and air all around it; cool, damp, and gray. It came offering what seemed to be a new, virtuous part in life...a new beginning, a new clean slate when compassion was just what was needed.

Lingering overnight rain clouds were what made the morning cool, damp, and gray. And from the rain clouds, a 1962 silver and white Gulfstream jet aircraft dropped steadily but carefully, piercing thick fog along the way as well before landing safely on a small Louisiana airfield...Hammond North Shore Regional.

The skilled pilot, along with the aircraft, were both hired and chartered privately to fly only one passenger...Callie Devereaux.

William was on the tarmac, standing by the car, watching and waiting when the plane landed, and then taxied and stopped near where he was standing.

The stairs of the aircraft came down as soon as the door opened, and then Callie disembarked.

"Believe me when I say, nothin's easy 'bout chemotherapy," said Callie when she thought she and William were close enough to hear each other.

William was thinking, "I can tell… you don't look so good." the look on his face might've shown what he was thinking.

Callie had lost weight, lots of it. The black pants and sweater she was wearing both looked to be a size too big. She had a black shawl wrapped around both shoulders and on the top of her head as well. Underneath, Callie was completely bald with only stubble where locks of brunette hair once grew and hung long down Callie's back.

"I never wanna see another wheelchair or hospital bed ever again. Ugh…

"Please, just get me home," she said, climbing in the back seat of the car while William held open the door. He still didn't bother to say anything; that's because he was stuck between being happy that she was home and feeling sorry for her.

It had been almost four months since the last time they'd seen each other. In a desperate attempt at saving Callie's life, friends of Bob's from med school, now all seasoned doctors, had assembled at the Chicago Medical Center in Illinois. Callie was flown in. A nurse with a wheelchair and Steve Bart, a well-known surgeon and Bob's old college roommate, were there waiting at the hospital–the welcoming committee.

"How you feelin'?" Steve asked, smiling, taking hold of Callie's hand.

"Like shit," she told him, forcing a smile back not only to be polite but more so from trying to disguise how afraid she really was. The reality of it was that if Bob's friends, all of whom had flown there from various parts of the country as she had done, couldn't save Callie, then life for her would virtuously be over.

"Bob and I were the best of friends. It's the least I could do to be here and help. So, don't worry, we'll get through this together," he said, reassuring her.

It had been explained that there were no guarantees and that treatments could, at times, be as harsh and painful as how the disease itself could make you feel, which was why Callie insisted on going alone. Treatment was the only chance she had of seeing another birthday. Even so, Pride wouldn't let her show weakness, not even to William or anybody else, especially not while being considered terminally ill.

Callie's motto was,

*"I want nobody feelin' sorry for me just because I'm in a little pain."* Of course, the pain Callie was experiencing was far worse than she actually let on or was honest about. Nevertheless, this was a thought she had, and stuck to it.

In the end, the treatments, which, at times, were indeed difficult, turned out to be a success. The cancer was fought back and had gone into remission. It was all but gone, actually, and eventually, Callie got back to a point where she was feeling well and strong enough to get out of bed again and go home.

*"What a hard-fought battle, though,"* she thought on the plane ride home,

*"...even you might've been proud, Luke,"* she thought, thinking courageously of the great grandfather she never knew.

"Have the girls and Todd gotten there yet?" she asked, breaking the awkward silence that plagued the car's interior. Before leaving, she'd made William promise not to call and tell anybody about what was going on with her. And he didn't, actually. William very rarely used the phone to call anybody. However, later the same night, Dominique called, and William told her everything,

"Oh, my God... how is she now?" Dominique asked, on the verge of panic.

"She still gettin' around alright, but I can tell she's in pain," William said, expressing the seriousness of it.

"You know your momma, though. She ain't gon' tell nobody."

"Ok, I'm on my way. See you when I get there," she said and hung up. Four hours later, Dominique was pulling into the driveway.

She and Seth weren't living in the Seattle area anymore. After suffering a broken back, leg, arm, and ruptured spleen, Seth miraculously recovered from being run over by an Army truck. Even so...Seth was left permanently disabled. On some days, something as simple as walking to the bathroom could be a challenge.

After being medically discharged and as a civilian, the army offered Seth a job training recruits at an army base near Shreveport, three and a half hours away. So, Dominique rushing back home to see Callie wasn't a problem.

William kept his promise and waited until later to call

the other three children: Nora, Samantha, and Todd. Todd was still in Europe. He'd become a big success. He'd also discovered an impartial sexuality and was suddenly enjoying life to the fullest, being gay. Therefore, coming back to Louisiana, where homosexuality was greatly shunned, was not in the plans for Todd.

"No… not now...probably not ever," he told William when asked if he'd come home to visit.

"Yeah, Nora and Samantha got here yesterday," said William, glancing back at Callie in the rearview mirror.

"Todd's not comin', but Dominique's been here all week, cleanin' and rearrangin' things. Even went out and bought new furniture… says she wants you to come home to a clean house.

"But the house was already clean, me and Nikki clean up every day… and there definitely was nothin' wrong wit' the old furniture we had.

"If you ask me, I think all she did was waste time and money."

A smile broke on Callie's face, and then she laughed. She couldn't remember the last time she'd laughed or felt so good, but she laughed now, and cheer spread amongst them.

*"It's good to be home,"* she thought with an approving smile, staring out a window while William drove along.

She later told William,

"I think it bothered Dominique when I gave my opinion about who this so-called friend of hers is… you know, the old lady in the swamp… the one you, Emma, and Mary decided not to tell me about," said Callie, still smiling and staring out the window.

"Didn't think I'd find out, huh?" she asked, finally turning to look, catching a glimpse of William's eyes in the rearview mirror again.

"I'm not surprised, though; that's just like Momma, comin' back from the dead to keep an eye on her one and only grandchild."

"Who you talkin' 'bout? Bessie, your momma?" William asked, not so much in disbelief as it was in surprise that somebody other than him knew about and actually believed that a ghost had been in existence amongst them.

"That doesn't bother you?" William asked, turning his attention now on Callie and the mental state she might be in.

"Child, please… maybe you didn't know my momma as well as you thought you did.

"Momma was heavy into the legends of black magic. Before movin' to Shreveport, she took on the last name McIntrye, the last name of the man her mother was married to. But actually, her name was Ladeaux, granddaughter of Ms. Ladeaux, the voodoo woman."

\* \* \* \*

**Five months earlier**

"Where's Momma?" Dominique asked, coming through the door as if out of breath and with a look of anxiety after driving three and a half hours to get there from Shreveport. It was the night before Callie's flight out to Chicago, the same night when Dominique and William talked on the phone. Judging by the way Dominique was breathing, you'd think that instead of driving, she might've run all the way there to catch Callie before the flight took off.

"She's up in her room," said William in a noncommittal tone, unphased by Dominique's excitement. "…went to bed a while ago, I think."

"How is she?" Dominique asked with deep concern, catching a breath.

"As I told you earlier, she still gettin' around alright, but I can tell she in pain, which mean she ain't doin' so good," William said, head shaking, eyes tearful and sad,

"You know your mother, though, always tryin' to be strong. She won't admit and tell you how much she hurtin'. But I know her; I can look in her face and tell." With that, Dominique's eyes started to water as well.

"I'm'a go up and see her," said Dominique, pulling herself together, all the while thinking,

"First Seth, and now Momma," heartbreaking sentiments.

As if walking on eggshells, Dominique climbed the staircase easily and fast but tentatively on tiptoes. She did the same upstairs in the hallway and then eased Callie's bedroom door open. For years, Callie's bedroom had been off-limits. Dominique hadn't spent five minutes in Callie's room since the day she burst in, and Callie cursed at her for it–the same day she met Ms. Ladeaux.

Callie was lying still, asleep on one side, breathing steadily and peacefully. A tear ran down Dominique's face.

*"Oh, Momma,"* she thought, realizing how serious it was to be stricken, as Callie was, with such a form of deadly cancer. It was enough all together to break anyone's heart.

On the nightstand was an opened bottle of gin, a glass, and an ashtray half filled with ashes, Marlboro cigarette butts, and burned wooden match sticks. In the bedroom,

Callie still used old kerosene lanterns and usually kept one burning, which was the case on this particular night.

The flickering flame gave off just enough light for Dominique to see, find a chair, and pull it up close to where Callie was sleeping. When she did, she realized that on the nightstand was also some kind of book, leather bound with an inscription: Devereaux. The letters were all burned on as if the inscription had been done with a hot branding iron.

The book was big, an 8 x 11 edition, thick with a lot of weight to it.

*"Interesting,"* thought Dominique, the academic scholar; after four years, Dominique had graduated from the University of Washington with a 4.0 grade average. But after opening the book to its very first page, Dominique realized that the book was actually an old photo album.

*"Better and still interesting,"* thought Dominique, disappointed to learn that no words of wisdom were there to be read. But it became exciting just the same at the thought of venturing back in time and maybe learning something about the family history. William never shared much about the family, and neither did Callie. She'd soon find out why.

The first shock came after only flipping through the first few pages; every person in the book so far was all white, and mostly men in Confederate uniforms—Luke and the three sons he'd lost in the war. All of them were tall in stature, strong and lean, with full heads of hair, mustaches, and beards grown from pride and confidence to match the uniforms they were wearing.

And then there was George with his wife Connie, the only other Devereaux besides Luke who'd ever gotten married...implausibly different than his three brothers. Not only was he married, but George was also short and fat with very little hair.

And finally, a picture that included a background shot of two black people, William and Emma, the butler and cook. Of course, William was a much younger man back then, and well, Emma dearly missed.

"I still think your gumbo was the very best," said Dominique, taking a long look at the picture, whispering the complimentary sentiments in remembrance of a person she would always miss and love.

"Emma," she whispered before finally turning the page.

Next was Ted.

"I guess you're supposed to be my granddad," said Dominique, reading Ted's name inscribed and remembering that Callie had mentioned him once or twice.

Flipping through more pages, one after another, Dominique saw more pictures of Ted, childhood photos mostly of him dressed in some of what she thought were some of the most ridiculous outfits Dominique had ever seen,

"I'm glad nobody dresses their child like that anymore," she said, meaning it, thinking of Nora and how nicely she dressed Charlie.

A picture of Connie just before she died was in the album as well. The cancer had taken a serious toll; Connie looked like a totally different person from some of the other pictures… her eyes and body seemed sunk in from all the weight loss and pain she'd obviously been suffering through.

The next picture of her was in a casket, dead, her in one and George in another.

The photos from then on showed Ted partying a lot and with different women everywhere: Baton Rouge, New Orleans, Dallas, Miami… seemingly anywhere the wind blew.

The next pictures were of Bessie. Dominique didn't know who she was but thought,

*"What an exceptionally beautiful woman… and she's black."* The picture left Dominique in awe but with a smile.

However, there was something familiar about the woman, something that made Dominique feel as if maybe she'd seen her before.

*"Nah, no way,"* she thought and then kept on flipping pages...Ted and Bessie in Galveston, at Fort Walton Beach, and so forth.

Dominique started to put things together when she saw Callie as a baby.

"Oh, Momma," she said, in awe again and smiling, "...you were so adorable." There must have been at least thirty pictures of Callie, both as a baby and during the time she was growing up as a teenager.

"All of them's your kin folks, every last one of 'em," said Callie, startling Dominique, who hadn't yet noticed that Callie was awake,

"...even me," said Callie, sharing a warm smile.

But Dominique didn't smile, nor did she look up for very long to absorb the warmth and true feeling of love from Callie's smile. That's because there, on the page in front of her, was probably the most recent picture of Bessie. She was wearing a thick wool sweater, a long thick wool skirt, galosh boots, and was holding a shovel and a long cane fishing pole...and had on a hat,

*"...a red party hat,"* thought Dominique. The lady was a lot younger, but there was no mistaking her; the lady was Ms. Ladeaux.

"Momma... who's this?" Dominique asked, bringing the book over so Callie could see it,

"...are we somehow related, too?"

Callie, rising to rest on an elbow to see and get a better look, said, "Oh...Yeah, you are."

Callie then started to move around on the bed, gathering herself. And after a while, a moment or two later, told Dominique, "That's your Grandma Bessie. She was killed long before you were born."

"Uh uh, Ma... that's Ms. Ladeaux, and she lives somewhere back there in the swamp. She and I have been goin' fishin' since I was a little girl." Dominique then went on to tell Callie everything, all that she knew and could remember about Ms. Ladeaux.

Callie didn't seem phased or even very much surprised and went on and told Dominique a few things, too, about Bessie and a few of the other mystical women in the family before them.

Trying to digest and understand what Callie was telling

her was like a hard pill to swallow, especially the part about believing that for all those years, the person she took as a best friend had all along been a ghost.

"Maybe this might explain what happened at the market in Seattle," said Dominique, coming to terms and grasping it.

"Sure it does; it wasn't just a coincidence. She was there because you were there.

"You don't have to worry though; she ain't gon' ever try to do anything to hurt you," Callie explained, still with a warm smile,

"She's more like a guardian angel, here to love and protect you."

## Chapter 58

The next day, after Callie came home, was Samantha's 21st birthday.

"I'm not only a year older, but I'm finally OLD ENOUGH TO DRINK!!!" she said, landing a rather weak punch line, kidding with everybody just as Nora smiled and passed her a glass half filled with straight gin.

The joke was that the girls had all been stealing liquor from Callie all along, for as long as any of them could remember, and had long since become somewhat seasoned drinkers themselves.

"Uh oh, my sister's gettin' drunk… it's on now, y'all," said Nora, making everybody laugh.

"Happy birthday, Sammy," Dominique said, showing that she had a glass of gin too. "…and I wish you MANY MANY MORE!!!" she said, shouting and laughing, an even weaker punch line. Everybody laughed again anyway.

"Cheers," Callie said with a smile, sporting the short hair, jubilant and happy, holding a glass up for a toast, glad that they were all there together.

"Thank you, Jesus," she thought in prayer, speaking silently, all the while smiling in a way that showed how proud she was.

"These are all my girls, and I'm still here with 'em." Obviously, the thought of having cancer still weighed heavily on Callie's mind, and being alive was something she was more thankful for than anything,

"I'm still here!!!" she said in the testimony, no longer able to conceal the emotions, shedding a joyful tear, shouting out loud,

"...and it's only because of you, Lord...YES!!! THANK YOU!!!"

* * * *

A long time had passed since the last time Callie had driven the red convertible Cadillac.

"The good ole' days," she thought, driving and riding along, the windows up on the new Mercedes, air on, appreciating the serenity and peacefulness... they'd run out of gin and cigarettes, and Callie, despite how much

Dominique protested, decided to go and get more.

"No, Momma, you just got home from the hospital. You need to take it easy and relax.

"I'll go," said Dominique, insisting.

"That's the whole reason I wanna go; been cooped up for too long. I need to get out on my own and get some air," said Callie, wanting more than anything to just drive the car for a while.

"I won't be gone long, promise," she said on the way out the door.

\* \* \* \*

The new Silver 500SEL Mercedes was smooth and a road-dominating vehicle that handled better than any car Callie had ever driven, which was what made her switch automotive products… the European automobiles, Jaguar and Mercedes Benz in particular, were on the rise just as the Japanese automakers were; Honda, Nissan, and Toyota. The question was, were the American automobile makers up to the new challenge of overseas sales competition?

The difference between this day and any other day was that Callie wasn't burning up the road in the red convertible Cadillac, and instead of sunny skies, the skies were overcast and gloomy. Nevertheless, the day was just as pleasant and relaxing. The clouds kept out the sun and thoughts of most memories, good or bad, which were associated with the nonstop motion of time and how things once were, the inevitable blow of evolution. The dreariness only implemented the here and now.

"I'm still alive," said Callie to no one in particular, but in thanks again to a higher power she knew existed,

"...and that's all that matters."

In no time at all, Callie was passing a sign that said,

"Lafayette Parrish." It was pronounced "Paroisse de Lafayette" in French.

Next was the bridge over the Bayou Teche waterway and Breaux Bridge, Louisiana, home of General Sam Houston. The liquor store there was one of the largest in the area, where Callie usually went to buy alcohol, as they had the largest variety, whether for wine, liquor, or beer.

The clerk did a double take when Callie walked in, noticing not only the short hairdo but also that Callie had lost weight; she'd lost mostly all the hips and big boobs and curves that made up the voluptuous figure everybody had known her for. She'd become a shell of the old Callie.

At the counter, the clerk spoke politely, rang up what Callie came to buy, and after bagging it, in a polite manner, told Callie, "Have a good day, Ms. Devereaux."

After grabbing the bag, when Callie started to walk away, a woman in line behind her said,

"You too, huh?" which was startling at first until Callie noticed the woman's slender physique and hair; she had short hair too and looked a lot like Callie after having recently gotten over a bout with radiation treatment.

"The hair, a dead giveaway," the woman said, with a hand on her head, smiling after running a hand over what little stubble that had grown on her head as well. Until then, Callie looked confused.

"The good thing about it, though," the woman said, creating eye contact that bothered Callie in ways she hadn't been bothered about in a long time.

"…hair will always grow back."

The eye contact was hypnotic and alluring; it made things quite interesting, actually. Other than the loss of weight and short hair, the woman was very attractive: mid-thirties, white but with a serious tan, explicit facial features, and five foot six, if that, with a body outline that showed she was once a very curvaceous woman.

*"...like me,"* Callie thought, looking the woman over from head to toe, liking everything about her.

"Eliza Hunter," the woman said, extending a warm, soft hand. Callie took it, and the woman's smile disappeared, but the whites of her eyes sparkled.

"Callie Devereaux… You wanna get together later?" Callie asked, getting straight to the point after noticing that everybody else in line and around the store was either watching or listening, still not enough to deter the attraction.

"Sure, why not," the woman said, displaying courage and another killer smile that affected Callie even more than the first one had.

Outside, the two women exchanged numbers, all the while imagining all the sensual things the two could do to each other.

The woman, still with the same smile, although overwhelmed with excitement, told Callie, "This is probably the most erotic trip to the store that I've ever taken." The smile had widened.

Callie was taken with the way the woman laughed and smiled. She managed to maintain composure and smiled back before walking away, over toward the Mercedes that was parked nearby. She wouldn't admit it, but the feeling was mutual,

"...*absolutely*," she thought.

"I'll call you later," she said, nevertheless maintaining a cool, leveled demeanor, leaving the woman standing there in awe, watching her leave. A moment or two later, in the rearview mirror, Callie saw the woman still standing there watching with the same look on her face, a look that told it all.

"Call you later, babe," she said, amused, turning from the parking lot, speeding away down the street, smiling all the while, feeling a tingling sensation and moisture growing beneath the silk red panties she had on.

"It's gon' be me and you later, babe, all night long."

\* \* \* \*

The car was on "E."

"Let me get twenty on pump number five," Callie told the overweight, white male cashier at the Circle K that she stopped at for gas.

"Twenty on pump number five," the man said, repeating Callie, but in a voice so soft it sounded more like a woman's voice, which didn't fit the man's muscular, 6'3" body frame. He was obviously gay, wearing a white Circle K t-shirt and tight jeans, with a long ponytail falling down his back.

"Y… M… C… A," thought Callie, reciting a song from the new singing group, The Village People, a rather popular band of gay men.

"That'll be all," said Callie, sharing a smile before walking away.

"Callie Devereaux?" a woman asked a moment or so later. The woman was enormously pregnant and obviously, or so it seemed, only days away from giving birth.

"Oh, my God, it is you," said the woman rushing over, waddling actually, swaying from side to side in an awkward motion, trying to hurry over to get a better look.

"I heard you were dead."

"Not hardly," Callie said to get things straight.

The woman was Callie's dear friend, Beth Ellen, the hair stylist and former call girl.

"Let me tell you… Harold finally got fed up and grew some balls and courage enough to leave his wife and kids for me," she said, sporting a smile that ran from ear to ear.

"As you can see, we're building a family of our own. This will be our second. He's at home now with the baby girl

I had a year ago.

"But enough about me, how are you feelin'? I heard you had cancer," said Beth Ellen, talking fast, barely breathing.

"Had is exactly right," Callie told her, proud of the results she'd gotten from treatment, a little cocky about it as well.

"I kicked cancer square in the ass. Uh oh… look out, world, here I come. You know me, always tryin' to enjoy life… but thank God for it, you know what I'm sayin'?"

"Of course I do. Girl… I'm just so happy for you," Beth Ellen said, smiling but in a way that expressed seriousness.

"I forgot who told me, but I cried so hard when they said you were dead."

"Well, cry no more, babe… Callie Devereaux is still alive and kickin'."

Just then, the alarms sounded, and an older black gentleman, after pushing through one side of the double glass doors of the store, rushed in.

"A tornado's on the ground, headed this way," he said, eyes wide, a look of fear and terror on his face.

"A tornado? What?" Beth Ellen asked, suddenly terror-stricken as well.

"Callie… sorry, but I gotta get home," she said and turned to walk away. During certain times of the year in the area, deadly tornadoes formed and happened often, leaving paths of death and destruction. Therefore, a warning alarm was something those who lived in Louisiana took very seriously, especially those living in southern Louisiana; the closer to the gulf you were in Louisiana, the more susceptible you were to also experience the effects of a tornado or hurricane.

Outside, the clouds had darkened, a light downpour of rain had become torrential, and suddenly, the wind was wild and traveling at speeds too high to measure.

"Everybody… the safest place is in the cooler. Follow me," said the cashier, already leading the way to safety.

And then the windows started shattering,

"Come on, we gotta go," Callie yelled, helping Beth Ellen to hurry and walk faster, following the cashier toward the coolers at the back of the store.

Outside, a car was lifted off the ground and blown away, items on the store shelves were being sucked out, and then another car flew by.

"OH, MY GOD!!!" a woman screamed, "...WE'RE ALL GONNA DIE!!!"

Part of the roof was torn off, and the woman's screams were muffled by a roar that sounded more like a charging locomotive passing through, out of control. Debris, wreckage, and fragments of everything not securely bolted or tied down flew by, and the rain fell all over everything. Eventually, the cashier, with all his might, was finally able to close the door on the cooler, and all was relatively silent except the sound of heartbeats carrying a tune much faster than what was considered normal.

And in a few moments, what seemed like forever, the mayhem and pandemonium was over. The roar of a locomotive wasn't there anymore.

Callie and Beth Ellen were holding on to each other as if for dear life. The cashier had positioned himself against the door, adding extra security, and everybody else seemed to be in shock. Even then, nobody wanted the door to come open again, afraid of what might be on the other side of it.

The older black gentleman who'd first come in and warned them was the first to speak up.

"Ok, y'all, we can't stay in here forever... I need to go check on my family," he said, looking around at everybody else,

"I gotta go."

"Yeah… it's probably gone by now," said one of the other men, suggesting that they all gain a level of courage and leave,

"I'm sure there's nothin' else to worry about; the damage has already been done."

"Yeah, but sometimes the eye of the storm can be quiet too, though. Don't mean that it's gone yet," said another of the men in the store, huddled in a corner of the cooler, holding a woman everybody assumed was the man's wife.

"Oh God… what are we gonna do?" asked the hysterical woman, oozing fear, becoming vocal again. "We're all gonna die."

* * * *

The lights outside weren't usually on.

"Not this early… it's not even six o'clock," thought Samantha, standing by a window with a perfect view to see everything that was happening in front of the house.

But the overcast skies had suddenly turned and became as dark as night except at times when thunder and bolts of lightning struck loud and violently and lit everything up. And the wind was blowing so hard that trees were swaying.

"It's starting to look really bad outside, y'all," said Samantha, making everybody else aware of it, too.

"...and Callie's been gone over an hour.

"You think somebody should go out and look for her?" Samantha asked, worried about Callie.

"I was wondering the same thing," said Dominique, coming to take a peek out the window as well.

Nora came over.

"Maybe she ran into somebody she knew."

"Maybe," Dominique said, "...but maybe not."

"I sure hope she did," said Samantha, starting to worry even more.

A minute or so later, William came in.

"I think y'all should see this," William told them, turning a lamp on and then the television set.

The news was what he wanted them to see. An on-scene reporter was making a statement.

"Four tornadoes have been confirmed so far in Louisiana, the worst, an EF2 in St. James parish.

"EF0 tornadoes have also been sighted in St. Tammy parish near Lacombe, in St. Helen parish near Amite, and in Lafayette parish.

"Governor John Bel Edwards has issued a state of emergency for seven different parishes across the state, including St. Johns, Assumption, and Washington, following the destructive storms."

"I ask all Louisianans to pray for the victims of the terrible storms that touched down in Louisiana today and especially at the Sugar Hill RV park in Convent," said Governor Edwards.

"Be assured that we will do all that we can to help save lives and restore the families, businesses, and communities destroyed by the tragedy."

The reporter continued reporting,

"At least three people have been confirmed dead at a trailer park in Convent, according to the associated press, where dozens of trailers were destroyed by a confirmed EF3 tornado with wind speeds of at least 150 mph."

"We've never had anything like this happen before. We never had this many people injured or so much destruction in one event," said St. James parish sheriff Wily Martin to a reporter for WVUE News.

"We won't stop searching for survivors until we're satisfied we've searched every pile."

Just then, on television, behind the on-scene reporter, Dominique saw it first.

"Hey...there's Momma," she said, in total shock; Callie was there in Lafayette, on the scene of destruction, standing with an arm around, holding and understandably comforting a woman crying uncontrollably. The woman looked to be pregnant and possibly going into labor.

# Chapter 59

The cashier opened the door of the cooler, and everybody walked out, uncertain to what all they might find in what seemed like another world.

The destruction was devastating; buildings, including the one they were in, were hardly recognizable, a tragedy heightened through an incredible wrath of nature. Everything around them was destroyed, the entire town; every structure and building, car and automobile were affected, and just as quickly, the hopefulness, faith, and spirit of all who saw it were destroyed.

"Oh, my God," the hysterical woman said, but barely in a whisper; the hysterics and panic were all gone, lost in overwhelming astonishment.

"Oh…my…God," she said again. Those were the only words she could think to say, and everybody else felt the same way.

## Buckets, Shovels, Ghost and Worms

Tornadoes, on average, travel four to eight miles along the ground at about 60 miles an hour. This one, over a mile wide with winds in excess of 200 miles per hour, was on the ground for more than 22 miles. Luckily, for the most part, the tornado's path led through sparsely populated, rural areas. However, the death toll was high; in the end, 16 casualties were reported, and although Beth Ellen had yet to find out about it, two of the 16 lives that were lost were Beth Ellen's husband, Harold, and their one-year-old baby girl.

"No... No," said Beth Ellen once she and Callie walked out of the cooler and saw what everybody else saw.

"Uh Uh... I gotta get home NOW!!!" she told Callie, screaming, obviously falling apart.

Callie reached out to her,

"NO... MY BABY!!!" she said, screaming again before turning to walk away and leave, but barely, carrying such a heavy load from being almost nine months pregnant and not knowing which way to go either.

Debris from the destroyed buildings and overturned or scattered cars and automobiles littered almost every ground space around them, including the streets and sidewalks.

She screamed again.

"NO!!!" And then, more calmly, turning back again towards Callie, and then to some of the other people around her, asked,

"Will somebody please just help me?"

Everybody else seemed just as devastated, just not as vocal, but still just as worried.

Nobody came forward. People were scattering; a few were trying to help those who needed help immediately, but most were trying to get home to check on their loved ones as well.

Only Callie came to the rescue.

"Where do you live?" she asked, speaking up and stepping in, becoming the only resolution, attempting to at least give the help that Beth Ellen had asked for and needed.

"The Maximar trailer park in Convent," Beth Ellen said, gathering herself.

"…but how are we gonna get there?" she asked, still worried, looking around, seeing no clear path to walk or drive through, knowing good and well she wouldn't be able to walk around very much or climb over anything, not being as big as she was, eight months pregnant.

"Oh, my God," she said, bursting out in tears after

realizing the obvious and thinking the worst,

"My baby," she cried again as if in the worst pain imaginable, feeling helpless and doomed.

Callie really didn't know what to do either. So, for a while, the two women just stood there; both cried and held each other. However, it wouldn't be long before help started to arrive, police officers and firemen moving debris and making a way to get through. Even a news crew showed up. A reporter from WVUE News, standing not too far away, was already holding a microphone, speaking toward a cameraman filming with a live camera when Callie noticed them. That's when Beth Ellen screamed yet again, catching everybody off guard when she said,

"OH NO…MY WATER JUST BROKE!!!"

It was the cameraman who first took action and grabbed Beth Ellen,

"Ok… we're gonna sit you down right over here," he said, leading the way to where he thought would be a more comfortable spot on a wooden crate that had obviously been blown away from who knows where.

"I'm here to help you," he told Beth Ellen, giving her the compassion and comfort he thought she might need.

"My wife and I have delivered our last two babies together. So, be assured, I've done this before," he said before scrabbling around to find anything else that might be of use, if need be, to help deliver the baby.

An officer and a fireman came over to help as well. Eventually, Beth Ellen was made a priority and loaded in a squad car. Callie squeezed in beside her before the officer, sirens blaring, whisked them off, rushing toward the Southern Louisiana Medical Center.

"Hold on, ma'am… we'll be there shortly," he said once he'd gotten around a corner and the coast was clear, all along hoping that Beth Ellen wouldn't make a mess, giving birth on the back seat of the squad car.

Two hours later, Beth Ellen gave birth to Melissa Ann Bynes at the hospital. The baby was born a month earlier than expected but was born in the best of health.

"Awwwwww… she's absolutely gorgeous," Callie told Beth Ellen after the ordeal was over.

"She is, isn't she," Beth Ellen said, bubbling over with joy, typically of how a proud mother would feel. It wouldn't be until two hours later when another officer came in, spoiling things with the bad news that Harold and their other daughter had both been killed.

## Chapter 60

Days later, relatives came and took the baby away; that's because Beth Ellen, after hearing that Harold and their other child had died, remained traumatized and in a state of shock. Doctors and psychiatrists mostly kept her hospitalized for well over a month, where around-the-clock tabs were kept on her. The thought was that she might've been considering suicide.

On the other hand, Callie, although safe and sound at home, was still troubled, not only by the ordeal she'd suffered through in Chicago but also by what she'd gone through with the storm and Beth Ellen. She tried to hide it, but William and Dominique could both see straight through it.

"Momma… why don't you come and go to church with us?" Dominique asked, unwilling to just watch while Callie lay and gave in to being depressed. Seth had been the same way until they both got saved and joined a traveling ministry.

Every other weekend, a revival would be held in different parishes around the state of Louisiana or Texas and sometimes in Mississippi. Both Dominique and Seth had become devoted Christians, and the thought that Callie might be persuaded to become one, too, was the greatest challenge of all for Dominique.

"Momma… just come with us one time. Try it, please. I promise you'll be glad you came," she told Callie.

Surprisingly, it didn't take much convincing at all. Right away, Callie agreed to go. The following Sunday, they were all at a revival in Alexandria. Two weeks later, they were at a revival in Monroe and then a couple of weeks later, in Thibodaux. Callie was saved when the revival came closer to home in Lafayette, which quickly became the talk of the town.

"Naw…not Callie Devereaux…I know she ain't get saved," one woman said as if the possibility couldn't possibly exist.

"Naw…I ain't buyin' it," the woman said, totally unconvinced.

"You know she got cancer," another woman added.

"What that mean?" the first woman asked.

"...you must not know Callie Devereaux.

"Regardless of her havin' cancer, she ain't gon' ever change."

"But I was there when she did it, confess all her sins," the second woman said, not so willing to disbelieve.

"...she cried and everything," the woman said, more willing to believe what she saw rather than being like how she thought the other woman was being: mean and uncompassionate.

"Tell you what...I'll believe it when I see it," the first woman said.

Differences of opinion caused disputes like this took place all over town, but in the end, they were all convinced. Callie not only went to church on Sundays but also did volunteer work at the local hospital, homeless shelter, and orphanage. She donated money—lots of it—and became an active member of the community as well. The old Callie was gone; she'd changed completely, and those who'd known her couldn't do anything but admire and respect what she'd done.

\* \* \* \*

At the grocery store one day, Callie ran into Eliza

Hunter again… they'd talked on the phone a few times and shared lustful thoughts about one another but hadn't actually seen each other since meeting at the liquor store—the same day of the storm.

"Oh wow… if you're cooking, I'll put all this back and come eat with you then," Eliza said, kidding, referring to all the food in the grocery cart she was pushing. Being a flirt was just something extra, something that came naturally.

Callie smiled.

"Be nice," she said, flattered and somewhat turned on, but then, just as fast, the thought went away.

"You remember what I explained to you, right? About being saved?"

"Yeah, I do," said Eliza. She'd gained weight and had hair; as it had with Callie, the stubble had grown and was several inches longer. The smile was the same, though, just as warm and inviting as it had been the first time the two women had met.

"I'm kidding," she told Callie, being emphatic after noticing how uncomfortable Callie seemed to be.

"I shouldn't've said that, not after what you told me. I remember."

"Accept my apology?" she asked with kind eyes pleading for forgiveness.

"You're ok," said Callie, sharing a warm smile.

The last time they'd talked on the phone, Eliza invited Callie over to have drinks and dinner. Of course, the plan was to have things lead to a whole lot more.

Callie declined and went on to explain how things had changed for her.

"Girl… I got saved and turned my life over to Christ," she told Eliza. It was evident in the words she spoke and the way she said them that Callie was serious… these were all words coming from the heart.

"We can still be friends, though," she went on to tell Eliza,

"…and you're always welcome to go to church with me any time you want. Don't be bashful." And that was pretty much the end of the conversation. Since then, the two hadn't spoken to one another until this particular day in the supermarket, and even then, the conversation was short.

"It's good seein' you again," said Callie, pushing past also with a grocery cart.

"God bless."

It was a shock when, a few days later, Callie got a call from Eliza asking where the next revival would be. Not so shocking, though, as it was the first day when the revival started… and sure enough, Eliza was there too.

# Chapter 61

"Momma… The revival we're havin' this weekend is gonna be in Breaux Bridge," Dominique said, giving Callie a head's up. Nikki had made tuna sandwiches and Lobster Bisque Soup. William had a table set for them outside, in the yard on one side of the house, and that's where they were having their lunch.

"It won't bother you to be there again, will it?" Dominique asked, considering that Breaux Bridge was where the deadly tornado touched down.

Callie didn't answer right away. The sandwich, made merely from tuna and a few other simple ingredients, was, however, the best she'd ever tasted, and so was the Lobster Bisque Soup.

"It won't bother me if it don't bother you," she finally said between bites and spoons filled with soup, for the moment unwilling to be disturbed.

"We're supposed to be havin' a guest speaker, a Reverend Jenkins outta Baton Rouge. I heard he can preach," said Dominique.

"Good," said Callie, starting to slow down a bit with how much she was eating. "I sure hope he can.

"I was so disappointed with the preacher they had at the last church we were in… he couldn't preach worth nothing.'

"I kept dozin' off durin' the whole sermon… can't remember a thing he was talkin' about."

"Don't worry," Dominique said with reassurance. "I promise this one'll be a whole lot better. I've never actually heard him preach, but from what I've been told, we're in for a real treat."

\* \* \* \*

By the time Sunday came around, Callie was a nervous wreck and didn't know why,

"What the hell's wrong with me?" she asked, looking in the mirror that morning for the umpteenth time. After changing clothes for the third time, and changing hairstyles, looking in the mirror yet again, she told herself,

"You're goin' to church, girl, not out to some damn nightclub." Nevertheless, the nervousness remained vast and overwhelming. Three times after she'd gone outside, supposedly ready to go, Callie had to come back in the house to get things she'd forgotten: a Bible that she always took to church with her, money for the collections, and even the car keys.

"I guess you'd forget your head, too, if it wasn't sewn on, huh?" William asked. After the third time, Callie ran back into the house. She didn't actually come out and say what it was she wanted to say in response to William's comment, but she did throw up a middle finger, indicating it.

"Yeah, love you too," William told her and laughed.

Other than the fact that Callie had become more of a spiritual woman, everything else about her was back to normal; she had gained weight as well, her hair had grown, and the worrying thought of dying was slowly fading away. She'd even regained a sense of humor, laughing when William shouted out to her as she drove away,

"YOU KNOW WHAT YOU CAN DO WIT' THAT FINGER, DON'T YOU?" he asked.

"TAKE IT AND STICK IT WHERE THE SUN DON'T SHINE!!!"

It was a beautiful day already, and Callie Devereaux planned to enjoy it to the fullest.

## Chapter 62

"New Beginning Fellowship Baptist Church; it's one of the oldest in Breaux Bridge."

"Sounds nice," said Callie when Dominique gave directions and the name of the church where the revival was being held.

"A new beginning is exactly what God gave me, and I thank you for it, Lord," Callie said the next day, turning off Parkway Drive and pulling into the church parking lot.

Despite a congregation of mostly white parishioners, the traveling ministries, along with its all-black congregation, were all invited to fellowship and enjoy the services. Once inside, though, Callie quickly noticed that they were all still segregated; the white parishioners sat mostly on one side of the church while the black congregation sat opposite them. Nevertheless, it was still to be a great historical event, the first of its kind in the state of Louisiana, one that included a mixture of two different races of people all praying together, praising the one God they all supposedly believed in.

The place was packed—the sanctuary, pews, and pulpit had hardly any place else left to sit. From one of the middle rows of seats, Dominique stood and waved and then beckoned as soon as Callie walked in.

Callie waved back. One of the ushers noticed the exchange, and right away, Callie was ushered over and allowed to squeeze by other people who'd already taken a seat. Dominique and Seth were there, waiting in a place saved just for Callie.

"Was it hard to find?" Dominique asked, wondering why it took so long for Callie to get there.

"Wasn't hard to find at all," said Callie, after taking a seat, placing the bible she'd brought with her in the compartment in front of them where other bibles, hand-held fans, and books of hymns were held.

"…just kept forgettin' things… had to go back in the house three times."

The choir, made up of mostly black southern singers from The Traveling Ministries, had been belting out one gospel song after another until the reverend of New Beginning came to the pulpit.

## Alvin Bell

"It's another great day the Lord has blessed us with," the reverend said, expressing love and warmth in the smile he shared with everybody. And even with a black suit on, he shared a great resemblance to Santa Claus as well,

"...an exceptionally great day if you look around and notice all who are here," he said, harping on the historical event.

"What a blessing," he said, caught in the moment.

"But then, why shouldn't we all be here together? We're all God's children, aren't we?" he asked, going on to capture the attention of everybody there. The church had gone dead silent. Besides the reverend's voice, the only other sound you could hear was when one of the parishioners or somebody from The Traveling Ministries congregation coughed or hacked to clear a throat.

The Reverend kept at it for fifteen minutes or so, hoping to ease things and make sense of what they were all there doing... an open or public conversation about race was never a welcomed issue, but in this case, it warranted the attention of everybody in the room.

Next to speak was Reverend Leroy Thompson of The Traveling Ministries.

"There was once a man in the woods, hunting for food

to feed his family," the reverend said right off the bat, catching everybody off guard with what he was saying.

"The man had a small .22 rifle, which was all he thought he needed to hunt squirrel and rabbit," said the reverend, obviously as part of a story he was telling.

"The man started to head home after the basket he carried was filled. But then, out of nowhere, a big grizzly bear came along, growling and baring its teeth. At that point, the .22 rifle became useless; shooting it would only make matters worse. It definitely wasn't gon' kill no great big grizzly bear.

"So, the man dropped the gun and took off runnin' as fast as he could. Nevertheless, in no time, the bear was gainin' on him, growlin' even louder, Grrrrrrrrr, and a lot more....

"The man was scared half to death, knowin' good and well that a bear of this size with such massive weight could tear a man apart with just one swipe of a claw. Regardless, though, the more the man ran, the more the bear was gaining on him.

"Finally, the man did the only other thing he knew to do... he prayed.

"'Lord, please let this bear be a Christian. Please, Lord,

let this bear be a Christian,' he said over and over again.

"But still, the bear gained ground until the man, for sure, could feel the bear breathing down his back. That's when he made the mistake of looking over a shoulder, tripping on a log as he did.

"'Oh Lord... please let this bear be a Christian... please let this bear be a Christian,' he said, praying as loud and hard as he could after falling down on the ground.

"And for a moment, it seemed to work because the bear stopped and stood there over the man for a while.

"'Please, Lord, let this bear be a Christian,' the man said again, one last time.

That's when the bear, answering the man's prayer, put both front paws together, bowed its head, and said,

"'Lord... thank you for the food I am about to receive.'"

Everybody in the church burst out laughing. The joke had lightened the mood more than anybody could've ever imagined.

After a while, when the laughter died down, Reverend Thompson introduced the guest speaker,

"Ladies and gentlemen, from Baton Rouge, Louisiana.

It gives me honor and great pleasure to introduce Reverend Roy Jenkins."

Right away, the name registered, but never in a million years would Callie have believed it. She first assumed and expected to see the senior Roy Jenkins, but to her recollection, the senior Roy Jenkins had passed away years ago, and so had the wife of Roy Jenkins. And as far as she knew, Blu was dead, too.

The assumptions were put to rest when there, in the pulpit, wearing an all-white three-piece suit, a man as dark as night stood up and made his way toward the microphone.

The man was indeed "Blu." But he wasn't just "Blu" anymore; he was now the "Reverend" Blu Roy Jenkins Jr. It had been well over twenty years since Callie had last seen him, but there he was, undeniably so. And besides the bald head he now had, Blu still looked the same, still more handsome than any man she'd ever known.

* * * *

"Momma… do you two know each other?" Dominique asked after Callie and Blu had not only spoken and said hello but also given each other a big hug, leaving Dominique and Seth standing there confused, trying to figure things out. Dominique especially took notice of how unmistakably long and passionately Blu and Callie embraced and held on to each other.

"Me and this man here… we've known each other since we were kids," Callie said, leaving out the most important part about exactly how well they knew each other.

The sermon Blu gave was phenomenal, a real showcase of talent when it came to speaking the gospel. Blu preached and preached so well that everybody paid close attention and got involved, shouting Amen and spewing other words of appreciation, agreeing wholeheartedly with everything Blu preached about.

Afterward, not only was Blu given a big round of applause, but a standing ovation was given, which led to a record amount of cash being collected. What made it so surprising, though, was when Blu stepped out of the pulpit, came down off the stage, and walked straight through everybody standing, applauding him, to over where Callie was standing, admiring him.

"Hey stranger," he said, smiling from ear to ear, arms held out, barely able to wait while Callie, with open arms as well, walked toward him.

"Oh, Blu," she said afterward, after wrapping both arms tight around Blu's neck.

"Dominique… meet Blu, your daddy," Callie added a

while afterward, which took both Dominique and Blu by surprise.

On the other hand, it was clear that what Callie said might be true… other than one having and one not having hair, and one being an older man, of course, and the other being a young woman, they were nearly mirrored images of one another.

"Yeah...she's your daughter," Callie confirmed and told Blu, who suddenly seemed at a loss for words.

## Chapter 63

"I never thought somethin' like this would ever happen again," said Callie, with Blu lying there beside her, both bodies entwined and wrapped in sheets on a bed at a Holiday Inn near the Breaux Bridge, Herbert Avenue exit off I-10.

"It's funny. I should say that with how often the times are when I think back to when we were kids.

"You ever think back to those days?" Callie asked, reverting back so much until she even started to sound like a little girl again.

"Huh, Blu?" she asked, looking up just as Blu turned and took a gentle hold of her.

"Sure I do, quite often, especially the times when you and I were together," he said, squeezing Callie a little tighter, bringing her closer and closer, and then running a manly hand down her naked backside while kissing her full on the lips, sharing a wet, hot tongue.

"Back then, you were the only thing that mattered," he said, whispering in Callie's ear afterward.

"I would've died for you… and almost did," he said, finding it a little funny now after more than twenty years had gone by.

The hotel they were at was out in the open amongst all the other hotels and restaurants, right in the middle of traveler traffic going on and coming off the interstate in both directions. In other words, the location was busy with lots of people, which didn't make it the most inconspicuous alternative to where they should have had an affair.

Blu had not only become somewhat of a celebrity as a well-known and respected minister in and around the state of Louisiana, but he'd also been married to a well-known woman in the community who'd died recently. And with how hard Callie was trying to overcome the harmful views of past reputations, being inconspicuous should have been a main priority. But after only one look at each other, caution was thrown to the wind, and rekindled were all the old feelings, attraction, and reactions that never let anyone or anything interfere. The need to have one another was always so much stronger, so much greater.

"The night when that damn fool, Johnny Le Fleur, shot me, I rolled off the balcony and hit the ground hard, but I hit it runnin'. I ran and ran 'til I couldn't run no more.

"I must've passed out somewhere along the way because the next thing I knew, I was at Ms. Mildred's house… yes, the voodoo woman," Callie remembered Ms. Mildred distinctively, casting spells on people in and around the area.

"Don't know what she did, but when I came to, I felt fine, not like I'd been shot in the back with Johnny Le Fleur's .45."

"I remember when I was runnin' though, I swore to God that if I lived to see another day, I would change my life forever, give up all the foolishness, and live righteously.

"And that's exactly what I did.

"Until this day, you're the only other woman besides my wife, Mildred, who I've slept with.

"Yes, I married the voodoo woman," Blu said, showing not a bit of shame.

"From that point on, until this very day, I don't go out to clubs anymore, don't drink or smoke or do much of anything else, including fornication. I gave up all the foolishness and feel a lot better for it."

"I'm sure you do," Callie told him, "The voodoo woman's got you hooked."

"Not at all," Blu told Callie, smiling, revealing the same million-dollar smile he had when they were younger with a single gold tooth showing.

"If anything, it was the other way around... she started goin' to church and everything too," said Blu. He didn't know it, but actually, it was a spell on Blu that made him marry Ms. Mildred.

"Unfortunately, she passed away a few months ago."

"Sorry for your loss," Callie said without really meaning it.

"Thinkin' back on how I used to be, I used to think livin' a life of sin was what it was all about, havin' fun. But really, it wasn't. All that kind of fun did was bring on a lotta stress, which isn't very much fun at all.

"But, you know the sayin', 'it takes a fool to learn,' somethin' I now know very well."

"I'm proud of you, Blu, I really am," said Callie with a smile, meaning it sincerely.

"You seem to have changed your life completely and have done very well for yourself." When Blu talked about how he'd made changes in life, all it did was remind Callie about how she'd done the same thing.

"…yes, very proud," she said, just before Blu rolled over and the lovemaking began again.

Thirty minutes later, spent and left with nothing but good feelings about each other, Blu was the first to say something, breaking the ice.

"You asked if I ever think back to when we were younger.

"Thoughts from the past cross my mind all the time… like how crazy you and I was, for one," said Blu, smiling in a way that showed he was really enjoying himself.

"Yeah, but come on, tell the truth… who was the craziest, me or you?" Callie asked, firing right back, challenging Blu with a big smile and reason to think back even more on things that actually happened.

"Probably me," Blu told her after only a moment of thought as if the answer was easy and obvious.

"I'm surprised nobody ever found me hangin' from a tree with the way me and you used to like to fool around.

"You know for yourself…takin' them kind'a' chances wit' a girl like you was dangerous, especially wit' me bein' as dark as I am, and with how, for so long, that daddy of yours had everybody believin' that you was white. Messin' wit' a white woman would get a nigga killed in a hurry.

"Uh uh, no sir… they didn't play that back then... now either, really.

"I'm sure somebody would'a' found me hangin' from a tree for real if that had been him, your daddy instead of mine, who caught us in the barn that day. You do remember that, don't you? We was both butt naked, and I was all over you," said Blu, laughing at the memory. It made Callie laugh, too.

"I got my behind beat so bad for that...I mean, tore up. I couldn't sit down for a whole week.

"But at least I lived to see another day," said Blu, still laughing about it.

"I also remember how good you made me feel," Blu added a moment or so later, the smile slowly fading away, replaced by an unmistakable look of passion laced with a massive stack of sincerity.

"…and how every day I couldn't wait to see you. Never mind that whenever I did see you, all I wanted was to make love," said Blu, smiling again.

"Uh-huh," said Callie, eyebrows raised to match the painted-on smile she'd been wearing since earlier that day at the church when Blu came off the stage and said hello.

"All you wanted was to get between these legs," she said, smiling at Blu seductively.

"No, not at all," said Blu, dropping the smile while expressing the true feelings he had for her.

"It wasn't just lust. I really loved you… and still do. Always have and always will," he added, climbing his naked body out of bed, landing on the side of it down on one knee.

"Nothin' could've been more of a blessin' to me than when I looked out at the crowd today and saw you. Nothin'.

"And now that we're together again… well… I never wanna lose you."

He paused.

"I guess what I'm tryin' to say is… will you marry me?"

"Marry you?" Callie asked, barely able to speak; the question had taken her breath away.

"Blu… we haven't talked or seen each other for almost twenty-five years. And now, after only one day, you wanna get married?"

"Yeah, I do," Blu said without a moment's hesitation.

"Huh… it's funny; I was hoping those would be the

words you answered me with," he said afterward, smiling again, but only momentarily.

"I should've married you a long time ago," he said, being serious again. "…and should've had the courage to go tell that daddy of yours exactly what I had in mind."

"He probably woulda' shot you," said Callie, laughing afterward to lighten the mood.

"You know I'm kidding, right?" she said when Blu didn't smile.

"I'm not," Blu said, speaking softly but with all honesty. "…I've never been more serious."

"Oh, Blu…" said Callie, becoming unglued,

"I'm not the one you wanna marry," she said just before the floodgates came open and tears started to fall uncontrollably.

"I'm sick, Blu."

"Sick? What do you mean, sick?" Blu asked, positioning himself in front of her just right for a direct look deep into Callie's hazel-brown eyes,

"You look fine to me."

"Yeah, thanks...but I've got leukemia," she said, pausing to allow what she said to sink in.

"I put on a smile and a lil' makeup once in a while, and at times, I pretend that everything's alright. But inside, I'm really hurtin'." Clearly, it was evident in the sound of Callie's weak, tearful voice how hard the subject was to talk about. Nevertheless, while the tears fell, Callie smiled brightly, giving Blu an example of how strong she was trying to be.

"And to think, just a few months ago, I went through all that damn chemotherapy, and for what? Silly me to think I would be cured."

"Nobody lives forever, huh Blu?" she said, still trying to find humor in it.

"You're gonna be fine," Blu said before Callie interrupted him,

"We'll get a second opinion, and..."

"Blu... Baby... forget it... there's no hope," she said, creating eye contact and holding it longer than Blu.

"The cancer had gone into remission; they even thought it was gone altogether, but no, now it's back and attacking parts of my body faster and twice as much as before."

"Believe me, I've had second, third, fourth, and fifth

opinions given. They all say the same thing: that there's very little if anything at all, that they can do.

"I'm not expected to live another six months, Blu… SIX MONTHS!!!" said Callie, speaking out in horrible disbelief, the tears starting to fall all over again.

"I don't wanna talk or think about it anymore. Please... just make love to me again, Blu… make love to me over and over again until you can't anymore."

# Chapter 64

"The holy spirit passed through everybody tonight, right there in the house of the lord. And to think, the man God chose to anoint and deliver the word was none other than my father.

"All these years... I wonder why Momma kept him a secret for so long," Dominique said while she and Seth lay in bed.

"Every time I asked her about him, all she'd ever say was that she didn't know and that he was probably somewhere dead.... she ain't care if what she said hurt my feelins' or not... she used to stay drunk and was mean as hell back then."

"Ok, but maybe she did think he was somewhere dead," said Seth, yawning while giving in to the most relaxed feeling in the world—sleep.

"...look how long it had been since the last time they

saw each other, well over twenty years. Hell… he ain't even know about you."

"Yeah, but regardless of whether he knew about me or whether she knew where he was or not, why didn't she just tell me about him? That would've been better than not tellin' me nothin' at all.

"I remember she used to get so mad when I asked her about my daddy like I might've struck a nerve. She'd say somethin' like,

"'Don't be askin' me nothin' 'bout him no more. You hear?' and that would be it, no explanation or nothin'."

"Baby... maybe you did strike a nerve," said Seth, hoping, wishing, and praying that the conversation would end and he'd be allowed to fall fast asleep peacefully.

"…who knows how their relationship ended? I don't, and neither do you. The main thing is that now, since the two of you have finally met, you have a chance to get to know one another and close the gap that's been there for so long. I'd say that's somethin' to be thankful for. Wouldn't you?" Seth asked, hoping to put an end to what could've easily become something that Dominique went on and on about, something he wanted no part of.

Seth didn't know of or have contact with his father

either. Whoever he was, he'd gotten two women pregnant at the same time in the town where they lived, and instead of facing up to the responsibilities, he chose to run and leave the two pregnant women behind. Seth's grandparents took Seth's mom in, and the other woman's relatives took her in. Since then, no one had seen or heard from his father again, something that had always bothered Seth. Talking to Dominique about the situation she was in now only served as a reminder and made things worse.

\* \* \* \*

Dominique and Blu did get to know each other. Eventually, they became best friends and spent a lot of time together, especially after Seth got caught cheating... supposedly the other woman he'd cheated with had gotten pregnant. The timing of it all couldn't have been any worse; Dominique had just found out about how she was also pregnant.

Dominique cried for a while but quickly got over it. Unfortunately, it wasn't the first time she suspected Seth of cheating.

"Oh well... like father, like son," she said a week or so later.

Divorce was imminent, and Blu being there was right on time, giving him a chance to be the father Dominique never had and so desperately needed.

And just as the transformation happened when Luke died, and Ted was born, Callie held on, withstanding unbelievable pain, and lived past the six-month period she was given to live, only to die the day after Alexandria, Dominique's baby, Callie's first biological child and granddaughter was born.

# Epilogue

**Five years later**

Blu was to be one of many guest speakers at the Harlem National Gospel Convention. According to the amount of tickets they'd sold, over forty thousand people were expected to attend. To accommodate such a large crowd, the event was being held at Madison Square Garden in New York, a place where Dominique always dreamed of going.

She had become the director and organizing manager of the Roy Jenkins Ministry Organization and was privileged enough to be there with him. Alexandria, Dominique's five-year-old daughter, was spending a few days in Baton Rouge with Auntie Sammy, who, like Bob, had become a doctor.

The list of gospel singers and musicians was astounding, listing performers like the legendary Shirley Caesar, Regina Belle, the Winans, and many more. Tickets were sold out.

"You gotta excuse me if I seem a lil' nervous; it's my

first time in New York," said Blu, looking as worried and anxious as he sounded, glaring around at everything, all the people, and then up at all the tall buildings.

"Wow... this place is really somethin' else," he said after he'd stepped out of the taxi.

They'd flown in and landed at New York's famous LaGuardia Airport. A taxi took them downtown to the Waldorf Astoria Hotel. Only the best was afforded by the Roy Jenkins Ministry Organization.

Blu was somewhat of a celebrity, touring the country, preaching the gospel to millions of Christians and true believers, but mostly in the southeast region of the United States. Visiting a church or gospel convention on the West Coast or across the Mason-Dixon line was a rarity.

"I still can't believe I'm here either," Dominique said after she'd gotten out and was standing there beside him.

"I'm finally here in the Big Apple."

Like Blu, Dominique was captivated, busy taking it all in, the tall buildings and the many, many people walking the busy New York City sidewalks.

Not too busy was she, though, to notice when another car, a chauffeur-driven Lincoln Continental, pulled up beside them.

The passenger side rear door opened, and what came out first was an old, familiar sound, one that made Dominique's head snap around; it took her back to when she was a little girl again,

"Good mornin' heartache, you ole' gloomy sight.

"Good mornin' heartache, thought we said goodbye last night," the old Billie Holiday song was being played on the radio, New York's finest, WBLS. Although, what the song made Dominique think of was,

"Ms. Ladeaux."

Instead, a pantyless woman wearing nothing more than a stunning air of confidence, an extra short dress, a pair of tall, black leather boots, and a long mink coat came strutting out with lots of dark chocolate brown skin showing, along with a masculine styled box haircut, skinned on both sides.

The woman was none other than Ms. Grace Jones… she was staying right there at the very same hotel.

"Oh wow… I can't believe it," said Dominique, barely in a whisper, in awe but trying very hard to sustain a cool composure after seeing somebody so famous. Most young, black women admired the Jamaican-born actress, singer/songwriter, and supermodel. Grace had a style all her own and wasn't afraid to flaunt it regardless of what others might have said or thought of her, something that gave many other women of color courage.

A lot of them were thinking, *"If Grace can do it, whatever it may be, then I can do it too."* Mainly, what they were talking about was simply taking a chance to be themselves.

A doorman slammed shut the door of the car Grace was riding in just as she walked by. Nevertheless, the song kept playing,

"Good mornin' heartache, you ole' gloomy sight.

"Good mornin' heartache…"

Dominique looked back as the car sped away. When it did, across the street, amongst the hundreds, maybe even thousands of pedestrians moving along the sidewalk, there was Ms. Ladeaux. She had the same thick wool sweater on, a long skirt, galosh boots, and the same red Billie Holiday hat. She was standing there wearing a big smile as well, waving at Dominique.

Dominique, on instinct, waved right back, but upon the realization of it all, was taken aback, especially when she noticed, standing beside Ms. Ladeaux was Callie… she looked a lot younger and was standing there like a child in amazement, staring up at all the tall buildings.

At just the moment when Callie looked over and smiled at Dominique, a city bus came by and blocked the view. They'd only had eye contact for maybe a split second. The bus never stopped and passed right on by quickly. However, when it did, Dominique, still expecting to see Callie and Ms. Ladeaux, was disappointed because they weren't there anymore. They'd both vanished.

* * * *

At a hundred and four years old, William was still alive and doing quite well actually; there were no signs of him having diabetes, high blood pressure, or any other serious ailment or disease. And to top it all off, medical researchers had developed a new pill to stimulate the sex drive of old men like him.

"I still got it, baby," he told Nikki after the first time he'd taken one. Of course, he was lying through the skin of his teeth, but Nikki didn't know it; she knew nothing at all about the new Viagra pills.

With a monthly prescription, William never ran out and made it all seem natural. Nikki was just amazed that a man like William, at a hundred and four years old, could still fuck all through the day. The only worry was that he might have a heart attack and die.

"I ain't worried 'bout no heart attack. We all know I ain't gon' live forever. So, I might as well enjoy it while I can.

"Come here, baby," he'd say to Nikki, who'd gotten a whole lot thicker, close to three hundred pounds.

"Pleasingly plump" was how William described his wife after she'd gained so much weight. To him, having sex with her was still the best thing in the world,

"More for me to love," was how William looked at it.

\* \* \* \*

"Momma… you think she'll ever catch on?" asked Callie with both bare feet dangling down, touching the water from where they were sitting on the pier, the same place in the swamp where Dominique and Ms. Ladeaux used to sit and catch fish.

Ms. Ladeaux, suddenly now a decrepit old woman with snow-white hair and a smile of peace and contentment, never missed a beat.

"I think she's already figured it out," said Ms. Ladeaux. Every female descendant who came after the famous voodoo queen, Marie Catherine Ladeaux, whether practitioners or not, was born with a special mystical gift and knowledge of magic, witchcraft, and sorcery, the kind that gave them power for either good or evil. Like Callie, Dominique wasn't the kind of person who would ever wanna do anybody any harm; she was more interested in saving people's lives.

In the meantime, right alongside Blu, Dominique continued to attend conventions and revivals on a regular basis, a delight she'd taken in strengthening the allegiance of souls to the church.

And other than the one incident that happened when Seth mysteriously became impotent, Dominique was never again to blame for anyone else's misfortune.